The Shadow of the Past

A volume in the series

Cornell Studies in Security Affairs

edited by Robert J. Art, Robert Jervis, and Stephen M. Walt

A list of titles in this series is available at www.cornellpress.cornell.edu.

The Shadow of the Past

Reputation and Military Alliances before the First World War

Gregory D. Miller

Cornell University Press
Ithaca and London

First published 2012 by Cornell University Press
Printed in the United States of America

Library of Congress Cataloging-in-Publication Data

Miller, Gregory D., 1973–
The shadow of the past : reputation and military alliances before the First World War / Gregory D. Miller
p. cm. — (Cornell studies in security affairs)
Includes bibliographical references and index.
ISBN 978-0-8014-5031-0 (cloth : alk. paper)
1. Europe—Foreign relations—1871–1918. 2. Reputation (Law) 3. Alliances. I. Title. II. Series: Cornell studies in security affairs.
D453.M55 2012
940.3'112—dc23 2011027256

Cornell University Press strives to use environmentally responsible suppliers and materials to the fullest extent possible in the publishing of its books. Such materials include vegetable-based, low-VOC inks and acid-free papers that are recycled, totally chlorine-free, or partly composed of nonwood fibers. For further information, visit our website at www.cornellpress.cornell.edu.

Cloth printing 10 9 8 7 6 5 4 3 2 1

Dedicated to my parents, Daniel and Susan Miller,
and to my daughter, Brooke

Contents

List of Figures and Tables ix

Acknowledgments xi

1. Alliances and Reputation in International Relations 1
2. Reliability and Alliance Behavior 35
3. The End of Splendid Isolation: British Pursuit of an Ally, 1901–1905 63
4. The First Moroccan Crisis: Testing the Anglo-French Entente, 1904–1907 92
5. The Bosnia-Herzegovina Crisis: Expanding the Entente, 1907–1911 126
6. The Agadir Crisis: Rolling toward War, 1910–1914 152
7. Summary and Expansion of Findings 182

Appendixes

A. First Treaty of Alliance between Austria-Hungary, Germany, and Italy, 20 May 1882 209

B. The Anglo-Japanese Alliance, 30 January 1902 213

C. Declaration between the United Kingdom and France Respecting Egypt and Morocco, 8 April 1904 217

D. The Second Anglo-Japanese Agreement, 12 August 1905 221

E. Conventions between Russia and the United Kingdom Relating to Persia, Afghanistan, and Tibet, 31 August 1907 225

Index 229

Figures and Tables

Figure 1.1	The prisoner's dilemma	13
Figure 1.2	The chain store paradox	15

Table 3.1	The great powers in 1901	69
Table 3.2	Review of chapter findings	88
Table 4.1	The great powers during the First Moroccan Crisis (1905)	98
Table 4.2	Review of chapter findings	122
Table 5.1	The great powers during the Bosnia-Herzegovina Crisis (1908)	132
Table 5.2	Review of chapter findings	148
Table 6.1	The great powers during the Agadir Crisis (1911)	161
Table 6.2	Review of chapter findings	179
Table 7.1	Summary of results	187
Table 7.2	A reputation theory of conflict initiation (where states A and B are allies and states A and C are adversaries)	192

Acknowledgments

This book is the product of many years of work. The argument began as a seminar paper for Randall Schweller's International Security course at The Ohio State University, evolved into a dissertation, was sounded out early on in a journal article, "Hypotheses on Reputation: Alliance Choices and the Shadow of the Past," *Security Studies* 12, no. 3 (Spring 2003), 40–78, and is now being published as a book. As a result, I owe a great deal of gratitude to everyone who had a hand in its making in one form or another. To begin with, I am forever indebted to the faculty and to my classmates at The Ohio State University. The people who had the most direct influence on this project in its early stages are an intellectually diverse yet valuable group of advisers. John Guilmartin profoundly enhanced my appreciation for history. I hope that the history presented in this book lives up to the high standards of his own work. John Mueller pushed me the most conceptually, but in doing so he challenged me to think about my objectives, and I have no doubt that this resulted in a much better product. Alex Thompson was and continues to be an amazing resource, providing advice on nearly every paragraph I wrote (and today on the academic profession in general). Finally, Randy Schweller was the single greatest influence on how I research, write, and think about international relations. In sum, this product exists in large part because of the valuable contributions of each of these individuals.

In addition, Jonathan Mercer was a discussant on a conference panel at which I presented a very early draft of the original seminar paper. Despite my argument being, and remaining, somewhat critical of his own work on reputation, his constructive comments were encouraging at a time when

I had doubts about going forward with the project. For much the same reason, I owe a debt of gratitude to Benjamin Frankel, the editor of *Security Studies*, as well as the reviewers who provided tremendous feedback on that early article and who confirmed that there was some validity to my work on reputation.

More recently, I thank Roger Haydon of Cornell University Press for being an advocate for this book from the beginning and displaying a great deal of patience with me. I also thank the series editors, Robert Art, Robert Jervis, and Stephen Walt, who offered excellent feedback, and the anonymous reviewers whose input dramatically improved the final product. One reviewer in particular read two different versions of the manuscript, and I am extremely grateful for his or her willingness to devote time and energy to the book. I am also extremely grateful for the work of Susan Specter, the manuscript editor at Cornell University Press, and Katy Meigs, the copy editor.

I thank Eric Heinze for being a good friend during my time at the University of Oklahoma, and I thank Keith Gaddie for proofreading nearly every page of the manuscript and offering suggestions and continued encouragement on several of my research projects. I also want to thank the Department of Political Science at the University of Oklahoma for reminding me that states are not the only actors that renege on commitments and fail to follow through on promises.

More important, I thank my family, to whom I dedicate this book. My parents, Dan and Sue, have always pushed me to reach my academic potential. They continue to provide me with invaluable stability and encouragement and are a source of unending support. Finally, I thank my daughter, Brooke, who gives me endless joy and who reminds me on a daily basis what is really important in life.

The Shadow of the Past

1

Alliances and Reputation in International Relations

Worry more about your character than your reputation. Character is what you are, reputation merely what others think you are.

DALE CARNEGIE/JOHN WOODEN

It is widely accepted in business that a positive reputation is a valuable commodity, both for individuals and for firms, and there is significant evidence to support this view. Individual reputations, often measured in the form of a credit report, influence whether someone will qualify for a loan, an apartment, or sometimes even a job. Similarly, firms value good reputations as a way to attract top employees, charge premium prices for products, and preserve customer loyalty. After one partner at an accounting firm was found to have taken bribes, the *Wall Street Journal* reported that "the nation's 11th-largest accounting firm is having problems obtaining new clients and partners, retaining current clients, and keeping its executive suite intact. . . . The firm's travail illustrates the pressures on a professional firm—whether it be in accounting, law, architecture or another field—when its reputation is threatened."[1] Reputations have become so important in business that in many industries the concept of public relations has been replaced with reputation management. A logical question to ask, and the one addressed in this book, is whether reputations are as valuable for states in international politics as they are for firms in the marketplace.

1. *Wall Street Journal*, 4 April 1986, cited in Keith Weigelt and Colin Camerer, "Reputation and Corporate Strategy: A Review of Recent Theory and Applications," *Strategic Management Journal* 9, no. 5 (September/October 1988), 450.

The Puzzle

National political leaders have traditionally believed that reputations matter. Monarchs such as Louis XIV and Philip II saw a direct connection between their reputation and the power of the state. The historian Geoffrey Parker writes, "The rulers of every European state believed that to 'lose face,' whether by failing to make good a claim or through military defeat, damaged their international standing."[2] Similarly, U.S. leaders during both the Cuban Missile Crisis and the Vietnam War believed that a failure to stand up to the Soviet Union would weaken U.S. reliability in the eyes of its European allies and potentially weaken the North Atlantic Treaty Organization (NATO). Dean Rusk and Robert McNamara, President John F. Kennedy's secretaries of state and defense respectively, believed that the loss of South Vietnam to Communism would destroy the Southeast Asia Treaty Organization (SEATO) as well as undermine the credibility of other U.S. commitments.[3] And according to the presidential biographer Robert Dallek, after a 1961 visit to South Vietnam, Vice President Lyndon Johnson believed that "if we did not make 'a major effort to help these countries defend themselves' . . . it would signal to the world that we 'don't live up to our treaties and don't stand by our friends.' "[4] Johnson's beliefs not only ensured U.S. involvement in Vietnam for the rest of the decade but contributed to the expansion of the U.S. commitment in Southeast Asia.

Likewise, international relations scholars have generally accepted the value of a state having a positive reputation: much of the deterrence literature relies on the idea that a reputation for resolve is necessary for preventing war;[5] game theorists typically assume that reputation can be manipulated;[6] and regime scholars emphasize how a state's reputation

2. Geoffrey Parker, "The Making of Strategy in Habsburg Spain: Philip II's 'Bid for Mastery,' 1556–1598," in *The Making of Strategy: Rulers, States, and War,* ed. Williamson Murray, MacGregor Knox, and Alvin Bernstein (New York: Cambridge University Press, 1994), 126; also see Parker, *The Grand Strategy of Philip II* (New Haven: Yale University Press, 1998).

3. "1961 Rusk-McNamara Report to Kennedy on South Vietnam," *The Pentagon Papers* (New York: Bantam Books for the *New York Times,* 1971), 150.

4. Cited in Robert Dallek, *The American Style of Foreign Policy: Cultural Politics and Foreign Affairs* (New York: Oxford University Press, 1983), 232–233. Also see Robert McNamara, *In Retrospect: The Tragedy and Lessons of Vietnam* (New York: Vintage, 1996).

5. Thomas Schelling, *Arms and Influence* (New Haven: Yale University Press, 1966); Patrick Morgan, "Saving Face for the Sake of Deterrence," in *Psychology and Deterrence,* ed. Robert Jervis, Richard Ned Lebow, and Janice Gross Stein (Baltimore: Johns Hopkins University Press, 1985), 125–152; Barry Nalebuff, "Rational Deterrence in an Imperfect World," *World Politics* 43, no. 3 (April 1991), 313–335.

6. Richard Selten, "Chain Store Paradox," *Theory and Decision* 9, no. 2 (April 1978), 127–159; David Kreps and Robert Wilson, "Reputation and Imperfect Information," *Journal of Economic Theory* 27, no. 2 (August 1982), 253–279.

influences its ability to form and preserve international institutions.[7] Other scholars adopt the view that reputations are valuable and suggest using them to explain various aspects of international relations, such as the effects of hegemonic stability,[8] as well as attempts by states to develop successful policies against terrorism.[9]

Today there is a growing challenge to the conventional wisdom held by policymakers and academics regarding reputation. Relying on sociopsychology, Jonathan Mercer claims that allies always perceive one another to be irresolute, whereas enemies always perceive one another to be resolved. He concludes that because states cannot change their reputations, they should never go to war out of concern for developing or preserving a reputation.[10] Other scholars are similarly critical of reputation. Making an argument related to Mercer's, that commitments are independent of each other rather than interdependent, George Downs and Michael Jones contend that reputation has a weaker effect on treaty compliance than is commonly assumed.[11] Daryl Press argues that the credibility of a threat made during a crisis is shaped more by power and interests than by the prior behavior of a state.[12] Finally, Shiping Tang argues that reputations for resolve cannot form because of the anarchy that pervades the international system and that reputations are the result of what he refers to as a cult of reputation or—consistent with Mercer—a mistaken belief by policymakers that reputation matters more than it really does.[13]

This apparent disconnect between traditional assumptions and later findings leaves us with a lingering puzzle: Do reputations matter in international politics? If so, then it is important to understand how. If they do not matter, then the crucial question is, why not? In this book, I suggest that Mercer's findings, and those of other critics, though important, provide an incomplete picture of reputation. All of these critics focus on just one type

7. Robert Keohane, *After Hegemony: Cooperation and Discord in the World Political Economy* (Princeton: Princeton University Press, 1984).

8. James Alt, Randall Calvert, and Brian Humes, "Reputation and Hegemonic Stability: A Game-Theoretic Analysis," *American Political Science Review* 82, no. 2 (June 1988), 445–466.

9. J. L. Scott, "Deterring Terrorism through Reputation Building," in *Defense Spending and Economic Growth,* ed. James Payne and Anandi Sahu (Denver: Westview Press, 1993), 257–268; Claude Berrebi and Esteban Klor, "On Terrorism and Electoral Outcomes: Theory and Evidence from the Israeli-Palestinian Conflict," *Journal of Conflict Resolution* 50, no. 6 (December 2006), 899–925.

10. Jonathan Mercer, *Reputation and International Politics* (Ithaca: Cornell University Press, 1996).

11. George Downs and Michael Jones, "Reputation, Compliance, and International Law," *Journal of Legal Studies* 31, no. 1 (January 2002), S95–S114.

12. Daryl Press, *Calculating Credibility: How Leaders Assess Military Threats* (Ithaca: Cornell University Press, 2005).

13. Shiping Tang, "Reputation, Cult of Reputation, and International Conflict," *Security Studies* 14, no. 1 (October 2005), 34–62.

of reputation: that for resolve or credibility. Yet states, like firms, have many different kinds of reputations, and an emphasis on *resolve* fails to account for other reputations that should still concern states even if the critics are correct. My contention is that states perceived to be *reliable* allies—a different reputation from being resolute adversaries—will have greater freedom of action in choosing their alliance partners and in the design of their alliances than states perceived to be unreliable allies. In particular, I suggest that a state's reputation influences alliances in two general ways. As a state is perceived to be more reliable, not only will it have to give up less autonomy to attract an ally but its allies will give up more of their own autonomy to be in an alliance with it. Alternatively, as a state becomes less reliable, its allies will wish to retain more autonomy while demanding that more constraints are placed on the less reliable state.

This book specifically focuses on a state's reputation for reliability for three reasons. First, most critical work on reputation focuses on credibility, or resolve, defined as a state's willingness to follow through on its threats. Although scholars claim to test the effect of reputation on states, they often ignore the importance of other types of reputations, such as a state's willingness to honor its promises. So this book examines a different type of reputation from most of the existing literature. Second, a state's reputation for reliability closely approximates the types of reputations desired by firms. Since my hypotheses are all derived from the business literature, reliability provides the most valid test of those hypotheses. Finally, a better understanding of reliability helps us fill some of the holes in our existing theories of alliance behavior, specifically related to the formation, termination, and variation of alliances.

Theories of Reputation

The concept of reputation has garnered attention in several disciplines, including anthropology and sociology. But it receives the most significant treatment in the business literature. As a result, it is useful to point out how reputation is dealt with there before discussing its role in the international relations literature. The business literature also provides me with my hypotheses, which I discuss in chapter 2.

Reputation and Business

Corporations readily understand the value of a good reputation: economic actors profit from having positive reputations and suffer from negative ones. Adam Smith alluded to reputation by suggesting that cooperation occurs because of repeated interactions. For him, actors in the market must be concerned with dishonest behavior translating into a loss of future profits, because any cheating that is detected or even perceived will have negative effects on business.[14] If true, actors will do all they can to at least maintain the appearance of honesty. More recently, Douglas Diamond and Steven Sharpe examined how reputations enforce nonbinding contracts in debt markets.[15] Similarly, Benjamin Klein and Keith Leffler focused on the importance of reputation for assuring product quality and found that a reputation for quality allows firms to earn rents on their reputation, basically enabling them to charge higher prices than firms without a positive reputation.[16]

Perhaps the best example of reputation at the microeconomic level is a person's credit report. Credit reports are used by banks, employers, and landlords to determine who is worthy of a loan, job, or apartment. In essence, credit reports are used to gauge a person's financial reputation. They show the prior economic behavior of an individual and are used to predict that person's future reliability. Individuals with good credit are more likely to get the loan, the job, and the apartment than those with poor credit.

Investors and consumers use similar concepts to evaluate corporations and their products. Stock reports exist to provide investors with information about how a stock performed in the past. Companies with a steady history, or with rising value, are preferred investments; they are more likely to have secure futures, and thus they attract greater amounts of capital. Similarly, companies with falling stock value lose money in the market, often because of prior actions.

Since 1983 *Fortune* magazine has conducted an annual "corporate reputation survey" that ranks the reputations of companies across sixty industries. One analysis of the stock market, taking into consideration a company's placement in either the top ten or the bottom ten of *Fortune*'s rankings, indicates that stocks provide a higher rate of return for those companies in the top ten than for the market average. In addition, stocks for companies in the bottom ten tend to return at lower rates than the market average (and in many cases lose value).[17] These results suggest that reputation is a good

14. Adam Smith, *Lecture on Jurisprudence,* ed. Ronald Meek, David Raphael, and Peter Stein (New York: Oxford University Press, 1978 [1790]).

15. Douglas Diamond, "Reputation Acquisition in Debt Markets," *Journal of Political Economy* 97, no. 4 (August 1989), 828–862; Steven Sharpe, "Asymmetric Information, Bank Lending and Implicit Contracts: A Stylized Model of Customer Relationships," *Journal of Finance* 45, no. 4 (September 1990), 1069–1087.

16. Benjamin Klein and Keith Leffler, "The Role of Market Forces in Assuring Contractual Performance," *Journal of Political Economy* 89, no. 4 (August 1981), 615–641. Also see Carl Shapiro, "Premiums for High Quality as Returns to Reputations," *Quarterly Journal of Economics* 98, no. 4 (November 1983), 659–680.

17. Roger Vergin, "Corporate Reputation and the Stock Market," *Business Horizons* 41, no. 1 (January/February 1998), 19–26. In a similar study, Keith Chauvin and James Guthrie analyzed stock market reactions to firms being placed on the list of the best employers for working mothers, published by *Working Mothers* magazine. They found that market returns on those firms are higher than the predicted returns on the day the list is published. Keith Chauvin and James Guthrie, "Labor Market Reputation and the Value of the Firm," *Managerial and Decision Economics* 15, no. 6 (November/December 1994), 550.

indicator of performance, or at minimum that investors pay attention to those companies with positive reputations.

While a corporate reputation is difficult to quantify, it is widely believed among scholars and corporate officers that companies gain numerous benefits for having a positive reputation, ranging from higher profits to better employees, or even greater freedom to take risks. The business scholar Charles Fombrun outlines seven such benefits—what he refers to as reputational capital—that firms receive for having a good reputation. He finds that well-regarded companies generally

- entice top recruits to apply for positions;
- experience greater loyalty from consumers and employers;
- face fewer risks of crisis;
- are given greater latitude to act by their constituents;
- command premium prices for their products;
- pay lower prices for purchases; and
- have more stable revenues.[18]

Other scholars identify different benefits of a favorable reputation, such as enhanced access to capital markets and greater attraction for investors.[19]

It is clear that business scholars follow the conventional wisdom that reputation matters. Does the same wisdom apply to international relations? One critical point is whether it is valid to compare corporate reputations with state reputations. Several studies already apply economic analogies to international politics. According to Kenneth Waltz, the domains of states and markets are structurally similar and therefore allow for the application of analogy.[20] Moreover, those in business frequently draw comparisons between corporate competition and war.[21] However, there are potential

18. Charles Fombrun, *Reputation: Realizing Value from the Corporate Image* (Boston: Harvard Business School Press, 1996), 73.

19. Randolph Beatty and Jay Ritter, "Investment Banking, Reputation, and Underpricing of Initial Public Offerings," *Journal of Financial Economics* 15, no. 1–2 (January/February 1986), 213–232; Paul Milgrom and John Roberts, "Relying on the Information of Interested Parties" *RAND Journal of Economics* 17, no. 1 (Spring 1986), 18–32. Also see Charles Fombrun and Mark Shanley, "What's in a Name?: Reputation Building and Corporate Strategy," *Academy of Management Journal* 33, no. 2 (June 1990), 233; Paul Milgrom and John Roberts, "Price and Advertising Signals of Product Quality" *Journal of Political Economy* 94, no. 4 (August 1986), 796–821; Klein and Leffler, "Role of Market Forces"; George Stigler, "Information in the Labor Market," *Journal of Political Economy* 70, no. 5 (October 1962), 94–105.

20. Kenneth Waltz, *Theory of International Politics* (New York: McGraw-Hill, 1979), 89–99. See also Robert Gilpin, *War and Change in World Politics* (New York: Cambridge University Press, 1981); Robert Keohane, "The Demand for International Regimes," *International Organization* 36, no. 2 (Spring 1982), 325–355.

21. Alan Axelrod, *Patton on Leadership: Strategic Lessons for Corporate Warfare* (Paramus, NJ: Prentice Hall, 2001); Gerald Michaelson and Steven Michaelson, *Sun Tzu Strategies for*

problems in applying economic analogies to international relations, particularly in dealing with the concept of reputation.

For one thing, nothing in international politics is comparable to a credit report. States cannot evaluate the past behavior of other actors as easily as economic actors can. In addition, economic transactions occur much more frequently than political actions. A company interacts with its customers every time a product is purchased or used, and this occurs more often than states interact with one another.

However, one could argue that if a company has thousands of customers, it can afford to alienate one or two, whereas the loss of one or two allies because of bad practices can be extremely damaging to a state's security. Every state action should be very important precisely because the number of actors and interactions is limited in international politics. Thus, if reputation matters at all, it should visibly influence the behavior of states.

Another problem has to do with the difference between firms and states as each operates within its own environment. The political scientist Duncan Snidal points out two important distinctions. The first is that firms can be eliminated by competition in the market, but the destruction of a state is rare. In addition, he suggests that outcomes in the market are evaluated according to systemic properties, while "international systems are evaluated fundamentally in terms of the impact they have on individual states."[22] What he means is that we tend to evaluate markets as a whole, such as the Dow Jones industrial average or other market indices, when evaluating the health of an economy, whereas the health of the international political system is usually measured in terms of stability (or the absence of war between the great powers). Although Snidal is correct about the differences, they are not critical enough to abandon the analogy. For one thing, states may not often be destroyed, but when security breaks down, people lose their lives. Corporate eliminations are more common but rarely result in fatalities. So, while the likelihood of elimination is lower for states, it is balanced by the greater consequence of such events.[23] Second, alliances are a collection of states, just as a market index is a collection of corporate stock prices. Therefore, at least in this respect, alliances are similar enough to the market to make comparisons worthwhile.

Winning the Marketing War: 12 Essential Principles for Winning the War for Customers (New York: McGraw-Hill, 2003); Kenneth Allard, *Business as War: Battling for Competitive Advantage* (Hoboken, NJ: Wiley, 2003).

22. Duncan Snidal, "The Game Theory of International Politics," *World Politics* 38, no. 1 (October 1985), 25–57.

23. Tanisha Fazal contends that state death depends on political geography and the growing norm against conquest, present since 1945, but asserts that state death is more common than generally assumed. Tanisha Fazal, *State Death: The Politics and Geography of Conquest, Occupation, and Annexation* (Princeton: Princeton University Press, 2007).

The political scientist Bruce Russett suggests that "to compare a certain kind of market situation . . . with a particular real-world international system is sure to involve major simplifications and even distortions." But he then says that "no comparison of two situations is ever strictly comparable; no man steps twice into the same river. The European balance of power in 1890 was not the same as in 1905, though that fact has not prevented historians and political scientists from drawing or applying some general principles to both."[24]

In the end, whether the analogy is appropriate depends, as with all uses of analogy, on the question being asked. For my purposes, I have shown that a firm's reputation has value, even in a realm where contracts are legally binding and actors have legal recourse for inappropriate action. As Keith Weigelt and Colin Camerer contend, reputations are important not just because of repeated interaction, as Adam Smith believed, but because information about an actor's preferences and intentions is often incomplete.[25] Similar conditions of uncertainty exist in the anarchic international political system. Kenneth Abbott and Duncan Snidal suggest that "in domestic societies, legal commitments are credible because aggrieved parties can enforce them, with the power of the state if necessary. [But] even 'hard' international law falls short of this standard."[26] Similarly, Hans Morgenthau claimed that the "rules of international law embodied in general treaties must often be vague and ambiguous, allowing all the signatories to read the recognition of their own national interests into the legal text agreed upon."[27] It is logical to presume, then, that reputation should matter more in international politics than it does in the market, since there is little else to enforce international agreements.

Ultimately, however, it is an empirical question, and if reputation does matter in international relations, then we should see certain behavior when a state is perceived to be a reliable ally that we would not see when it is perceived to be unreliable. Under conditions of anarchy and uncertainty, which define international politics, the best way to predict an actor's future behavior is based on its past actions. If a state has a reputation for always coming to the aid of an ally, its promises will be more believable than those of a state that has failed to honor its prior commitments. As such, it will have an easier time attracting allies and preserving its autonomy. On the other hand, states that have reneged on past commitments will have difficulty finding

24. Bruce Russett, ed., *Economic Theories of International Politics* (Chicago: Markham, 1968), 8.

25. Weigelt and Camerer, "Reputation and Corporate Strategy," 447.

26. Kenneth Abbott and Duncan Snidal, "Hard and Soft Law in International Governance," *International Organization* 54, no. 3 (Summer 2000), 42.

27. Hans Morgenthau, *Politics among Nations: The Struggle for Power and Peace,* brief edition, rev. Kenneth Thompson. (Boston: McGraw-Hill, 1993 [1948]), 260.

reliable allies, or at least they will have to pay greater costs or give up more concessions to make themselves an acceptable ally.

Reputation and International Relations

The connection between reputation and politics is not new. Thucydides and Machiavelli both believed that reputation was a crucial element of leadership. Machiavelli dealt directly with the benefits of a good reputation and the consequences of a bad one, illustrating two different types of reputation—resolve and reliability. In *The Discourses* he discusses resolve, writing, "If you yield to a threat, you do so in order to avoid war, and more often than not, you do not avoid war. . . . On the other hand, you will find your supporters growing cooler towards you, since they will look upon you as weak and pusillanimous."[28] In this, he implies that appearing resolute is beneficial, not only because it is more likely to deter war but also because it reassures allies about one's willingness to follow through on threats.

In *The Prince* he contends that reliability is also important for both allies and adversaries: "A prince is also respected when he is a true friend and a true enemy; that is, when he declares himself to the side of one prince against another without any reservation. . . . If you do not declare your intentions, you will always be the prey of the victor . . . because whoever wins does not want reluctant allies who would not assist him in times of adversity; and whoever loses will not give you refuge since you were unwilling to run the risk of coming to his aid."[29] He implies here that it is better for a state to honor its commitments and lose a war than to stand on the sidelines and lose its reputation.[30]

In the modern period, reputation has been a critical component of many international relations studies, such as that by James Alt, Randall Calvert, and Brian Humes, who discuss the importance of a hegemon maintaining its reputation.[31] Early scholarship on international regimes by Robert Keohane also accepted reputation as an important component of the development and maintenance of international institutions. He wrote: "The dilemmas of collective action are partially solved through the device of reputation. . . .

28. Niccolò Machiavelli, *The Discourses* (London: Penguin, 1998 [1531]), 313.

29. Niccolò Machiavelli, *The Prince* (Oxford: Oxford University Press, 1979 [1532]), 75.

30. The concept of reputation has also been applied to American politics. Richard Neustadt argues that professional reputation is one of the three requirements of a successful president. David Romero examines the benefits of a politician's reputation during elections. Richard Neustadt, *Presidential Power: The Politics of Leadership* (New York: John Wiley, 1960); David Romero, "The Case of the Missing Reciprocal Influence: Incumbent Reputation and the Vote," *Journal of Politics* 58, no. 4 (November 1996), 1198–1207.

31. James Alt, Randall Calvert, and Brian Humes, "Reputation and Hegemonic Stability A Game-Theoretic Analysis," *American Political Science Review* 82, no. 2 (June 1988), 445–466.

As long as a continuing series of issues is expected to arise in the future, and as long as actors monitor each other's behavior and discount the value of agreements on the basis of past compliance, having a good reputation is valuable even to the egoist whose role in collective activity is so small that she would bear few of the costs of her own malefactions."[32]

But reputation typically played the largest role in the study of deterrence. There are three requirements for deterrence to be successful, according to much of the literature: communication, credibility, and the interdependence of commitments.[33] Deterrence depends on the defender signaling to another state that the cost of attacking outweighs any potential benefits. Sending a signal to an adversary communicates the state's intention to retaliate for an attack and thus raises the costs of attacking. The range of possible commitments a state can make run from the relatively costless statement by a leader to signing a formal agreement or even positioning military forces in a way that makes one's intentions obvious. States do not always honor their commitments,[34] but for deterrence to exist, much less for it to be effective, a commitment must be communicated. Moreover, as Robert Jervis and James Fearon both argue, costly signals reveal more about a state's intentions than do cheap signals.[35]

Signaling is also a means of tying one's reputation to a commitment. Deterrence scholars believe that a state that signals its interest in honoring a commitment risks losing its reputation if it backs down. The economist and

32. Keohane, *After Hegemony*, 105.

33. See Thomas Schelling, *The Strategy of Conflict* (Cambridge: Harvard University Press, 1960); Schelling, *Arms and Influence;* Alexander George and Richard Smoke, *Deterrence in American Foreign Policy: Theory and Practice* (New York: Columbia University Press, 1974); Patrick Morgan, "Saving Face for the Sake of Deterrence," in Jervis, Lebow, and Stein, *Psychology and Deterrence*, 125–152,; Alexander George and Richard Smoke, "Deterrence and Foreign Policy," *World Politics* 41, no. 2 (January 1989), 170–182.

34. Evidence concerning how often states do honor their commitments is mixed. Alan Ned Sabrosky, "Interstate Alliances: Their Reliability and the Expansion of War," in *The Correlates of War II: Testing Some Realpolitik Models*, ed. J. David Singer (New York: Free Press, 1980), 161–198; and Brett Ashley Leeds, Andrew Long, and Sara McLaughlin Mitchell, "Reevaluating Alliance Reliability: Specific Threats, Specific Promises," *Journal of Conflict Resolution* 44, no. 5 (October 2000), 686–699.

35. Robert Jervis, *The Logic of Images in International Relations* (New York: Columbia University Press, 1970); James Fearon, "Domestic Political Audiences and the Escalation of International Disputes," *American Political Science Review* 88, no. 3 (September 1994), 577–592. Anne Sartori takes a more optimistic view of "cheap talk." Anne Sartori, "The Might of the Pen: A Reputational Theory of Communication in International Disputes," *International Organization* 56, no. 1 (Winter 2002), 121–149. Jeong-Yoo Kim's study of pretrial negotiations similarly suggests that when repeated interaction is likely, concern about reputation makes even so-called cheap talk meaningful: "If the players are concerned about their reputation, cheap talk cannot be taken as meaningless even in a game where the interests of the players are so conflicting that cheap talk would be meaningless if they met only once." Jeong-Yoo Kim, "Cheap Talk and Reputation in Repeated Pretrial Negotiation," *RAND Journal of Economics* 27, no. 4 (Winter 1996), 788.

political scientist Thomas Schelling stated, "A potent means of commitment, and sometimes the only means, is the pledge of one's reputation."[36] However, signaling a commitment is a necessary but not sufficient condition for deterrence to work. A second requirement is that the commitment must be credible, and much of deterrence theory is predicated on states needing to develop a strong reputation in order to deter future attacks. As Barry Nalebuff suggests, "one primary component of communication is the use of reputation. . . . The cost-benefit calculation that leads to certain behavior in the present reflects on how one will act in future cases."[37] Therefore, the defender must convince the other side that it has not only the ability but also the will to punish aggression. This is often referred to as resolve. Deterrence scholars argue that if a state fails to punish an aggressor, its reputation will suffer. As a result, its future deterrent threats will be less believable, since a reputation for being irresolute makes its commitments less credible. This is evident in Jervis's claim that "deterrence theory . . . assumes that states are—and should be—terribly concerned about their reputations for living up to their commitments. . . . If a state defaults on one commitment, other states will be less likely to believe it in the future."[38]

Finally, Franklin Weinstein asserts "that the deterrence theorists think of commitments in terms of the maintenance of the principle that all commitments must be kept is manifest from their position on the interdependence of commitments."[39] He implies that deterrence depends on the previous behavior of the state. If it stood its ground in past crises, having that reputation for resolve will increase the credibility of its future deterrent threats. However, the concept goes beyond that to suggest that a state's actions in one case signal its resolve in all future cases, regardless of any differences that exist from one case to the next. This was a critical component of U.S. foreign policy during the cold war and is an important assumption concerning reputation. As Schelling asserted, "the main reason why we [the United States] are committed in many of these places is that our threats are interdependent. Essentially we tell the Soviets that we have to react here because, if we did not, they would not believe us when we say that we will react there."[40]

Some scholars have tried to evaluate the validity of this assumption. For instance, Paul Huth, Christopher Gelpi, and Scott Bennett claim that "previous capitulation by either the challenger or defender appears to be a sign of

36. Schelling, *Strategy of Conflict*, 29.

37. Nalebuff, "Rational Deterrence," 315.

38. Robert Jervis, "Introduction: Approach and Assumptions," in Jervis, Lebow, and Stein, *Psychology and Deterrence*, 9.

39. Franklin Weinstein, "The Concept of a Commitment in International Relations," *Journal of Conflict Resolution* 13, no. 1 (March 1969), 46.

40. Schelling, *Arms and Influence*, 55.

general weakness on their part."[41] Whereas this general weakness may or may not affect the behavior of other states, deterrence scholars and policymakers alike have traditionally feared the negative effects that accompany such a reputation, just as firms fear a decline in their corporate reputations.[42]

As a result of these three components of deterrence—communication, credibility, and the interdependence of commitments—the conventional wisdom among the majority of deterrence scholars is that reputation is critical. As Schelling put it: "This kind of 'face' [a state's reputation for action] is one of the few things worth fighting over."[43] If a state threatens war to defend itself or to defend others, it must follow through on its threat or else its resolve will be called into question when it makes future threats. The implication of this is that states might have to wage war in the present to prevent larger wars in the future.

Reputation and Game Theory

One area that also deserves some attention is game theory because it incorporates reputation into many of its models. One historical problem with the game-theoretic use of reputation, as Mercer points out, is that it makes the same mistakes as the deterrence scholars by treating the importance of reputation as a given, rather than testing the concept itself.[44] Despite this failing, the logic behind the game-theoretic view of reputation is important for the development of any study in which reputation is a central theme.

Every repeated game assumes that actors develop reputations over time and, more important, that these reputations influence the behavior of other actors. For example, in the "chicken" game actors have an interest in not backing down so that others will be forced to back down.[45] Two models in particular are relevant for studying reputation in game theory as it relates to international politics: the prisoner's dilemma (PD) and the chain store

41. Paul Huth, Christopher Gelpi, and Scott Bennett, "The Escalation of Great Power Militarized Disputes: Testing Rational Deterrence Theory and Structural Realism," *American Political Science Review* 87, no.3 (September 1993), 618.

42. Jonathan Mercer in particular denies that commitments are interdependent and suggests instead that they are *independent* of one another. If so, this means that one's willingness to back down in a particular situation would not necessarily signal a similar willingness to back down elsewhere.

43. Schelling, *Arms and Influence,* 124.

44. Mercer, *Reputation and International Politics,* 28–42.

45. The chicken game is described as follows: "Two drivers race down the center of a road from opposite directions. If one swerves and the other does not, then the first will suffer the stigma of being known as a chicken (CD) while the second will enjoy being known as the hero (DC). If neither swerves, both will suffer grievously in the ensuing collision (DD). If both swerve, damage to the reputation of each will be limited (CC)." Kenneth Oye, "Explaining Cooperation under Anarchy: Hypotheses and Strategies," in *Cooperation under Anarchy,* ed. Kenneth Oye, (Princeton: Princeton University Press, 1986), 8.

		Player 2	
		C	D
Player 1	C	3, 3	0, 4
	D	4, 0	1, 1

Figure 1.1. The prisoner's dilemma

paradox. The PD is one of the most frequently used games in international relations, and like many games it simply assumes that reputation matters. In the traditional version of the game (illustrated in figure 1.1) players have an individual incentive to defect, which usually results in mutual defection even though that is the worst possible outcome for both players.[46]

The PD is analogous to the moment when an ally must decide whether to honor a commitment or not. Within an alliance, the information flowing between the partners is imperfect and asymmetric. There is a mutual benefit to cooperation, but there is also an incentive to defect, because honoring a commitment is potentially costly; it may mean getting involved in a war that results in a loss of lives and money.[47] To offset that risk, there must be some advantage or benefit to honoring a commitment. In a game with multiple turns, the benefit of a cooperative strategy comes from the development of a trustworthy reputation and the way in which that reputation influences the behavior of other players.

As we know from studies of the PD, players who have a long shadow of the future—who expect to repeatedly interact with each other—are more likely to cooperate because the repeated interaction allows both sides to generate expectations about how the other is likely to behave in the future.[48] Charles Lipson suggests that "not only does repetition permit players to make threats and commitments, it also makes reputation important—all the

46. The prisoner's dilemma is described as follows: "Two prisoners are suspected of a major crime. The authorities possess evidence to secure conviction on only a minor charge. If neither prisoner squeals, both draw a light sentence on the minor charge (CC). If one prisoner squeals and the other stonewalls, the rat will go free (DC) and the sucker will draw a very heavy sentence (CD). If both squeal, both will draw a moderate sentence (DD)." Oye, "Explaining Cooperation under Anarchy," 7.

47. Glenn Snyder, *Alliance Politics* (Ithaca: Cornell University Press, 1997).

48. Robert Axelrod, *The Evolution of Cooperation* (New York: Basic Books, 1984); Robert Jervis, "From Balance to Concert: A Study of International Security Cooperation," in Oye, *Cooperation under Anarchy,* 58–79; Duncan Snidal, "The Game Theory of International Politics," *World Politics* 38, no. 1 (October 1985), 25–57.

more so since there is no external guarantee that promises will be kept."[49] Therefore, the shadow of the future is important. However, whereas iteration may be a necessary condition for cooperation to emerge, it is not a sufficient condition—one can imagine a game in which both players are aware that the game will be played an infinite number of times. This will not produce cooperation unless information is public. In fact, infinitely played games in which one's actions will not be made public may lead to less cooperation, since there is no danger of other actors being made aware of defections, which means that punishment is unlikely. As such, another necessary condition for cooperation is information about prior behavior, because when information is public one can be held accountable for past actions. Therefore, reputation influences behavior, and this "shadow of the past" helps states mitigate some of the effects of uncertainty by developing expectations about the future behavior of one another.

A variation of the PD helps explain reputation further by altering the payoffs to make mutual cooperation more likely. In the story of the prisoner's dilemma the two suspects are held and questioned separately. If both suspects are virtual strangers having no shadow of the past or expecting little interaction in the future, they are unlikely to cooperate with each other, and both will suffer the effects of mutual defection. However, if both prisoners are members of an organized crime family, where defection is costly (death is often the punishment for being a "rat") and where cooperation has added benefits within the organization, then the prisoners are more likely to cooperate with each other and stay quiet. In other words, the criminal's behavior will create a reputation for being either a rat or a stand-up guy, and both reputations have consequences.

More generally, PD scenarios in international politics can be altered to make cooperation more likely. One way to do this is for each player to receive a secondary payoff for cooperation (representing the benefits of establishing or preserving a reputation for reliability). Another way is to reduce the gains from obtaining the sucker's payoff (defecting when the other player cooperates, akin to abandoning an ally in war). The possibility of defection still exists, especially if both actors are concerned about relative gains.[50] However, the likelihood of cooperation increases when there are

49. Charles Lipson, "International Cooperation in Economic and Security Affairs," *World Politics* 37, no. 1 (October 1984), 5.

50. For a discussion of absolute versus relative gains, see Michael Mastanduno, "Do Relative Gains Matter?: America's Response to Japanese Industrial Policy," *International Security* 16, no. 1 (Summer 1991), 73–113; Duncan Snidal, "Relative Gains and the Pattern of International Cooperation," *American Political Science Review* 85, no. 3 (September 1991), 701–726; Duncan Snidal, "International Cooperation among Relative Gains Maximizers," *International Studies Quarterly* 35, no. 4 (December 1991), 387–402; Robert Powell, "Absolute and Relative Gains in International Relations Theory," *American Political Science Review* 85, no. 4

secondary payoffs for cooperation and when one reduces the risk of being suckered and/or increases the cost of defecting. Therefore, when a game's time horizon is sufficiently long enough to allow reputations to form, and when the incentives to defect are offset by either the costs of losing one's reputation or by the advantages of mutual cooperation, then cooperation is more likely to occur.

In one experiment, Gordon Tullock complicated the PD in this way, by allowing subjects to choose their partners and communicate their results. He found that "if some individual player did . . . play a noncooperative strategy he would find it very difficult to get people to play with him in the future. Almost certainly, he would have to offer some side-payments until he had established something in the way of reputation."[51] This fits perfectly with two of the arguments that I test in this book: first, that an unreliable state will have difficulty attracting allies; second, that even though states with bad reputations may find allies, they will have to make some form of payment to attract and keep them.

Another game, which deals more directly with reputation, is the chain store paradox.[52] In this game (illustrated in figure 1.2), an established chain store, the incumbent, faces new entrants into a market, with each new competitor taking away business. Whenever a new competitor emerges, the chain store has the choice of cooperating (doing nothing) or fighting (undercutting the new challenger).

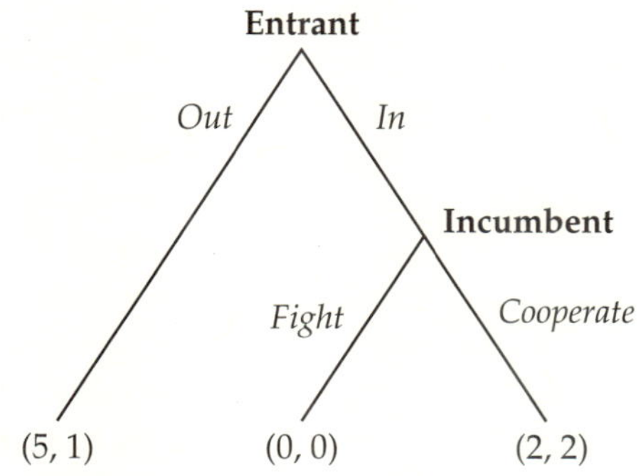

Figure 1.2. The chain store paradox

(December 1991), 1303–1320; James Morrow, "When Do 'Relative Gains' Impede Trade?" *Journal of Conflict Resolution* 41, no. 1 (February 1997), 12–37; Suzanne Werner, "In Search of Security: Relative Gains and Losses in Dyadic Relations," *Journal of Peace Research* 43, no. 3 (August 1997), 289–302.

51. Gordon Tullock, "Adam Smith and the Prisoners' Dilemma," *Quarterly Journal of Economics* 100, supplement (1985), 23.

52. Selten, "Chain Store Paradox," 127–159; Kreps and Wilson, "Reputation and Imperfect Information," 253–279.

According to the deductive logic of the game, when faced with a challenge, the chain store will always cooperate because it is the least costly option in the short-run. However, a chain store receives the greatest long-term profit when no challengers exist. If the chain store acts aggressively toward new entrants it will initially lose, but it will develop a tough reputation and prevent future competitors from entering the market. On the other hand, if the chain store acts cooperatively, it gains a soft reputation, which invites more competitors to enter the market, further reducing its profits. Therefore, the chain store will accept short-term losses to deter future competitors, because a tough reputation will provide it with greater profits in the long run. As Basil Yamey shows, firms adopt predatory pricing to eliminate existing rivals and also to signal their reaction to future entries, thus influencing the behavior of potential rivals.[53]

Although this game is more about earning a reputation for acting tough, comparable to resolve in the deterrence literature, the lessons learned from the game are applicable to other situations involving reputation. The most important lesson from this game (and the reason for the name "paradox") is that the psychological effect that one actor's reputation has on the behavior of other actors negates the logic of the scenario. In a one-shot game, the chain store would have no reason to undercut a competitor, because it would profit more from cooperation. But if reputation is relevant, the chain store will accept—in fact, prefer—short-term losses in order to gain more in the long run.[54] If comparable to international politics, then a state should accept the short-term costs of honoring an alliance commitment. This is especially true if there are long-term benefits associated with a reputation for reliability, such as greater freedom of action in making alliance decisions about which states to ally with and the design of alliances.

Critiques of Reputation

Several scholars have challenged the position that states should take actions to develop or preserve their reputation.[55] The first and still most significant of these critics is Jonathan Mercer, who challenges not only the deterrence

53. Basil Yamey, "Predatory Price Cutting: Notes and Comments," *Journal of Law and Economics* 15, no. 1 (April 1972), 129–142.

54. Patrick James attempted to use this concept in the political realm by applying it to Canadian politics. Patrick James, "The Chain Store Paradox and Constitutional Politics in Canada," *Journal of Theoretical Politics* 11, no. 1 (January 1999), 5–36.

55. Ted Hopf, *Peripheral Visions: Deterrence Theory and American Foreign Policy in the Third World, 1965–1990* (Ann Arbor: University of Michigan Press, 1994); Daryl Press, *Calculating Credibility: How Leaders Assess Military Threats* (Ithaca: Cornell University Press, 2005); George Downs and Michael Jones, "Reputation, Compliance, and International Law," *Journal of Legal Studies* 31, no. S1 (January 2002), S95–S114.

scholars' assumptions about the importance of reputation and the notion that commitments are interdependent but also the wisdom of a state basing its decisions on concerns about reputation.[56] Mercer's focus on sociopsychological factors is an important addition to the growing literature on reputation in international relations. He challenges the traditional view, largely on the basis that different actors assign different reputations during the same event and that decision makers, state motivations, and international structure all have a tendency to change. The implication of this is that the actions a state takes in one situation give little indication of how it will act in the future. In other words, for Mercer, a state's behavior is explained better by the situation, such as the state's strategic interests, than by its character or disposition.

By examining three crises from the early part of the twentieth century, Mercer finds that states cannot change their reputations—a state's allies will always see it as irresolute while its adversaries will always see it as resolute. As he claims, "even when observers used an ally's irresolution to explain its behavior, they did not expect their ally to be similarly irresolute in the future."[57] Therefore, he concludes that states should never go to war out of a concern for reputation, because doing so will not change anyone's mind. Not only does this invalidate many of the arguments made by deterrence theorists but it flies in the face of what policymakers historically have believed about reputation.

Mercer's critiques are a valuable step toward improving our understanding of reputation, but his analysis is incomplete. According to Mercer, failing to honor a commitment does not create a reputation for being unreliable unless such behavior causes other states to refuse alignment based on that unreliability: "Evidence that an observer believes a state behaved irresolutely . . . is not evidence that a reputation has formed. Only if the observer then expects the state to be irresolute in the future should we say that a reputation has formed."[58] This is an important point, and based on his three case studies, Mercer contends that reputations are not worth fighting for. However, by focusing on the nature of the alliances that form (rather than just whether or not they form), as well as how alliances change as a result of reputation, I contend that states do alter their behavior based on another state's reputation, but in ways that Mercer is unable to capture given his emphasis on resolve.

Mercer points out that not only do actors possess different types of reputations but that perceptions of these reputations vary from one actor to

56. Mercer, *Reputation and International Politics.*

57. Ibid., 228.

58. Jonathan Mercer, "Reputation and Rational Deterrence Theory," *Security Studies* 7, no. 1 (Fall 1997), 108.

another: "Because different people think differently about me, I can have different, even competing, reputations."[59] Mercer also makes the distinction between the threats made to an adversary (which may lead to a test of one's credibility or resolve) and the promises made to allies (which can test one's reliability or trustworthiness).[60] He is correct that reputations are gained in a number of different ways, and there are a variety of different types of reputation. The irony is that he fails to take this into account within his own work. Like earlier works on deterrence, he focuses exclusively on a state's reputation for resolve. From this, he concludes that reputations are not worth fighting for. However, if states have multiple reputations, then even if we accept Mercer's findings about the irrelevance of being resolute, it is conceivable that other types of reputations *are* worth fighting for.

While Mercer's focus is on resolve, he does make claims about how a state's reputation influences its alliances. For example, he writes that "although the Algeciras defeat influenced German policy-makers in many ways, it did not lead them to put more faith in their Austrian ally. Because they made situational explanations for Austrian support in 1906, they should not—and did not—credit the Austrians as reliable allies in 1908. This reaction . . . illustrates one of my four propositions: allies rarely get reputations for having resolve."[61] Yet a critical element that Mercer ignores is that when we compare this to German attitudes toward its other ally, Italy, which sided with France at Algeciras, we see very different behavior corresponding to the different levels of support.

Mercer also claims that "victory in war does not guarantee a reputation for resolve—especially among those who are strongly motivated to view a state as irresolute."[62] However, this misses the point. Whether victorious or not, a reputation for reliability forms when a state goes to war to honor a commitment to its ally. And, if commitments are interdependent, then, all else being equal, a state that has honored prior commitments and therefore has a reputation for being reliable will be a more attractive ally than one perceived to be unreliable.

Understandably, Mercer's critique of the conventional wisdom has itself come under fire from some scholars. In one review, Dale Copeland suggests that Mercer fails to explain why states are labeled as an ally or adversary in the first place (which Copeland attributes to reputation).[63] Mercer, though, dismisses this criticism, arguing that "unless one chooses an ally or an ad-

59. Mercer, *Reputation and International Politics*, 7.

60. Ibid. Schelling also discusses the differences between threats and promises. Schelling, *Strategy of Conflict*, 35–46; 175–178.

61. Mercer, *Reputation and International Politics*, 124.

62. Ibid., 220.

63. Dale Copeland, "Do Reputations Matter?" *Security Studies* 7, no. 1 (Autumn 1997), 55.

versary on the basis of its reputation for resolve . . . then the designation of ally or of adversary is unrelated to its reputation for resolve."[64] This very issue lies at the heart of my puzzle. Do states choose allies on the basis of their reputations? Nobody has addressed this question yet, and I suggest that if reputation matters it will have some bearing on a state's alliance choices.

Paul Huth's review of Mercer's work addresses the level-of-analysis problem in studies of reputation. Are reputations assigned to states or to leaders?[65] This is important because reputations assigned to states are conceivably more durable than those given to leaders. Even though a full assessment of the different levels of reputation is beyond the scope of this book, both states and leaders can get reputations, and any future study of reputation must at least acknowledge that fact.

Huth also asks how generalizable reputations are.[66] There are two issues here: whether reputations are based on the most recent case or on a pattern of behavior across time, and whether a state's reputation is applied dyadically, regionally, or globally. On the issue of measurement, Mercer bases his analysis on only the most recent situation. Though recent behavior may influence our perceptions more than actions in the more distant past, evidence from sociology suggests that "reputations are . . . based on accumulating patterns of evidence which societies constantly process and reprocess."[67] The business literature on reputation generally confirms this view.

As to the generalizability of reputation, the business literature is also useful here as a starting point. Keith Chauvin and James Guthrie's examination of how a firm's reputation for human resource management reduces the cost of labor turnover suggests that reputations are "global" because they send signals not only to those currently interacting with a firm but also to anyone who may interact in the future. Likewise, as Stewart Macaulay puts it, "not only do the particular business units in a given exchange want to deal with each other again, they also want to deal with other business units in the future. And the way one behaves in a particular transaction, or a series of transactions, will color his general business reputation."[68]

64. Mercer, "Reputation and Rational Deterrence Theory," 110.

65. Paul Huth, "Reputations and Deterrence: A Theoretical and Empirical Assessment," *Security Studies* 7, no. 1 (Autumn 1997), 78–80.

66. Ibid., 80–82.

67. Nicholas Emler, "A Social Psychology of Reputation," in *European Review of Social Psychology*, vol. 1, ed. Wolfgang Stroebe and Miles Hewstone (New York: John Wiley and Sons, 1990), 178.

68. Chauvin and Guthrie, "Labor Market Reputation," 543–552; Stewart Macaulay, "Non-Contractual Relations in Business: A Preliminary Study," *American Sociological Review* 28, no. 1 (February 1963), 64.

Finally, Huth suggests that states develop reputations for both a willingness to use force and for having an effective military.[69] The majority of existing works concentrate only on willingness, but focusing on the reliability of an ally is a way to incorporate both of these forms of reputation, because a state will be a better ally if it has an effective military as well as the will to use it. Daryl Press is another critic who tests reputation against capabilities and finds that capabilities are a more important determinant of state behavior.[70] But his work suffers from two significant weaknesses as a test of reputation. The first is that, like all the other critics of reputation, he limits his analysis to reputations for resolve. The second is that his analysis is restricted to crises, during which it could be argued that capabilities should be more important than reputation because of the greater likelihood of war. Although many of my cases also take place during crises, my concern is less about whether or not states honor their commitments than explaining the consequences of a state's behavior during a crisis or war. An advantage of focusing on reliability is that my findings not only contribute to the reputation debate but also fill gaps in the literature on military alliances.

Theories of Alliance Behavior

Alliances are one of the most studied aspects of international relations. As George Liska offers, "It is impossible to speak of international relations without referring to alliances."[71] However, despite the attention given to the subject, there are still large gaps in our understanding of several aspects of alliances. In applying reputation to the study of alliance behavior, I focus on three areas of the literature in which there are either gaps in our understanding or a lack of scholarly attention. These areas include the formation and termination of alliances and the institutional differences between alliances.

For the purposes of this book, I adopt the definition of military alliances used by Leeds et al.: "written agreements, signed by official representatives of at least two independent states, that include promises to aid a partner in the event of military conflict, to remain neutral in the event of conflict, to refrain from military conflict with one another, or to consult/cooperate in the event of international crises that create a potential for military conflict."[72] Although alliances are a type of international institution, scholars

69. Huth, "Reputations and Deterrence," 75–78.

70. Press, *Calculating Credibility*.

71. George Liska, *Nations in Alliance: The Limits of Interdependence* (Baltimore: Johns Hopkins University Press, 1962), 3.

72. Brett Ashley Leeds, Jeffrey M. Ritter, Sara McLaughlin Mitchell, and Andrew G. Long, "Alliance Treaty Obligations and Provisions, 1815–1944." *International Interactions* 28, no. 33 (January 2002), 237–260.

generally treat them separately from other types of institutions because of their potential effect on state security. States give up some sovereignty on joining any international institution, but alliances present states with unique risks and challenges, both because an alliance can embroil a state in conflicts it might otherwise avoid, and because allies may fail to live up to their commitments when a state is threatened. As a result, alliances are a significant part of the international relations literature; yet there are several gaps in our understanding of alliance behavior, some of which can be filled with a better understanding of reputation. For simplicity, I divide my discussion of the alliance literature into three categories: alliance formation, alliance termination, and alliance variation.

Alliance Formation

There are three fundamental questions regarding alliance formation: Why do states form alliances? How do states choose their partners? And when do states prefer neutrality over an alliance? To date the majority of work on alliance formation focuses on the first question. However, our understanding of alliances is incomplete because we cannot sufficiently explain how states choose their allies out of all the possible partners, nor can we explain why states sometimes choose to remain unaligned, distancing themselves from potential threats (though more work is now being done on the question of neutrality, or "underbalancing").[73] A closer examination of the literature reveals some of these weaknesses and also shows where reputation can improve our understanding of both the decision to form an alliance and the choice of a particular ally or a decision for neutrality.

Most explanations of alliance formation rely on a predominantly realist view of the international system, in which states form alliances to increase their military capabilities. The basic idea is that alliances combine the capabilities of states, thus making them more powerful—even if the capability of the alliance is less than the sum of the parts, each member of an alliance is more powerful for having an ally. As Alexander Groth and Richard Randall suggest, "states enter alliances in order to be stronger, safer, and generally better off presumably than they would be alone."[74] The classic theory fitting this perspective is that of balance of power, in which states form alliances to prevent another state from becoming too powerful.[75]

73. For an explanation of buck-passing or distancing behavior, see Randall Schweller, *Unanswered Threats: Political Constraints on the Balance of Power* (Princeton: Princeton University Press, 2006).

74. Alexander Groth and Richard Randall, "Alliance Pathology: Institutional Lessons of the 1930s," *Political Science Quarterly* 106, no. 1 (1991), 109–110.

75. Morgenthau, *Politics among Nations;* Edward Gulick, *Europe's Classical Balance of Power: A Case History of the Theory and Practice of One of the Great Concepts of European Statecraft* (New York: W. W. Norton, 1955); Inis Claude, *Power and International Relations* (New York:

Balance of power theory is criticized on a variety of fronts. For one thing, as many scholars point out, states often bandwagon, or align *with* the most powerful state in the system, as Italy did with Nazi Germany before the Second World War.[76] Similarly, states may align *with* threatening states to manage the threat.[77] Sometimes states even choose not to align at all, buck-passing or distancing themselves from a potential threat.[78] A bigger problem is that balancing theories tell us which states will be aligned against, but they say little about which states will make up the balancing coalition. This is where reputation can help. If states balance to improve their power or security, they will logically prefer to ally with other states that honor their commitments. If a state has multiple potential allies, all else being equal, it should prefer to ally with a state that is most likely to support it in a conflict and that is least likely to drag it into an unwanted conflict. In other words, if given a choice, states will prefer to ally with the most reliable state. If nobody is perceived to be reliable, then the state may prefer to bandwagon.

States will bandwagon, or ally with the most powerful state, for a variety of reasons, ranging from trying to avoid being attacked (Walt) to sharing the spoils of victory (Schweller).[79] But even this decision is subject to reputation, because, regardless of why a state bandwagons, if the more powerful state is itself unreliable, then buck-passing, or neutrality, may be preferable to incurring the costs and risks of forming any alliance.

Random House, 1962); Waltz, *Theory of International Politics;* Evan Luard, *The Balance of Power: The System of International Relations, 1648–1815* (New York: St. Martin's Press, 1992). Another theory based on a similar principle is balance of threat, in which states align against the most threatening state in the system rather than against the most powerful. Stephan Walt, *The Origins of Alliances* (Ithaca: Cornell University Press, 1987).

76. This is most commonly referred to as bandwagoning. Deborah Larson, "Bandwagon Images in American Foreign Policy: Myth or Reality?" in *Dominoes and Bandwagons,* ed. Robert Jervis and Jack Snyder (New York: Oxford University Press, 1991), 85–111; Paul Schroeder, "Historical Reality vs Neo-Realist Theory," *International Security* 19, no. 2 (Summer 1994), 108–148; Randall Schweller, *Deadly Imbalances: Tripolarity and Hitler's Strategy of World Conquest* (New York: Columbia University Press, 1998).

77. Paul Schroeder, "Alliances, 1815–1945: Weapons of Power and Tools of Management," in *Historical Dimensions of National Security Problems,* ed. Klaus Knorr (Lawrence: University of Kansas Press, 1976), 227–262; Patricia Weitsman, *Dangerous Alliances: Proponents of Peace, Weapons of War* (Stanford: Stanford University Press, 2004).

78. Thomas Christensen and Jack Snyder, "Chain Gangs and Passed Bucks: Predicting Alliance Patterns in Multipolarity," *International Organization* 44, no. 2 (Spring 1990), 137–168; Steven David, "Explaining Third World Alignment," *World Politics* 43, no. 2 (January 1991), 233–256; Eric Labs, "Do Weak States Bandwagon?" *Security Studies* 1, no. 3 (Spring 1992), 383–416; Robert Kaufman, " 'To Balance or to Bandwagon?': Alignment Decisions in 1930s Europe," *Security Studies* 1, no. 3 (Spring 1992), 417–447; John Mearsheimer, *The Tragedy of Great Power Politics* (New York: W. W. Norton, 2001), esp. 157–162.

79. Walt, *Origins of Alliances;* Randall Schweller, "Bandwagoning for Profit: Bringing the Revisionist State Back In," *International Security* 19, no. 1 (Summer 1994), 72–107.

Existing theories of alliance formation also have some difficulty explaining neutrality. One way this problem is addressed is by incorporating the value that states assign to their autonomy. Michael Altfeld points out that states form alliances at the expense of autonomy, and James Morrow builds on this to show that states value different levels of autonomy and security and that these preferences also change over time. This helps explain why some states prefer not to align—presumably because they value their autonomy more than any security gains they would receive from an ally.[80] However, it is difficult to determine a priori how each state assesses the relative value of security and autonomy and then chooses an optimum level of both. For one thing, it is not easy to identify how much autonomy states desire, nor can leaders always know how much autonomy their public will demand. More important for the purposes of this book, states cannot be certain about the amount of security they will gain from an alliance. Therefore, while the logic of the security-autonomy trade-off explains why states may in some cases prefer neutrality to an alliance, it cannot provide specific explanations either for alliance formation or for the selection of a particular ally.

Domestic factors may also influence a state's alliance choices. While not inconsistent with the security-autonomy view (since autonomy may be important for domestic reasons), the domestic-politics approach may help explain the particular partner choices of some states. It is a virtual law of politics that leaders want to stay in power, so if a domestic public has strong opinions, positive or negative, about a potential ally, leaders will consider those opinions when making alliance choices. Michael Barnett and Jack Levy argue that, similarly, domestic preferences for isolationism may prevent states from forming an alliance, and factors such as ideology, religion, and economics may prevent alliances between certain states.[81] Prior to the Second World War, U.S. isolationism and unwillingness to commit to formal agreements was a function of domestic attitudes about European power politics. Only during the cold war, when Americans perceived Communism to be a threat to the homeland, did the United States begin to form permanent alliances.

80. Michael Altfeld, "The Decision to Ally: A Theory and Test," *Western Political Quarterly* 37, no. 4 (December 1984), 523–544; James Morrow, "Alliances and Asymmetry: An Alternative to the Capability Aggregation Model of Alliances," *American Journal of Political Science* 35, no. 4 (November 1991), 904–933. Also see Alvin Saperstein, "Alliance Building versus Independent Action," *Journal of Conflict Resolution* 36, no. 3 (September 1992), 518–545; James Morrow, "Arms versus Allies: Trade-offs in the Search for Security," *International Organization* 47, no. 2 (Spring 1993), 207–233; Gerald Sorokin, "Arms, Alliances, and Security Tradeoffs in Enduring Rivalries," *International Studies Quarterly* 38, no. 3 (September 1994), 421–446; John Conybeare, "Arms versus Alliances: The Capital Structure of Military Enterprise," *Journal of Conflict Resolution* 38, no. 2 (June 1994), 215–235.

81. Michael Barnett and Jack Levy, "Domestic Sources of Alliances and Alignments: The Case of Egypt, 1962–1973," *International Organization* 45, no. 3 (Summer 1991), 369–395.

Likewise, the conventional wisdom is that states tend to ally with states with similar government types. Stephan Walt refers to this as "ideological solidarity" and hypothesizes that the more similar two states are ideologically, the more likely they are to ally.[82] There are several reasons why this might be true: it is a way of defending those ideological principles; similar states are less likely to fear each other; and an alliance may lend legitimacy to a weak regime. This idea is supported in some empirical tests,[83] but there are those who question whether a state's regime type affects its choice of partners. Michael Simon and Erik Gartzke find that states prefer to align with states of *other* regime types, since this provides a sort of comparative advantage.[84] What these arguments all ignore is that leaders may also take a state's reputation into account, regardless of its regime type.

The institutional perspective sees alliances as a means of solving problems that individual states might have trouble dealing with on their own. The main theory that falls within this category is referred to as either the "economic theory" or the "collective theory" of alliances. This view perceives alliances as a way of solving the collective-action problem that states might otherwise face in the security realm.[85] This approach might help explain some aspects of partner choice, given that states would generally prefer to ally with at least one stronger state so that they can free ride off the efforts of that state. However, a collective-goods approach is much better at explaining the behavior of states within existing alliances than explaining why an alliance would form in the first place.

82. Walt, *Origins of Alliances*, 33–40. Morgenthau also addresses the role of ideology on alliances. Morgenthau, *Politics among Nations*, 199–200.

83. Randolph Siverson and Juliann Emmons, "Birds of a Feather: Democratic Political Systems and Alliance Choices in the Twentieth Century," *Journal of Conflict Resolution* 35, no. 2 (June 1991), 285–306; Ole Holsti, T. Hopmann, and J. D. Sullivan, *Unity and Disintegration in International Alliances: Comparative Studies* (New York: John Wiley and Sons, 1973).

84. According to them, each government type has different advantages and disadvantages—autocracies can mobilize faster than democracies, but democracies can sustain support for a conflict much longer—and states prefer a good mix of these benefits. Michael Simon and Erik Gartzke, "Political System Similarity and the Choice of Allies," *Journal of Conflict Resolution* 40, no. 4 (December 1996), 617–635.

85. Mancur Olson and Richard Zeckhauser were the first to develop this model, applying it to the NATO case. See Mancur Olson and Richard Zeckhauser, "An Economic Theory of Alliances," *Review of Economics and Statistics* 48, no. 3 (August 1966), 266–279. Others who have applied or tested this theory include: Todd Sandler and Jon Cauley, "On the Economic Theory of Alliances," *Journal of Conflict Resolution* 19, no. 2 (June 1975), 330–348; Wallace Thies, "Alliances and Collective Goods," *Journal of Conflict Resolution* 31, no. 2 (June 1987), 298–332; John Conybeare and Todd Sandler, "The Triple Entente and the Triple Alliance 1880–1914: A Collective Goods Approach," *American Political Science Review* 84, no. 4 (December 1990), 1197–1206; Todd Sandler, "The Economic Theory of Alliances," *Journal of Conflict Resolution* 37, no. 3 (September 1993), 446–483; and Avery Goldstein, "Discounting the Free Ride: Alliances and Security in the Postwar World," *International Organization* 49, no. 1 (Winter 1995), 39–71.

One theory from the economic realm that might provide some insight into the nature of alliance formation is "hegemonic stability" theory. This is directly related to the collective theory of alliances because, as Charles Kindleberger suggests, public goods can be provided, despite incentives to free ride, if a hegemon exists and is willing to pay the costs.[86] Because defense is a public good, and because there are a large number of states in the international system, states sometimes will not provide that good because they have individual incentives to free ride.[87] According to hegemonic stability theory, though, if a hegemon exists, it will provide defense and simply extract payments from other states so that it is not taking the entire burden on itself. This could be useful for understanding alliance formation, because if a large state is willing to provide for the defense of a region, then that explains why smaller states would be willing to align with it—they receive the benefits of a security alliance without having to give up much autonomy. Yet such arrangements will only be effective if the hegemon has a reputation for following through with its promises. A hegemon that fails to provide the public good can quickly lose supporters and see its leadership position challenged by a coalition of states.

Even though each of the current perspectives on alliance formation adds to our knowledge of state behavior, there are clearly gaps. To be of value, a reputation-based theory of alliance formation need not displace any of the above theories, but it should enrich them. Incorporating reputation into many of the theories discussed above adds to those theories, improving our ability to explain why alliances form, as well as which states will ally with each other or choose neutrality.

Before turning to alliance termination, it is useful to briefly discuss the two concerns states have when forming an alliance—entrapment and abandonment.[88] Entrapment refers to a state's fear of being dragged into an unwanted conflict, whereas abandonment is the fear that one's allies will not honor their commitments when the state is threatened. Reputation can be a factor in both of these fears and, therefore, a state's willingness to form an alliance. If a potential ally has behaved aggressively in the past (that is, dragging its allies into unwanted conflicts), then concerns about entrapment will be higher because of that state's reputation. And we would expect

86. Charles Kindleberger, "Dominance and Leadership in the International Economy: Exploitation, Public Goods, and Free Rides," *International Studies Quarterly* 25, no. 2 (June 1981), 242–254.

87. Defense of an alliance is, for the most part, both nonexcludable and nonrival, although there could be exceptions. One study that addresses this issue is William Gates and Katsuaki Terasawa, "Commitment, Threat Perceptions, and Expenditures in a Defense Alliance," *International Studies Quarterly* 36, no. 1 (March 1992), 101–118.

88. Glenn Snyder, *Alliance Politics* (Ithaca: Cornell University Press, 1997); Christensen and Snyder, "Chain Gangs and Passed Bucks," 137–168.

such alliances to be different from those formed between states without such reputations. Similarly, fears of abandonment will be higher if an ally historically has failed to honor its alliance obligations. When a state has previously reneged on commitments, that reputation may prevent other states from allying with it altogether, or it is at least grounds for creating a more binding alliance to ensure compliance.

Alliance Termination

Another topic of interest in the alliance literature has to do with the conditions under which alliances end. When a firm suffers from a loss of reputation, the consequences will depend on the nature of the reputation that declines. Poor customer service can cost a firm its clients, poor product quality might cause investors to withdraw funds, and poor work conditions will lead to a loss of employees. If reputation matters in international politics, the parallel is that when a state becomes less reliable it should suffer the loss of its allies. If states can ignore their commitments and not lose allies, then that validates some of the critics' arguments about reputation not being worth fighting for. On the other hand, if abandoning one ally leads to the loss of several other allies, then that challenges the critical view of reputation and confirms that a state's reputation is valuable. Therefore, studying reputation not only addresses an area of alliances that is understudied and has important implications for the scholarly debate over reputation, it is also relevant for policymakers.

Relatively few theories focus specifically on alliance termination, and most of the work done in this area focuses on factors that affect how long a typical alliance will last. For the most part, arguments about the conditions under which alliances end must be inferred from theories of alliance formation, since logic suggests that if one knows the origins of an alliance, then the removal of that condition will bring the alliance to an end. For example, balance of power theory generally posits that alliances end either when the partnership is no longer necessary to prevent another state from becoming too powerful or when one member starts to gain too much power. However, many of these theories are unable to explain the end of some alliances and the continuation of others. Fortunately, reputation provides a way to fill this critical gap in the literature.

For example, theories that expect alliances to form in response to imbalances of power or threats to state security should expect alliances to end with improvements in either of those conditions. If a threatening state is defeated, most of these theories expect the alliance to end. We know, for instance, that British alliance policy in the nineteenth century sought first to achieve a balance of power in Europe and then to return to isolationism once the balance was restored. Scott Bennett tests several propositions related to this perspective and finds that (1) alliances are more likely to end as the allies' security improves; (2) the more security benefits that are given to members of an alliance, the less likely the alliance will end; and (3) when mutual threats to members of an alliance are reduced, it is more likely that the alliance will end.[89]

Another way of thinking about this is that as a state's capabilities increase relative to a potential adversary, it will value its alliances less. Following this logic, many expected the demise of NATO once the Soviet Union collapsed.[90] That the organization continues to exist, and continues to grow despite the absence of an obvious challenger, cannot easily be explained by balancing theories alone.

James Morrow also suggests that a change in a state's capabilities will influence the duration of an alliance. But his argument is that as a state increases its capabilities, it will require less security while demanding more autonomy. In contrast, a state with diminishing capabilities will demand greater security from the alliance.[91] In either case, a state's partner may be unable or unwilling to provide for the change in demands, increasing the probability that the alliance will end.[92] When Europe narrowed the post–Second World War power gap with the United States, many European states demanded more autonomy. France, for instance, withdrew from NATO's integrated military command in 1966. This decision was made largely on the basis of France's ability to produce its own nuclear weapons, the result of which was a French demand for greater autonomy. Morrow's theory, however, cannot explain why NATO persists after the cold war. For the alliance to continue—and in fact grow—the allies would have to be experiencing diminished capabilities. If anything, though, NATO capabilities have increased since the end of the cold war, though this has not been accompanied by widespread demands for greater autonomy.

From the domestic perspective, there are several plausible arguments about the end of an alliance. For one, alliances may end as a result of regime change, such as the transfer of power to a new leader who does not want to maintain the same commitments.[93] Having similar government types may

89. D. Scott Bennett, "Testing Alternative Models of Alliance Duration, 1816–1984," *American Journal of Political Science* 41, no. 3 (July 1997), 846–878.

90. John Mearsheimer, "Back to the Future: Instability in Europe after the Cold War," *International Security* 15, no. 1 (Summer 1990), 5–56; John Mearsheimer, "The False Promise of International Institutions," *International Security* 19, no. 3 (Winter 1994–95), 5–49; Kenneth Waltz, "The Emerging Structure of International Politics," *International Security* 18, no. 2 (Autumn 1993), 44–79.

91. Morrow, "Alliances and Asymmetry," 904–933.

92. Morrow also contends that asymmetric alliances, in which one state gains security and another gains autonomy, are likely to last longer than symmetric alliances, in which both states gain the same thing.

93. Randolph Siverson and Harvey Starr, "Regime Change and the Restructuring of Alliances," *American Journal of Political Science* 38, no. 1 (February 1994), 145–161.

also affect the duration of an alliance. Kurt Gaubatz and William Reed both find that alliances between liberal democracies tend to last longer than alliances between states with other forms of government, even though power changes hands more frequently in democracies than in nondemocratic states. The basis for their argument lies in the domestic institutions and norms that exist in democratic societies. According to Gaubatz, democracies are more likely than nondemocracies to maintain their alliance commitments over time.[94] In other words, many alliances end because of one actor's failure to honor its commitments, but commitments from democratic states are more likely to be honored, and therefore their alliances endure longer on average. If alliances between democratic states last longer because their commitments are more reliable, then this may explain NATO's continued *existence.* This approach, however, still cannot explain NATO's *expansion.*

Another argument is that alliances are institutionalized over time and become difficult to destroy. As such, the longer an alliance lasts, the longer it is likely to continue to exist.[95] Yet this fails to account for the alliances that do end. Economic theories of alliances might also be useful for explaining alliance failures. If small states free ride too much, the alliance may fall apart from an inability to provide the necessary resources. Generally, one large state will pick up the largest burden of an alliance, but its willingness to do so may change over time, especially if its capabilities decline. For example, according to hegemonic stability theory, an alliance is most likely to end if the largest state is unable or unwilling to carry most of the financial burden. The most likely cause of this change is a shift in the hegemon's capabilities. Unlike the situation envisioned in balancing and security-autonomy trade-off theories, in which the shift in capabilities occurs relative to an adversary, this shift in capabilities exists vis-à-vis the other members of the alliance. As the U.S. position in the world economy has diminished relative to many of its allies, the United States has put pressure on Europe to bear more of the NATO burden.[96] So far Europe has been reluctantly willing to do this, but this also explains the decision to expand the alliance, with the new members paying much of the added costs. However, this view suggests that, in spite of its institutionalization, NATO could fall apart if this collective-action problem becomes too great.

94. Kurt Gaubatz, "Democratic States and Commitment in International Relations" *International Organization* 50, no. 1 (Winter 1996), 109–130; William Reed, "Alliance Duration and Democracy: An Extension and Cross-Validation of 'Democratic States and Commitment in International Relations,'" *American Journal of Political Science* 41, no. 3 (July 1997), 1072–1078.

95. Robert Keohane and Celeste Wallander, "Contending Approaches on Security Institutions," presented at the International Studies Association meeting in Chicago (1995), cited in Bennet, "Testing Alternative Models of Alliance Duration," 850, 855, 877.

96. Keith Hartley and Todd Sandler, "NATO Burden-Sharing: Past and Future," *Journal of Peace Research* 36, no. 6 (1999), 665–680; Alan Tonelson, "NATO Burden-Sharing: Promises, Promises," *Journal of Strategic Studies* 23, no. 3 (September 2000).

As with theories of alliance formation, a greater understanding of reputation can supplement the existing explanations for the termination of alliances. Incorporating reputation shows that not every alliance will continue to persist indefinitely. However, as long as the members are reliable, and as long as the organization itself is perceived to be reliable, then it is likely to continue long after its initial purpose is satisfied. As Geoffrey Blainey states, "The alliance or friendship might have existed for ten or twenty years of peace and survived much strain, but the ultimate test of an alliance is action rather than promises."[97] Moreover, if we accept that alliances are costly to create, then it is plausible that as long as a state is a reliable partner, remaining in the alliance is much less costly than forming new alliances. That NATO members showed themselves to be reliable during the cold war helps explain why the alliance did not fall apart after the collapse of the Soviet Union. This argument also suggests that as states become less reliable, the chance of an alliance falling apart increases. Even if the alliance does not end, it may be transformed as a result of a decline in one or more member state's reliability.

Alliance Variation

In spite of the large amount of literature on alliances, few works deal with the institutional variation that exists across alliances, though there have been several attempts to create typologies of the characteristics that distinguish alliances from one another. Alexander George and Richard Smoke mention three ways in which defense obligations vary: the nature of the threat; the scope of the commitment; and the circumstances in which the commitment will be fulfilled.[98] Earlier works addressing the same issue include Morgenthau's characterization of alliances along five dimensions: (1) multilateral vs. unilateral, (2) temporary vs. permanent, (3) operative vs. inoperative, (4) general vs. limited distribution of benefits, and (5) complementary vs. identical vs. ideological scope of interest.[99] Singer and Small distinguish among ententes, neutrality and nonaggression pacts, and defense pacts as variations in the character and strength of a commitment.[100] Perhaps the most comprehensive attempt to distinguish alliances is Bruce Russett's coding of forty-four alliance characteristics.[101] Although each of these typologies effectively identifies some of the ways in which alliances

97. Geoffrey Blainey, *The Causes of War* (New York: Free Press, 1973), 52.

98. George and Smoke, *Deterrence in American Foreign Policy,* 554.

99. Morgenthau, *Politics among Nations,* 197–209.

100. J. David Singer and Melvin Small, "Formal Alliances, 1815–1939: A Quantitative Description," *Journal of Peace Research* 3, no. 1 (1966), 1–32.

101. Bruce Russett, "An Empirical Typology of International Military Alliances," *Midwest Journal of Political Science* 15, no. 2 (May 1971), 262–289.

vary, few studies examine why these differences exist when alliances form. Nor does the literature examine how and why alliances change over time.

Although there are few studies of the institutional variation among alliances, regime scholars do address differences in the design of various international institutions, and these typologies are applicable, since alliances are one specific type of institution. Moreover, if reputation can improve our understanding of the differences among alliances, then it should also be generalizable to explain institutional variation outside of the security realm.[102] Stephan Haggard and Beth Simmons, for example, define four ways in which regimes vary: (1) strength, meaning the degree of compliance with regime injunctions; (2) form, based on the level of administration as well as how the members are represented; (3) scope, referring to the range of issues covered; and (4) allocation mode, or whether resources are market oriented or authoritative.[103]

Regime scholars also attempt to explain the causes of these variations. Charles Lipson explores the distinction between formal and informal agreements, suggesting that states sometimes prefer informal agreements because they avoid the ratification process that can be politically costly to a democratic leader, they are easier to modify as situations change, and they are easier to negotiate so they can be formed more quickly.[104] Ultimately, this implies that states prefer informal agreements when they do not want or need to commit their national reputation to the agreement. In contrast, Kenneth Abbott and Duncan Snidal claim that "by using hard law . . . actors reduce transactions costs, strengthen the credibility of their commitments, expand their available political strategies, and resolve problems of incomplete contracting. Doing so, however, also entails significant costs: hard law restricts actors' behavior and even their sovereignty."[105]

In addition, Barbara Koremenos, Charles Lipson, and Duncan Snidal assert that states construct and shape institutions to advance their goals. According to them, differences between institutions are the result of calculated choices by states as to how to solve their problems.[106] One such problem

102. It is conceivable that such generalization is inappropriate, since the dangers of being abandoned in other areas—trade, the environment—are not as costly as being abandoned by an ally while involved in a conflict. In other words, if reputation matters anywhere in international politics, it should matter in the security realm. For a discussion of the differences between security and economics in this sense, see Lipson, "International Cooperation in Economic and Security Affairs," 1–23.

103. Stephan Haggard and Beth Simmons, "Theories of International Regimes," *International Organization* 41, no. 3 (Summer 1987), 491–517.

104. Charles Lipson, "Why Are Some International Agreements Informal?" *International Organization* 45, no. 4 (Autumn 1991), 495–538.

105. Abbott and Snidal, "Hard and Soft Law," 38.

106. Barbara Koremenos, Charles Lipson, and Duncan Snidal, "The Rational Design of International Institutions," *International Organization* 55, no. 4 (Autumn 2001), 762.

could be having an unreliable ally. Although space prevents me from evaluating all of the ways in which alliances vary, I can explore the effect that reputation has on some of the most relevant aspects of institutional design. In particular, Abbott et al. focus on three dimensions in which institutions vary: obligation, precision, and delegation. They define these in the following way: "*Obligation* means that states or other actors are bound by a rule or commitment or by a set of rules or commitments. . . . *Precision* means that rules unambiguously define the conduct they require, authorize, or proscribe. *Delegation* means that third parties have been granted authority to implement, interpret, and apply the rules; to resolve disputes; and (possibly) to make further rules."[107]

I apply these same terms to alliance design but conceptualize them slightly differently, which I discuss in detail in chapter 2. By examining reputation and how it affects these three dimensions of alliance variation, we can improve our understanding of the institutional differences between alliances, as well as at least one source of those differences. Just as important, reputation explains why these dimensions sometimes change over the course of an alliance.

Outline of the Book

I address these gaps in the alliance literature by examining the role of reliability. In chapter 2 I discuss how I define and measure reputation in this book. In that chapter I also outline my assumptions and discusses the hypotheses and competing theories that are tested in the case studies, as well as the conditions under which reliability should have the greatest influence on alliance behavior. Reputation will not always determine state behavior; under certain conditions, strategic factors such as capabilities, geography, and the number of potential allies will affect the relative importance that states assign to reputation. These are also discussed in some detail in chapter 2.

Chapters 3 through 6 present the case studies that test my hypotheses; they focus on several different incidents prior to the First World War. Chapter 3 examines the period from 1900 to 1905, focusing on the British government's decision to abandon its historical policy of "splendid isolation" and pursue an alliance. I initially examine British negotiations with Germany as an attempt to balance against the growing Franco-Russian threat to British naval and colonial interests and to prevent Russian expansion into Asia.

107. Kenneth Abbott, Robert Keohane, Andrew Moravcsik, Anne-Marie Slaughter, and Duncan Snidal, "The Concept of Legalization," *International Organization* 54, no. 3 (Summer 2000), 401, emphasis in original.

The British ultimately rejected the alliance offer from Germany and signed an alliance with Japan instead. As I show, this decision was heavily influenced by Germany's reputation as an unreliable ally. The Anglo-Japanese alliance was then quickly tested during the Russo-Japanese War and later renewed on favorable terms as a result of Britain's "benevolent neutrality." England and France also signed an agreement during the Russo-Japanese War, largely because of France's fear that British reliability could drag both states into a war because of their alliance commitments.

Whereas chapter 3 focuses on British negotiations for an alliance and then the behavior of allies after a war, the remaining three case study chapters examine the behavior of allies, and the consequences of their behavior, when faced with crises short of war: the First Moroccan Crisis (1905–1906), the Bosnia-Herzegovina Crisis (1908–1909), and the Agadir Crisis (1911). One reason for studying crises is that the number of wars that test alliance obligations is relatively small, particularly when we focus only on the great powers. By examining conflicts short of war, I expand the number of potential tests and can more easily focus on the same states over a short period of time, providing a more accurate test of reputation. In addition, wars are not the only test of a state's reliability. The level of support a state provides to its allies during near wars should also influence its reputation, since a state that does not support its allies in a dispute could be considered even less reliable if the dispute were to escalate. Although expectations may differ between conflicts and wars, a lack of allied support during a crisis should have a similar effect on a state's reputation as failing to honor an obligation to go to war.

A second reason for looking at these cases is that if I find that a state's behavior during a crisis influences its reputation, and therefore its autonomy, then it is even more likely that a state's behavior in war would have similar consequences. These are also historically important cases because these crises helped divide Europe into two armed camps, with Germany, Austria-Hungary, and Italy on one side and England, France, and Russia on the other. This helped contribute to the outbreak of the First World War. I do not claim that they caused the war, but the behavior of the allies helped create an environment in which a general war became more likely.

Another reason for using these three particular crises is that they are the same cases Mercer uses to critique the conventional wisdom on reputation. Therefore, these should be difficult tests for reputation. However, I not only examine these crises from a different perspective—allied reliability rather than resolve—but I provide new information and evidence about the relevance of reputation to these cases. Mercer's is the most critical analysis of reputation to date, so testing my hypotheses on the same cases is a useful way to show how a state's reputation for reliability can affect alliance behavior, even if one accepts his findings that reputations for resolve have little influence on the behavior of states.[108]

One advantage of studying these cases is that all three crises involved the same six participant states. In addition, the primary belligerents in each case received different levels of support from their allies. This has allowed me to directly compare how relationships changed after the crises as a result of the level of support the states gave to their ally. In chapter 4, for example, I examine the First Moroccan Crisis (1905–1906), which involved a dispute between France and Germany and tested Britain's recently formed entente with France, as well as the Dual Alliance of France and Russia and the Triple Alliance of Austria-Hungary, Germany, and Italy. This case allows me to compare the different levels of support that Germany and France received from their allies and how each of the relationships changed in the aftermath of the crisis.

France received more support from England than it did from Russia, which suggests that after the crisis, all things being equal, French perceptions of British reliability should rise while perceptions of Russia's reliability should decline. If so, then there should be observable differences between British and Russian autonomy after the crisis. Not only did British support for France lead to the formation of the Triple Entente but the Franco-Russian alliance changed as a result of Russian behavior during the crisis. Likewise, Austria-Hungary supported Germany, but Italy chose to side with France in the crisis, suggesting that Germany should trust Austria-Hungary more than Italy after the crisis and that, again, we should see observable differences in Germany's relations with its allies.

In chapter 5 I look at the Bosnia-Herzegovina Crisis (1908–1909) between Austria-Hungary and Russia. This case focuses on how the crisis contributed to changes in the nature of both the Triple Alliance and the recently formed Triple Entente. Specifically, it examines the degree to which Britain and France backed their Russian ally, as well as the amount of support that Italy and Germany provided to Austria-Hungary. Because the six main actors in this case are the same as in the First Moroccan Crisis, even though the primary disputants are different, it allows me to test whether reputations are influential only as they pertain to specific situations—for example,

108. Although I challenge many of Mercer's arguments and findings with respect to a state's reliability and reputation more generally, I do not dismiss the possibility that Mercer and the other critics may be right about the lack of importance a state's reputation for resolve has on the behavior of its adversaries. But my findings suggest that even if a reputation for resolve is not worth fighting for, a reputation for reliability may be worth it. To his credit, in his conclusion Mercer concedes the possibility that reputations for keeping promises are more influential on state behavior than reputations for following through on threats. Mercer, *Reputation and International Politics*, 224–226.

n between France and Germany over Morocco—or if reputations ore widespread influence, including a state's behavior in other crises or with respect to other allies.

For the final case study in chapter 6 I focus on the Agadir Crisis (1911). As in the First Moroccan Crisis, France and Germany are once again the primary belligerents. This case not only allows for another test of Russian and British support for France, and Italian and Austro-Hungarian support for Germany, but since this crisis occurred just three years before the outbreak of the First World War, it is a particularly difficult test of reputation. Much has been made of the tight alliances and how they contributed to the outbreak of the war. But the evidence I present in this chapter suggests that at least part of the story is the reputation of the allies, because the alliances became tighter in response to perceived losses of reliability.

Chapter 7 provides a conclusion and is divided into three parts. First is a review of my findings. Although there are summaries of the cases at the end of each chapter, it is useful to provide a final review to determine the overall success of my claims. The successful hypotheses are then applied to two other cases to illustrate that the results are not exclusive to the pre–First World War era or to multipolar international systems. Specifically, I discuss how allied reliability affected the formation and transformation of NATO during the cold war and the role of allied reliability in the post-9/11 environment. Finally, the conclusion addresses some unanswered questions, assesses the specific policy implications of my findings, and provides some suggestions for future reputation research.

It is logical to presume that a state's reputation should matter in international politics, given the absence of a central authority to punish unacceptable behavior (what international relations scholars refer to as anarchy). Nowhere do I claim that reputation will explain all alliance behavior. A more appropriate standard, and the one adopted here, is simply whether reputation improves our understanding of alliance choices. What my findings suggest is that a state's reliability is an important factor that influences the behavior of other states and should not be overlooked by states that care about their alliance autonomy, particularly with respect to alliance formation and variation. I find much less support for reliability affecting the durability of an alliance, which is interesting because it fits with Mercer's claims about reputation. I also find an unexpected connection between a state's reliability and the willingness of its allies to challenge their adversaries.

2

Reliability and Alliance Behavior

We judge ourselves by what we feel capable of doing, while others judge us by what we have already done.

HENRY WADSWORTH LONGFELLOW

In the opening chapter I detailed how scholars have dealt with reputation, and I explored some of the major theories of alliance behavior. I also explained how the business literature treats the effects of a firm's reputation on its success and have suggested that the influence of a firm's reputation on the market is comparable to the effect that a state's reputation has on other states in the international political system. In this chapter I discuss my assumptions as well as the methods used for studying reputation in this book, and then I lay out the hypotheses that are tested in the case study chapters that follow. In general, I contend that a state's reputation affects its ability to attract new allies and keep existing allies and that it can also influence the design of the alliances it is able to form. First, however, it is necessary to define reputation.

Defining Reputation

The definition of reputation used here borrows from Jonathan Mercer's work, but it also identifies some problems with his definition. Defining reputation is relatively simple: the Oxford dictionary says that reputation is "a widespread belief that someone or something has a particular characteristic."[1] Synonyms include credit, repute, and regard. However, defining

1. Angus Stevenson, ed., *The Oxford Dictionary of English*, 3rd ed. (Oxford: Oxford University Press, 2010).

the concept in a way that is useful for studying reputation in international politics is more complicated. Other disciplines provide some sense of how reputation is commonly defined by scholars. In the anthropology literature, John Hutson contends that "a man's reputation is what is said about him. It is the overall response of people to both actor and role performance; an assessment not only of the results achieved but also of the manner in which they were achieved."[2] And one article from the business literature defines reputation as "information about an agent that develops over time from observed behavior about some characteristic of the agent."[3]

Despite the slight differences between disciplines, definitions of reputation are generally similar. As such, Mercer's definition is an appropriate starting point: "Reputation is a judgment of someone's character (or disposition) that is then used to predict or explain future behavior."[4] One problem is that Mercer's definition biases his work against reputation. For one thing, he argues that reputations only form out of an actor's character (disposition) and not as a result of situation. He claims that "because a reputation is a judgment about another's character, only dispositional attributions can generate a reputation."[5] Although he uses this as part of his definition, it is more realistically an assumption, and one that does not appear to be valid. In fact, there are both logical and empirical reasons to relax this assumption and believe that reputations do form out of situations, particularly in international relations. First of all, because of uncertainty actors may be unaware of the situational constraints that influence another actor's behavior. Consequently, a lack of information might lead observers to attribute situational behavior to a person's character. Or observers may simply ignore the situation. The fundamental attribution error asserts that people often "underestimate the extent to which behavior is shaped by the constraints of the situation and overestimate the extent to which it is shaped by people's underlying dispositions."[6] If true, then even if observers are aware of the situational constraints, they could underestimate the power of a situation and therefore assign a reputation to a state.

One can also think of practical reasons for relaxing this assumption. Two actors that frequently interact, such as firms and their clients, will have an easier time distinguishing between situation and disposition. As the frequency of contact decreases, the ability to make that distinction also

2. John Hutson, "A Politician in Valloire," in *Gifts and Poison: The Politics of Reputation*, ed. F. G. Bailey (Oxford: Basil Blackwell, 1971), 79.

3. Keith Chauvin and James Guthrie, "Labor Market Reputation and the Value of the Firm," *Managerial and Decision Economics* 15, no. 6 (November/December 1994), 544.

4. Jonathan Mercer, *Reputation and International Politics* (Ithaca: Cornell University Press, 1996), 6.

5. Ibid.

6. Ziva Kunda, *Social Cognition: Making Sense of People* (Cambridge: MIT Press, 1999), 429.

declines. Because interactions occur less frequently in international politics than in other areas, each action provides relatively more information to observers. Mercer states that "because a situational attribution does not have cross-situational validity, it cannot be used to predict behavior in a different situation and so cannot generate a reputation."[7] But, in the absence of other information, actors will ignore the importance of a situation and assign a reputation anyway.

A simple anecdote illustrates how my definition differs from Mercer's. If I leave a restaurant without tipping the server, according to Mercer's definition I would develop a reputation for being cheap *only if* someone witnessed my failure to leave a tip and then used that information to expect me to not leave a tip the next time I eat out. But Mercer assumes that the observer takes into account any situation that may have caused me to not leave a tip—for instance, if the service was bad or if I am a struggling academic who cannot afford to leave a tip. If, in that situation, the average person would do the same thing, then for Mercer a reputation does not form. Finally, because reputations are based on perception, Mercer would expect others in the restaurant to assign different reputations to me—perhaps one might be absentmindedness. Although all of these contingencies are conceptually valid, they fail to capture the common usage of reputation, and they are therefore less useful, because even situational attributions are relevant for creating a reputation in international politics, and dismissing them out of hand overly biases Mercer's results against reputation.

In this book, reputation is simply a shared perception about one state's prior behavior that is used to predict future behavior. To gain a reputation for being cheap in the above anecdote requires at least one person witnessing my failure to tip and then communicating it so that at least two people share the same judgment.[8] Although the situation (poverty, bad service, etc.) might explain my behavior better than my character would, an observer may not be aware of the circumstances or may choose to ignore them. As a result, in the anecdote above, observers will use my actions to predict that I will not leave a tip the next time.

Mercer assumes that perceptions of a state's reputation vary from one observer to the next.[9] Although this helps us understand that reputations are not consistently applied, it is not enough for one state to assign a reputation to another, because one actor's belief about another actor's character is

7. Mercer, *Reputation and International Politics,* 6.

8. Because we are talking about international relations, these perceptions need not be shared by states; they need only be shared by individuals having the power to make decisions for a state. In other words, the sharing can be done at the state level or at the individual level of analysis.

9. Mercer, *Reputation and International Politics,* 7.

an opinion, not a reputation. Works in anthropology and sociology suggest that there must be agreement for a reputation to exist. Nicholas Emler, for instance, argues that reputations "are *social, not individual judgments* . . . [that are] created collectively through processes of social communication, and are not to be confused with one individual's perception of another."[10] Therefore, a reputation only forms when multiple actors have the same opinion about the person's character. In the simplest case, at least one observer must share a judgment with at least one other actor (either by both making the same judgment from observing the behavior, or else by one observer communicating their judgment to a third party, who then accepts that judgment).[11] In the cases discussed in this book, this means that multiple states, or multiple actors within a state, must share a perception of another state's reliability. Perceptions need not be unanimous—the case studies reveal some examples where individuals disagreed about the reliability of a state—but they must be held by more than one actor to be a valid indicator of a reputation, as opposed to simply one actor's opinion.

One of Mercer's main points is that a state cannot change its reputation—allies will always be viewed as irresolute, while enemies will always be seen as resolute.[12] In some respects this is an empirical question that I test in this book—if alliances change because of a state's behavior during a conflict or war, then the state's reputation may be one cause of that change. However, Mercer's assumption that reputations do not change is also a function of his definition, which requires that the source of the reputation be an actor's character or disposition.[13] In contrast, my definition accepts that reputations can be situational and therefore are subject to change.

Assumptions

In this book I examine whether a state's reputation affects its ability to attract and keep allies, and whether it influences the types of alliances it is able to form. To develop my hypotheses using the market analogies discussed in chapter 1, I have three basic assumptions that are consistent with studies of reputation across disciplines. First, actors have a variety of reputations simultaneously. Second, reputations exist at different levels of analysis,

10. Nicholas Emler, "A Social Psychology of Reputation," in *European Review of Social Psychology*, vol. 1, ed. Wolfgang Stroebe and Miles Hewstone (New York: John Wiley and Sons, 1990), 181, emphasis added. See also M. A. Heppenstall, "Reputation, Criticism and Information in an Austrian Village," in *Gifts and Poison*, ed. Bailey, 139–166, esp. 153–154.

11. The anthropology literature refers to this form of communication as "gossip." Heppenstall, "Reputation, Criticism and Information," esp. 153, 166; F. G. Bailey, "The Management of Reputations and the Process of Change," in *Gifts and Poison*, ed. Bailey, esp. 288.

12. Mercer, *Reputation and International Politics*, 67, 212–213.

13. Ibid., 6.

including the unit (e.g., the firm or the state) and the unit's leader (e.g., the CEO or the prime minister). Finally, I assume that observers are skeptical about the ability of others to learn from their mistakes.

Actors Possess a Variety of Reputations

All actors, be they individuals, firms, or states, possess a variety of different reputations. Sometimes these complement each other, such as when a firm has a positive reputation for both customer service and for the treatment of its employees. Other times reputations may be incongruous, for instance, if a firm has a reputation for innovation but also for poor management. It is difficult to conduct a study that accounts for all the different types of reputations. Instead, we must be content to focus on a specific type of reputation, while recognizing that overgeneralizations about reputation are dangerous.

Mercer agrees that states have a variety of reputations, although he then focuses almost exclusively on resolve. The problem is that once he concludes that a state cannot change its reputation for resolve, he posits that reputations are not worth fighting for.[14] While his findings may be correct with respect to reputations for resolve, his conclusion ignores other reputations that are also worthy of scholarly attention and that may even be worth fighting for.

As I mentioned in chapter 1, there is already a consensus among firms that reputations matter. The emphasis now is on how they can develop and preserve positive reputations. Sociology also focuses on how reputations can be maintained. As Emler suggests, "we . . . have constantly to work to defend and repair reputations, both by providing visible behavioral evidence that is consistent with the qualities and identities we wish to claim and by explaining away apparent inconsistencies."[15] There also seems to be an understanding that it is easier to destroy a positive reputation than it is to create one. If applicable to international politics, then a state's reputation will suffer more by failing to honor a commitment than can be gained by honoring the commitment. The point is that states can behave in ways that will change other states' perceptions of their reputations.

Reputations Exist on More than One Level of Analysis

It is obvious who is responsible for an individual's reputation. The task of assigning a reputation grows more difficult when dealing with groups of individuals, such as firms or states. Is Microsoft's reputation for innovation a function of the performance of its employees, or is it based solely

14. Ibid., 7, 15, 228.
15. Emler, "Social Psychology of Reputation," 184.

on the company's creator, Bill Gates? For the most part, a firm's reputation is assigned to both the group and to the leader. A change in management sometimes alters a firm's reputation; in fact, changing CEOs is a common business strategy for minimizing the reputational costs of a mistake.[16] However, some reputations are difficult to alter, even by a change in leadership.[17]

It is logical to assume then that in international politics reputations are assigned to both the state and its leaders. A change in leadership may have some effect on a state's reputation (as with Mikhail Gorbachev taking over the Soviet Union or Barack Obama taking over the U.S. presidency), but some reputations will persist, even after a change (Iran and North Korea continue to be considered "rogue states" regardless of changes to the leadership).

A related assumption is that reputations are more diffused in a democratic state. This means that the reputation of a nondemocratic state is more strongly tied to its leader, whereas the reputation of a democratic state is less connected to an individual. There are two reasons for this. First, nondemocratic leaders are generally in power longer than democratically elected leaders. As a result, there is more opportunity for a nondemocratic leader's reputation to be perceived as interchangeable with that of the state.[18] Second, because democratic leaders must answer to an electorate, their reputations are more likely to fluctuate or to be perceived as constrained by domestic institutions.

Furthermore, reputations may be assigned to substate actors, such as a political party or a legislative body. If reputations are assigned to political parties, then a change in leadership will have a limited effect on the state's reputation as long as the same party maintains control.[19] Similarly, certain

16. Tyco International is one firm that hired a new CEO with a positive image to improve the firm's reputation. On 26 July 2002, Tyco's stock gained almost 46% ($3.78) only one day after announcing the replacement of its former CEO, who was indicted the month before on charges of tax evasion. Gregory Zuckerman, "Calm Will Follow the Storm, Bulls Forecast—Volatility Barometer Tells Analysts Market Bottom is Just around the Corner," *Wall Street Journal*, 29 July 2002.

17. Because of its involvement in producing Agent Orange during the Vietnam War, Dow Chemical continues to suffer from reputation costs even though it is currently one of the more environmentally conscious companies. Kathleen Dechant and Barbara Altman, "Environmental Leadership: From Compliance to Competitive Advantage," *Academy of Management Executive* 8, no. 3 (August 1994), 7–27; Giovanni Azzone and Giuliano Noci, "Seeing Ecology and 'Green' Innovations as a Source of Change," *Journal of Organizational Change Management* 11, no. 2 (1998), 94–111.

18. Louis XIV's claim "l'etat, c'est moi" (I am the state) is an example of how the reputations of states and individuals are interconnected, especially in a nondemocratic state.

19. Examples of dominant political parties, in which a change in leader may have brought little change to the state's reputation, include the KMT in Taiwan and the PRI in Mexico (which controlled the presidency for seventy-one years). Dorothy Solinger, "Ending One-Party Dominance: Korea, Taiwan, Mexico," *Journal of Democracy* 12, no. 1 (January 2001), 30–42; Kenneth Greene, "Dominant Party Strategy and Democratization," *American Journal of Political Science* 52, no. 1 (January 2008), 16–31.

national legislatures may have a reputation of their own that influences the behavior of other states, particularly in situations where an alliance must be ratified or when approval is necessary before a state can go to war in support of an ally.

Observers Are Skeptical that States Learn from Their Mistakes

Although the concepts of reputation and learning are similar, there is an important difference. According to Dan Reiter, states learn from their past behavior and from the behavior of others and adjust how they act in the future.[20] An example of learning is the Clinton administration choosing not to intervene in Rwanda because of the United States' experience in Somalia the year before—if indeed that is the case.[21] This is similar to the idea of reputation in that expectations about future behavior are based on historical experiences (information becomes more complete as states learn more about the behavior of others).

But learning implies that states are able to alter their behavior based on previous experiences and can therefore avoid repeating mistakes. In other words, if France learned from its mistakes at the Munich conference in 1938, then other states should have jockeyed to ally with France, believing that it was an attractive ally because it learned its lesson and would never again appease aggression. Robert Jervis calls this the paradox of deterrence, suggesting that if a state backs down from one challenge, it will redouble its efforts next time: "Damage to a state's reputation in one instance need not weaken its attempts at deterrence, indeed, it may even enhance them."[22]

In contrast, reputation implies that whether or not actors learn from their mistakes, others will act as if someone is likely to repeat their previous behavior, regardless of whether it was successful or not. As such, states should be less likely to align with France after the Second World War because of Munich (regardless of what lessons it may have learned). For this book, I assume that a state may alter its behavior through learning but that the behavior of *other* states will be a function of that state's reputation rather than of lessons that the state may have learned.

20. Dan Reiter, *Crucible of Beliefs: Learning, Alliances, and World Wars* (Ithaca: Cornell University Press, 1996).

21. Charles Stevenson, "The Evolving Clinton Doctrine on the Use of Force," *Armed Forces & Society* 22, no. 4 (Summer 1996), 511–535; Michael Barnett, *Eyewitness to a Genocide: The United Nationals and Rwanda* (Ithaca: Cornell University Press, 2002), 40; Gregory Stanton, "The Rwandan Genocide: Why Early Warning Failed," *Journal of African Conflicts and Peace Studies* 1, no. 2 (September 2009), 6–25.

22. Robert Jervis, *Perception and Misperception in International Politics,* (Princeton: Princeton University Press, 1976). See also Robert Jervis, "Deterrence and Perception," *International Security* 7, no. 3 (Winter 1982–83), 12–13.

Economic analogies are again useful to illustrate this point. If a person defaults on a loan, banks will not give that person another loan in the belief that such a person will act more responsibly in the future. Instead, banks will refuse the loan, acting according to the person's reputation. Even if the previous loan was from a different bank, such behavior negatively affects one's credit report. Likewise, investors do not easily forgive struggling companies under the assumption that the firm learned its lesson and will turn things around. Instead, companies with problems suffer penalties based on their previous behavior. Recent examples include the cases of Enron and WorldCom. Investors are unlikely to forgive mistakes on the assumption that the leadership learned its lesson.[23] Therefore, learning is what (we hope) states do. Reputation, however, is the behavior that other states expect, and it is this expectation that I contend leads to various alliance choices.

Variables

My independent variable is a state's reputation for reliability. In the absence of perfect information, reputation is a state's best tool for gauging the sincerity of another state's commitments. If I am testing the correct hypotheses, then states should behave differently toward those with reliable reputations than they do toward those that are perceived to be unreliable.

Measurement is one problematic feature of any study of reputation. Although some scholars have begun to address the issue of measuring reputation,[24] each measurement can only deal with one specific type of reputation. The business literature has gotten around this problem by publicizing surveys of people familiar with particular business sectors. For instance, the reputations of MBA programs are largely based on nationwide surveys of people who run MBA programs. A survey, however, is unlikely to provide useful information for international politics.

Most scholars choose a shortcut to measuring reputation that emphasizes a state's most recent actions, based on the recognition that actors tend to remember recent events more readily than older events.[25] Mercer suggests that "a state that yields should be viewed as irresolute and a state that

23. Even replacing those who caused the problems may not immediately improve the firms' reputations.

24. Jean-Sebastian Rioux, *The Reputation-Building Behavior of States, 1918–1988* (PhD diss. Florida State University, 1996).

25. For example, Daniel Ellsberg made the argument that U.S. decision makers got involved in Vietnam precisely because they had strong recollections of Korea. Daniel Ellsberg, "The Quagmire Myth and the Stalemate Machine," *Public Policy* (May 1971), 217–274; Daniel Ellsberg, *Papers on the War* (New York: Simon and Schuster, 1972).

stands firm should be viewed as resolute; however a state behaved in the last crisis should govern others' expectations of that state." For instance, he claims that the French continued to doubt British reliability even after the British opposed Germany at the 1906 Algeciras conference, which he uses to support his argument that states cannot change their reputations.[26]

Although this is a compelling shortcut to take because it allows for an objective measurement, it fails to assess an actor's true reputation. Reputations develop over time, not from a single act. The business literature shows us that a positive reputation is costly and difficult to build. Therefore, in the example above, we should not expect the French to suddenly trust the British, with whom they had almost gone to war only seven years earlier. In addition, measuring reputation according to a single prior act creates a dichotomous variable: either the state honored its commitment (reliable) or it failed to do so (unreliable). It is more accurate to view reputation as a continuum from completely reliable to completely unreliable. For this reason I use a more subjective measurement, an analysis of statements and writings by key decision makers that I contend is appropriate to assess how one state's behavior is influenced by its perceptions of another government's reputation. Failing to support an ally does not make a state completely unreliable, but it does decrease its reliability, especially when compared to other states that provided support. As a result, I expect its autonomy to decline. Although supporting an ally does not instantly create a reliable reputation, it will give a state more alliance autonomy.

One potential problem with the use of decision makers' statements is that some leaders may use claims about reputation as a cover for less popular arguments. The solution to this problem is to pay attention to the intended audience. Comments from a leader's personal papers are less likely to be misleading than statements made to a reporter. Another solution is to accept that even if someone uses a reputation argument for political purposes, the state must have done something to earn that reputation—if a state has always acted reliably then an argument about its reputation cannot be used against it, even for political purposes. As a result, the intention behind a decision maker's reference to reputation is less important than the fact that reputation is cited at all. This also illustrates the importance of a perceived reputation being shared by more than one actor, so that we do not incorrectly identify one person's opinion or political argument as a reputation.

The next issue is to identify what constitutes an unreliable state. There are, in fact, few instances in which states completely renege on their formal

26. Mercer, *Reputation and International Politics*, 43, 104–106. See also John David Orme, *Deterrence, Reputation, and Cold-War Cycles* (London: Macmillan, 1992), 6.

ns. One study, using the Alliance Treaty Obligations and Provi- (TOP) dataset, finds that states honor their alliance commitments percent of the time.[27] ATOP includes cases in which a state fails to hen it is obligated to do so, as well as cases in which a state signs a separate agreement with an enemy. ATOP does not, however, include two other instances in which a state may prove unreliable: if it drags its ally into an unwanted conflict, or if it fails to support an ally during a crisis short of war. Although such actions may not damage a state's reputation as much as those represented in ATOP, they should nevertheless be included in any study of reputation and alliances because they will affect perceptions of a state's reliability.[28]

My dependent variable is state behavior, specifically the behavior of states considering an alliance or in an existing alliance. In examining alliances, I incorporate all four types of formal agreements identified by David Singer and Melvin Small—defense pacts, neutrality and nonaggression pacts, and ententes—since a state's reliability should affect the behavior of its allies regardless of the type of alliance.[29] In terms of alliance formation, either a state is able to form an alliance or not. With respect to alliance termination, I focus on whether alliances end or are renewed, and even whether one state threatens to withdraw from the alliance. Finally, the behavior I am concerned with regarding alliance variation is the design of the institution, specifically regarding the precision, obligation, and delegation of the alliance. This includes both new alliances that are being negotiated and alterations to an existing alliance because of perceived changes in an ally's reliability. These changes need not be reflected in the design of the institution itself, because doing so would require significant time and energy. Instead, the changes I expect to see in allied relations will be specific to both the past behavior and the needs of the states. As an example, if a state fails to support an ally but the alliance persists, I expect the ally to demand that the unreliable state give up more autonomy in some way, either as a costly signal of its future intent to be reliable or in some area that specifically aids the ally.

27. Brett Ashley Leeds, Andrew Long, and Sara McLaughlin Mitchell, "Reevaluating Alliance Reliability: Specific Threats, Specific Promises," *Journal of Conflict Resolution* 44, no. 5 (October 2000), 686–699. For information on the ATOP dataset, see Brett Ashley Leeds, Jeffrey M. Ritter, Sara McLaughlin Mitchell, and Andrew Long, "Alliance Treaty Obligations and Provisions, 1815–1944," *International Interactions* 28, no. 3 (2002), 237–260.

28. I use these four measures because they seem to be the most common reasons a state suffers a loss of reliability. But since reputation is subjective, a state could cite a variety of actions as evidence of another state's unreliability.

29. J. David Singer and Melvin Small, "Formal Alliances, 1815–1939: A Quantitative Description," *Journal of Peace Research* 3, no. 1 (1966), 1–32.

Hypotheses

One underlying question in this puzzle is whether reputation is rational or psychological. Mercer believes that it is psychological (and in fact suggests that it is irrational for states to be concerned with their reputations). In contrast, I contend that reputation can be both rational and psychological. Reputations are psychological because they are based on the perceptions of others and because they influence expectations about future events. However, a concern about reputation is rational if, as I show here, states benefit for having a reliable reputation and suffer costs for having an unreliable one.

In essence, I suggest that a state's reputation influences alliances in two general ways. As a state is perceived to be more reliable, not only will it have to give up less autonomy to attract an ally but its allies will give up more of their own autonomy. Alternatively, as a state becomes less reliable, its allies will wish to retain more autonomy while demanding that more constraints be placed on the less reliable state. Breaking these arguments down into smaller components provides testable hypotheses to deal with the three primary aspects of alliances discussed in chapter 1: formation, termination, and variation.

Alliance Formation

There are three fundamental questions regarding alliance formation: Why do states form alliances? How do states choose their partners? Why do states sometimes prefer neutrality over an alliance? To address the gaps in our understanding of alliances, I draw from the literature on corporate reputation to develop my hypotheses. The business literature tells us that a company's reputation will, for one thing, affect the quality of employees it can attract: "The firm's return to its reputation . . . is the ability to attract and retain higher-quality workers at a lower cost than would be incurred absent the reputation."[30] According to Charles Fombrun: "Just as a top school's reputation draws the brightest students, so do esteemed companies more easily recruit the finest candidates for their jobs."[31] Similarly, products with a reputation for high quality attract more consumers, and firms with a reputation for effective management attract more investors. On the other hand, banks refuse loans to individuals with poor credit, and firms that mistreat employees have trouble finding high-quality applicants.

30. Chauvin and Guthrie, "Labor Market Reputation," 544.

31. Charles Fombrun, *Reputation: Realizing Value from the Corporate Image* (Boston: Harvard Business School Press, 1996), 76. See also Chauvin and Guthrie, "Labor Market Reputation," 544.

If reputations matter in international relations, then we should see certain behavior when a state is perceived to be an unreliable ally that we would not see when it is perceived to be reliable. For example, if states balance to improve their security, they would logically prefer to ally with states that can be trusted to honor their commitments. If a state has multiple potential allies, all else being equal, it should prefer to ally with the state that is most likely to support it in a conflict or war. If no potential allies are perceived to be reliable, then the state will prefer neutrality over an alliance with any of them. Therefore, the first hypothesis is that unreliable states will not be able to attract new allies.

> HYPOTHESIS 1: An unreliable state will be unable to attract new allies.

The institutions literature already assumes that this is true, as Robert Keohane suggests: "International regimes alter the information available to governments and the opportunities open to them; commitments made to support such institutions can only be broken at a cost to reputation."[32] That literature rarely takes the next step, to ask what effect the loss of reputation would have. But this argument can be tested by focusing on alliances as one type of institution. At minimum, incorporating reputation into our theories of alliance formation clarifies why some states are perceived to be more attractive allies than others. More specifically, incorporating reputation into our theories helps explain how states choose their partners and, just as important, why states sometimes prefer neutrality.

A fundamental reason for creating an alliance is to improve security; states typically will not enter into alliances that make them worse off. It is especially dangerous to ally with a state that will not honor its commitments, because doing so could provoke an adversary without improving one's own security. As Michael Altfeld argues: "It can never be rational for a government to form an alliance which does not increase its security since some increase is always necessary to offset the loss in autonomy which is assumed to occur."[33] There is asymmetric information to every agreement, however, because one actor cannot know if the other will honor its commitment. In fact, an alliance is unnecessary if a state is *certain* that it will

32. Robert Keohane, *After Hegemony: Cooperation and Discord in the World Political Economy* (Princeton: Princeton University Press, 1984), 26.

33. Michael Altfeld, "The Decision to Ally: A Theory and Test," *Western Political Quarterly* 37, no. 4 (December 1984), 529. See also Alastair Smith, "Alliance Formation and War," *International Studies Quarterly* 39, no. 4 (December 1995), 415; Hans Morgenthau, *Politics among Nations: The Struggle for Power and Peace*, brief ed., rev. Kenneth Thompson (Boston: McGraw-Hill, 1993 [1948]), 197.

receive support.[34] A state's reputation is useful, then, because it provides information to other states so they can determine the probability that a state will honor its commitments. A state that has consistently reneged on its commitments will add little to an ally's security because of the high likelihood that it will defect. On the other hand, a state that repeatedly honors its commitments will be perceived to be a valuable ally. As a result, it is logical to expect reliable states to be able to find willing partners, while unreliable states will have a more difficult time doing so.

Although this hypothesis is plausible, there are instances in which unreliable states are able to find willing allies. Italy was undoubtedly perceived to be one of the least reliable states in Europe during the interwar period, but it was courted by everyone prior to the Second World War, including Germany, which Italy abandoned during the First World War. Because of the limited number of states in the international system, and because states are often forced to ally out of strategic necessity (disregarding reputation under certain circumstances), this first hypothesis is unlikely to always hold true. Nevertheless, because it is a basic argument regarding the connection between reputation and alliance formation, it is worth testing and may help identify those situations in which other strategic considerations are more important than reputation for determining state behavior.

The reality is not that unreliable states will never find allies but simply that they will have more difficulty doing so. And when unreliable states are able to find allies, their autonomy will be reduced through alliance formation because their reputation limits their choice of allies to other unreliable states. This assumes that reliable states tend to ally with each other, but this is logical based on findings in the business literature; reputable firms interact with other reputable firms or risk damaging their reputation by association. For example, top department stores sell only high-quality products, because failing to do so would hurt the store's reputation. As a result, firms that produce low-quality products are forced to sell their goods to less-respected vendors. Wujin Chu and Woosik Chu show that "reputable retailers have an incentive to correctly represent the quality of the products they sell in order to protect their investment in reputation. Discounters who have no reputation to lose, have no such incentive."[35] Applying this logic to international relations improves our understanding of alliance formation by suggesting that reliable states ally with other reliable states, leaving

34. Unless, of course, the sole purpose of the alliance is to threaten or deter others. Thomas Schelling makes this argument in discussing the reason strategy involves states that have some conflicting interests and some common interests. Thomas Schelling, *The Strategy of Conflict* (Cambridge: Harvard University Press, 1960), 4–5.

35. Wujin Chu and Woosik Chu, "Signaling Quality by Selling through a Reputable Retailer: An Example of Renting the Reputation of Another Agent," *Marketing Science* 13, no. 2 (Spring 1994), 187.

unreliable states to ally with one another. Therefore, even if the first hypothesis does not hold true, hypothesis 2 is based on the similar premise that an unreliable reputation reduces a state's autonomy, not by preventing it from finding an ally, but by limiting its choice of allies.

HYPOTHESIS 2: States tend to ally with states of similar reliability.

Clearly, a better understanding of how states use reputation to make their alliance decisions will improve our ability to explain why alliances form, as well as how states choose their allies, or choose neutrality. Taken together, these two hypotheses help identify whether unreliable states are able to find allies and, if they are, whether their options are limited because of reputation.

Another important question within the alliance literature has to do with alliance termination, and reputation should improve our understanding of this aspect of alliances by examining whether alliances end as a result of one or more members suffering a loss of reliability. Particularly if hypothesis 2 is valid, then when one member of an alliance loses reliability, we should expect it to have trouble keeping its allies.

Alliance Termination

According to the business literature, a company that develops a bad reputation will lose profits. William Rogerson finds that, "owing to the effect of reputation, high quality firms have more customers, because *they have fewer dissatisfied customers who leave,* and word-of-mouth advertising results in more arrivals."[36] Not only do reputable firms attract more customers, top job seekers, and investors, but a positive reputation also helps firms gain repeat customers and maintain employee loyalty. Fombrun claims that "a good reputation builds employee loyalty by increasing the willingness of employees to cooperate with unusual requests and by fostering teamwork and a sense of shared destiny."[37]

Although several variables have been used in international relations to explain the downfall of an alliance, neorealists have the most basic prediction: alliances end when the geostrategic circumstances that led to their creation disappear. In other words, if a threatening state is defeated, the alliance formed to counter that threat should end. However, if reputation influences the behavior of states the same way it affects economic actors, then we should also see alliances ending when states perceive a decline in

36. William Rogerson, "Reputation and Product Quality," *Bell Journal of Economics* 14, no. 2 (Autumn 1983), 508, emphasis added.

37. Fombrun, *Reputation*, 77.

their ally's reliability. In fact, there are two possibilities in which a change in reputation affects the existence of a state's alliances. The first is a dyadic explanation of reputation, suggesting that if one state fails to honor its commitment to another (or drags the other into an unwanted war), that particular alliance is likely to end. This provides the third hypothesis.

> HYPOTHESIS 3: An unreliable state will lose the ally that it entrapped or failed to support.

A more difficult test for reputation is whether a state's reliability affects its alliances more broadly. If commitments are interdependent, and if reputation is generalizable beyond the dyad, then any decline in a state's reputation should affect all of its alliances. If state A is in separate alliances with states B and C, and state A fails to honor a commitment to state B, then not only should the alliance between A and B end (as suggested by hypothesis 3) but I also expect the alliance with state C to end.[38] This, then, is the next hypothesis using reputation to help explain alliance termination.

> HYPOTHESIS 4: An unreliable state will lose its allies generally.

These two hypotheses on alliance termination are useful, not only because they provide different tests for reputation but also because they parallel the debate in the deterrence literature concerning whether a state's credibility deters only those directly affected by the state's resolve or rather deters states more generally.[39] If international politics mirrors the corporate world, I expect support to be greatest for the more specific argument on alliance termination (hypothesis 3) than for the broader argument (hypothesis 4). In business even the least-reputable products do get purchased, and firms that treat their workers poorly do still have employees, though typically only those who have limited options.

38. It is conceivable that under some circumstances state C may have wanted state A to abandon state B, in which case A's reputation might not suffer (specifically if B and C are adversaries). But, as my cases show, welcome behavior by a state does not necessarily lead others to assign it greater reliability if it has failed to support one of its allies.

39. For example, see Glenn Snyder and Paul Diesing, *Conflict among Nations* (Princeton: Princeton University Press, 1977), 187; Paul Huth and Bruce Russett, "What Makes Deterrence Work?: Cases from 1900 to 1980," *World Politics* 36, no. 4 (July 1984), 496–526; Paul Huth, *Extended Deterrence and the Prevention of War* (New Haven: Yale University Press, 1988); Paul Huth, "Extended Deterrence and the Outbreak of War," *American Political Science Review* 82, no. 2 (June 1988), 423–443; Paul Huth and Bruce Russett, "General Deterrence between Enduring Rivals: Testing Three Competing Models," *American Political Science Review* 87, no. 1 (March 1993), 61–73; and Paul Huth, "Reputations and Deterrence: A Theoretical and Empirical Assessment," *Security Studies* 7, no. 1 (Autumn, 1997), 92–93.

Because states often ally for strategic reasons, such as power aggregation or to constrain another state's behavior, reputation is not always the primary factor in alliance behavior. But even when a state is willing to ally with an unreliable state for some strategic advantage, reputation will still affect the unreliable state's autonomy by influencing the institutional design of the alliance that is created. For instance, states that are increasingly perceived to be unreliable will have to make greater concessions to their allies to prevent an alliance from ending. The final hypothesis illustrates how reputation influences some of the variation that exists across alliances, both when they form and as they transform over time in response to changing perceptions of a state's reliability.

Alliance Variation

In spite of the large literature on alliances, there are few explanations for the variation that exists across military alliances, and reputation helps fill this gap. Someone with poor credit may be able to obtain a loan, but the conditions of that loan will be different from those given to an individual with good credit. Similarly, alliances will vary because of the reputations of the member states. If an unreliable state is able to find a willing ally, the agreement they make will differ from a commitment made between two reliable states. Just as trusted friends conducting a business transaction will accept an oral agreement while strangers require a more binding written contract, the language of an alliance with an unreliable state will be more binding and restrictive than an alliance between reliable states. Other institutional differences based on a state's reputation are likely to include the amount of up-front costs required of a state to form an alliance and the level of military integration within the alliance.

Many scholars suggest that a commitment to work together decreases the autonomy of all the states involved. James Morrow, in particular, argues that states choose between autonomy and security when forming alliances.[40] However, the degree to which a state's autonomy is reduced by an alliance depends on its reputation; reliable states can gain allies and still maintain their autonomy, while unreliable states will need to give up more autonomy to attract and keep allies, especially reliable ones. There are two reasons why an unreliable state's autonomy is reduced. On the one hand, a

40. James Morrow, "Alliances and Asymmetry: An Alternative to the Capability Aggregation Model of Alliances," *American Journal of Political Science* 35, no. 4 (November 1991), 904–933; Robert Jervis, "From Balance to Concert: A Study of International Security Cooperation," in *Cooperation under Anarchy*, ed. Kenneth Oye (Princeton: Princeton University Press, 1986), 58–79; Charles Lipson, "Why Are Some International Agreements Informal?" *International Organization* 45, no. 4 (Autumn 1991), 495–538; Kenneth Abbott and Duncan Snidal, "Hard and Soft Law in International Governance," *International Organization* 54, no. 3 (Summer 2000), 421–456.

state may demand greater control over an unreliable ally to offset the higher risk of being either abandoned or dragged into an unwanted conflict. On the other hand, an unreliable state can impose costs on itself to signal its interest in honoring an agreement, because giving power to other actors is one way in which commitments can be made to appear more reliable.[41]

Fombrun finds that "companies that are well regarded can benefit from charging premium prices for their products and so reimburse themselves over the long term for the front-end costs of building good reputations."[42] This means that firms with high-quality products are able to charge more because consumers are often willing to pay for assurances of quality. A positive reputation also "provides leverage in many negotiations, particularly with suppliers, creditors, and distributors. Suppliers would prefer to negotiate supply contracts with credible companies, companies unlikely to renege on orders. Likewise, before lending money, creditors want to believe that the company is good for it, that their money won't go down the drain. Studies show that a good reputation can reduce a company's cost of capital by improving its ability to raise money in the credit market."[43]

In contrast, firms with poor reputations incur greater costs because of the higher risks they pose for consumers and investors. Similarly, a person with bad credit who is seeking a loan may be able to find a willing lender, but greater control will be placed on the loan because of the higher risk: the loan may come with a higher rate, require more collateral, or require shorter repayment time. As a result, if there are states willing to ally with an unreliable state, I expect the alliance itself to reduce the unreliable state's freedom of action (increasing the likelihood that it will have to honor its commitments). If one advantage of being reliable is having more autonomy, then it logically follows that reliable states will have a freer hand within their alliances, while unreliable states will be restrained by the institutional design of an alliance.

> HYPOTHESIS 5: An unreliable state will be more constrained by the design of its alliances.

This hypothesis not only explains how reputation influences the initial alliance design but it also identifies one cause of institutional change

41. James Morrow, "The Strategic Setting of Choices: Signaling, Commitment, and Negotiation in International Politics," in *Strategic Choice and International Relations*, ed. David Lake and Robert Powell (Princeton: Princeton University Press 1999), 92. See also James Fearon, "Domestic Political Audiences and the Escalation of International Disputes," *American Political Science Review* 88, no. 3 (September 1994), 577–592; James Fearon, "Signaling Foreign Policy Interests: Tying Hands versus Sinking Costs," *Journal of Conflict Resolution* 41, no. 1 (February 1997), 68–90; and Andrew Kydd, "Trust, Reassurance, and Cooperation," *International Organization* 54, no. 2 (Spring 2000), 325–357.

42. Fombrun, *Reputation*, 75.

43. Ibid., 75–76.

discussed by many in the institutions literature. Barbara Koremenos, Charles Lipson, and Duncan Snidal assert that states construct and shape institutions to advance their goals. According to them, differences between institutions "are the result of rational, purposive interactions among states and other international actors to solve specific problems" (such as having an unreliable ally).[44] Although it is impossible here to evaluate all of the ways in which alliances vary, I can explore the effect that reputation has on some of the more relevant aspects of alliance design and transformation.

Abbott et al. focus on three dimensions in which institutions vary: obligation, precision, and delegation.[45] I apply these same terms to alliance design but conceptualize them slightly differently. For my purposes, *obligation* involves the costs that a state must pay to convince a potential ally that a commitment exists. I define *precision* as the level of explicitness in a treaty's language. Finally, *delegation* is the degree to which one state gives authority over its military to an ally.

Obligation

As the business literature tells us, firms generally seek to develop positive reputations so that they may acquire reputational capital. There are instances, though, where firms have an incentive to misrepresent low-quality products as being high quality in order to charge higher prices. These firms, however, will not have repeat customers; only those high-priced products that are in fact high quality will attract repeat customers. In other words, a positive reputation is not only advantageous to firms but it benefits consumers because it ensures that misrepresentation of quality is not possible over the long run. In contrast, only firms with high-quality products will spend a lot up front, such as in the development of a product or in its advertising, because they know they will profit from high prices and repeat customers. Therefore, consumers can often assess the quality of a product by the amount of money that is spent on publicity, or in the case of professional (e.g., medical or legal) services, on the amount of money spent on office furniture and equipment.[46]

44. Barbara Koremenos, Charles Lipson, and Duncan Snidal, "The Rational Design of International Institutions," *International Organization* 55, no. 4 (Autumn 2001), 762.

45. Kenneth Abbott, Robert Keohane, Andrew Moravcsik, Anne-Marie Slaughter, and Duncan Snidal, "The Concept of Legalization," *International Organization* 54, no. 3 (Summer 2000), 401–419.

46. Rogerson, "Reputation and Product Quality"; Franklin Allen, "Reputation and Product Quality," *RAND Journal of Economics* 15, no. 3 (Autumn 1984), 311–327; Keith Weigelt and Colin Camerer, "Reputation and Corporate Strategy: A Review of Recent Theory and Applications," *Strategic Management Journal* 9, no. 5 (September/October 1988), 443–454.

The lesson here is that for an obligation to exist, an actor must incur a cost if the commitment is broken. For international politics, if a state is perceived to be unreliable, one way it can strengthen its desirability as an alliance partner is to accept costs that will be imposed if the state fails to honor its agreements. Similarly, one way to distinguish between unreliable and reliable states is in the amount of up-front costs a state is willing to pay to participate in the alliance. States that intend to honor their commitments will pay up-front costs that will be lost if they renege on the commitment. These costs can be self-imposed, as a state attempts to signal its trustworthiness to its allies, or they can be demanded from a potential ally as a way to offset the risks of allying with an unreliable state. Among other things, these costs may be economic, as in the promise to provide preferential trade or financial aid, they may consist of a transfer of technology, or they could include a state's willingness to increase its military capabilities. The specific details depend on the international situation at the time and on the needs of the allies.

Regardless of the nature of the payment, cost is a strong signal of commitment, and the greater the up-front costs paid by a state, the stronger the signal of its commitment to the alliance.[47] On the other hand, states perceived to be reliable will not have to make such costly signals because they will have already paid the costs of developing a reliable reputation by honoring previous commitments.

Precision

In business, agreements made between parties that distrust each other (or that know very little about each other) are spelled out very carefully. In contrast, an oral promise is sometimes enough of a commitment between parties that know and trust each other. Likewise, there is a great deal of variation between military alliances concerning their level of precision. On one end of the spectrum are those that are specific about their nature, purpose, and target,[48] and at the other end are vague alliances that leave much open to interpretation;[49] most alliances fall somewhere between these two

47. This insight draws heavily from Fearon, "Domestic Political Audiences," 579–581; Fearon, "Signaling Foreign Policy Interests," 69; and Kydd, "Trust, Reassurance, and Cooperation," 326.

48. The Dual Alliance of Russia and France (1894) specifically outlined when one state would provide support to the other (Article I), discussed the terms in which both states would mobilize (Article II), provided for specific numbers of troops to engage Germany (Article III), called for cooperation between army general staffs (Article IV), ensured no conclusion of a separate peace (Article V), and set the duration of the alliance for as long as the Triple Alliance existed (Article VI). J. A. S. Grenville and Bernard Wasserstein, eds., *The Major International Treaties of the Twentieth Century: A History and Guide with Texts,* (London: Routledge, 2001), 39.

49. The Triple Alliance of Germany, Austria-Hungary, and Italy (1882) promised mutual support "within the limits of their own interests." Cited in Grenville and Wasserstein, *Major International Treaties,* 38.

extremes.[50] As Glenn Snyder suggests, "the more explicit and precise the verbal commitment, the greater the cost in nonfulfillment and the lower the credibility of the threat of nonfulfillment."[51] Therefore, allies of unreliable states should demand greater precision to alleviate fears of either abandonment or entrapment.

In particular, the nature of the commitment, whether there are provisions for the length of the treaty, and the target of the alliance will be more explicit when at least one of the signatories is perceived to be unreliable. Alliances among reliable states are more likely to have vague language, implying greater levels of trust, and providing greater autonomy to the allies.

Delegation

Although Abbott et al. use delegation to focus on the role of third parties to "implement, interpret, and apply the rules,"[52] I emphasize military integration, because that is one way in which military alliances are often implemented. Though states are typically unwilling to delegate authority to an international institution or some other third party, they do allow themselves to become dependent on other states if doing so means improving their security. I am not aware of any parallels with the business literature, although, given the legal nature of the economic market, third parties that take on this role are typically agents of the state. In international politics, however, anarchy allows states to interpret and apply the rules as they see fit. Even when states delegate that authority to a third party, such as an international institution, they still may choose whether or not to adhere to the interpretation. As a result, a state that is perceived to be unreliable is more likely to have to delegate authority over its military to an ally.

There are two primary types of military integration. One is the creation of a unified military command in which states have joint authority over each other's military. The other involves subordination, in which one state's military is under its ally's command. Both types of military integration should be more prevalent when an ally is perceived to be unreliable, because it reduces fears of abandonment by helping to ensure that an unreliable ally will fight when war occurs, since it is more difficult for a state to withdraw from battle when another state's commanders control its forces.

50. The Treaty of Brussels (1948) explicitly named Germany as the target of the alliance between France, Great Britain, and the Benelux countries and was designed to last for at least fifty years. The language, however, was ambiguous about what actions were to be taken: "To take such steps as may be held to be necessary in the event of a renewal by Germany of a policy of aggression." Treaty text available on the NATO website, www.nato.int/docu/basictxt/b480317a.htm, accessed 10 March 2010.

51. Glenn Snyder, *Alliance Politics* (Ithaca: Cornell University Press, 1997), 169.

52. Abbott et al., "Concept of Legalization."

It is also important to understand the reason for a state's particular reputation. The above claims apply to situations in which a state is deemed unreliable because it failed to support an ally in the past. However, if a state is unreliable because it previously dragged its allies into war, then an alliance with high levels of military integration can be disadvantageous to an ally, because the same conditions that make it more difficult for an unreliable state to abandon its allies also make it more difficult for a reliable state to avoid being dragged into a conflict. As a result, when a state is unreliable because it entrapped allies in the past, I expect integration to decrease or to be *lower* than an alliance formed between reliable states.[53]

I expect these three measures to be interchangeable—some alliances stress obligation, others emphasize precision, and so on—although I expect the most unreliable states to be bound by more than one type of constraint. The form of institutional variation that will be used is contingent on the international situation at the time and the needs of the allies. Although explanations for those decisions are beyond the scope of this book, I do discuss them as they arise in several of the case studies.

Competing Hypotheses

There are two literatures that this book addresses—the literature on reputation and the literature on alliance behavior. As a result, there are several competing arguments that can be compared to my reliability hypotheses. Although reputation is unlikely to be a more important factor than each of the alternatives in every situation, reputation frequently is an important variable, and when combined with other theories provides a stronger explanation than the existing theories alone. Therefore, within each case study I compare my five hypotheses with these alternative explanations, all of which suggest that strategic interests of some type are enough to explain a state's behavior and the consequences of that behavior on its alliance autonomy. The first is Mercer's argument that states cannot change their reputation and therefore will not benefit from supporting an ally or suffer for failing to honor a commitment. I also use three theories from the existing alliance formation literature.

One of these is a Waltzian version of balance of power theory, which relies primarily on state capabilities and suggests that states will work to prevent other states or alliances from growing too powerful. To measure

53. I do not expect the other two forms of institutional design examined here to exhibit this same characteristic. Greater obligation and greater precision are likely to be demanded of an unreliable state, regardless of whether it received its reputation for abandonment or for entrapment.

the balance of power, I use the Correlates of War (COW) capabilities score to identify the power of each of the states I examine.[54] Although such scores are typically better suited for large-n statistical analyses, other scholars have used them within case studies to gauge the relative capabilities of the great powers.[55] Next I look at Walt's balance of threat theory, which takes into account capabilities, much as balance of power theory does, but also incorporates geography and intentions to suggest that states will ally against those that threaten their interests the most.[56] Finally, I examine what I refer to here as "binding theory," which focuses on threat much the same way as balance of threat theory does but suggests that rather than ally against a threatening state, states will ally with the threat in order to manage its behavior.[57] There are, as we have seen, many other explanations for alliance behavior, but given the limited space I can devote to each case, I selected the three theories that seem to be the most prominent explanations for state alliance behavior in general, but especially prior to the First World War.

There are no prevailing theories of alliance termination, but we can rely on the alliance formation theories to derive counterarguments under the assumption that whatever condition leads to the formation of an alliance will also affect its continued existence. Using balance of power theory, if capabilities shift I expect the alliance to end. In the case of balance of threat theory, if a threatening state is defeated, the alliance formed to counter that threat should end. Finally, under binding theory, alliances formed with the threatening state will end if the state is no longer perceived to be the greatest threat. In other words, all three competing theories suggest that

54. J. David Singer and Melvin Small, *Correlates of War Project: International and Civil War Data, 1816–1992* [computer file] ICPSR09005-v1. Ann Arbor, MI: Inter-university Consortium for Political and Social Research [distributor], 1994.

55. William Wohlforth, "The Perception of Power: Russia in the Pre-1914 Balance," *World Politics* 39, no. 3 (April 1987), 353–381; Randall Schweller, "Tripolarity and the Second World War," *International Studies Quarterly* 37, no. 1 (March 1993), 73–103; Randall Schweller, *Deadly Imbalances: Tripolarity and Hitler's Strategy of World Conquest* (New York: Columbia University Press, 1998). Although Stephen Walt does not use the Correlates of War scores, he uses a similar composite of data to assess the relative power of states. Stephan Walt, *The Origins of Alliances* (Ithaca: Cornell University Press, 1987).

56. Walt, *Origins of Alliances.*

57. Throughout my case studies I use the term "binding theory," but my treatment of this behavior is a combination of Paul Schroeder's argument about using an alliance to manage the policies of another state and the concept of bandwagoning, which is allying with the source of greatest power or threat, either to avoid being attacked (Walt) or to obtain some profitable gain (Schweller). I treat alliances with the more powerful or threatening state the same, since the reason a state bandwagons is not particularly important for the puzzle in this book. Paul Schroeder, "Alliances, 1815–1945: Weapons of Power and Tools of Management," in *Historical Dimensions of National Security Problems*, ed. Klaus Knorr (Lawrence: University of Kansas Press, 1976), 227–262; Walt, *Origins of Alliances;* Randall Schweller, "Bandwagoning for Profit: Bringing the Revisionist State Back In," *International Security* 19, no. 1 (Summer 1994), 72–107.

alliances will end as a result of changing capabilities rather than as a function of a state's behavior.

There are also no dominant theories of alliance variation, so I rely on an interpretation of what Mercer might expect to see. Although Mercer's focus is on resolve, he does make claims about how a state's reputation influences its alliances. For example, he writes that "although the Algeciras defeat influenced German policy-makers in many ways, it did not lead them to put more faith in their Austrian ally. Because they made situational explanations for Austrian support in 1906, they should not—and did not—credit the Austrians as reliable allies in 1908. This reaction . . . illustrates one of my four propositions: allies rarely get reputations for having resolve."[58] This passage shows that Mercer uses the reputations of resolve and reliability interchangeably, even though they refer to fundamentally different types of reputation. That he claims to address the effect of reputation on the behavior of allies allows me to make inferences on his behalf about a state's reliability.

Mercer's basic argument is that reputation only forms through undesirable behavior, such as when an ally backs down, confirming a reputation for irresolution, or when an adversary stands firm, strengthening a reputation for resolve.[59] If Mercer is right, then states should not avoid alliances with unreliable states, especially if they benefitted from the state's prior bad behavior. Unreliable states should not lose allies because failing to support an ally does not decrease a state's reputation. And finally, Mercer would not expect alliances to change as a result of a state's reliability either rising or falling. He essentially believes that situational factors, such as capabilities, geography, and interests, will be the key determinants of state behavior.

To sum up, Mercer's argument that states cannot change their reputations and therefore should not be concerned about their reputations produces at least three hypotheses that one can compare to mine.

> MERCER 1: A state's reputation should not affect its ability to form an alliance.
>
> MERCER 2: As a state's reliability decreases, it should not lose existing allies.
>
> MERCER 3: As a state's reliability either declines or improves, its alliances should neither become more constraining nor less constraining, respectively.

The most significant difference between Mercer's test of reputation and the one in this book is that he examines whether a state's actions affects

58. Mercer, *Reputation and International Politics,* 124.
59. Ibid., 66.

its allies' expectations of the state's future behavior. In this book I examine whether a state's actions affect its relations with its allies—specifically, whether those allies alter their arrangements with a state based on its level of support. Because of this approach, state expectations are a less-important variable than the tangible change to the relationship between the states. Also, because I expect states to change their relations based on past behavior, I assume that states will generally expect to receive support from their allies—either because they received support in the past or because changes were made to bind a previously unreliable state to increase the chances that it will provide support in the future. I do discuss expectations when they appear relevant or when they do not conform to my assumption, but expectations are not critical for evaluating my argument to the same extent that they are for Mercer.

In general, my case studies ask three questions with respect to each state: How did the state behave? Did the state's behavior improve or weaken its reliability as an ally? And what effect did that change in reputation have on its relations with its other allies? In most cases, there are clear strategic interests, such as balancing power or threat, or even commercial interests, that explain a state's behavior. Consistent with Daryl Press's results, I rarely find evidence that states *act* out of concern for their reputation as an ally during crises.[60] However, I consider it a successful test of reliability if states that fail to support their allies either have trouble finding new allies, lose their existing alliances, or are forced to give up more autonomy than the states that support their allies. Failed tests of my hypotheses are those cases in which an unreliable state is able to gain a new ally, does not lose its allies, or does not lose autonomy within its alliances relative to the more reliable states.

Scope Conditions

I make no claims that reputation is more important for explaining alliance behavior than are any of the existing theories, only that reputation is an important factor despite much of the recent scholarship discounting it. As such, reputation need not be a better explanation than the alternatives; it merely needs to affect state behavior within alliances. Nevertheless, it is useful to discuss the conditions under which reputation should have the greatest affect on state behavior. There are several variables that should influence the degree to which reputation matters, including: the offense-defense balance, system polarity, the role of leaders, expectations of war, the

60. Daryl Press, *Calculating Credibility: How Leaders Assess Military Threats* (Ithaca: Cornell University Press, 2005). England appears to be unique, as being a reliable ally seems to repeatedly become a strategic interest for the British government upon forming an alliance.

number of states within an alliance, and whether a state has other alliance options. I am able to hold the first three variables constant because of the short time period examined across my four case studies. But they are still worth discussing briefly, along with the three factors that do vary.

Reputation should matter more when offense is believed to have the advantage compared to when defense is thought to be dominant.[61] If wars are expected to be quick and decisive (when offense has the advantage), having a reliable ally is critical because states will not have the time to search for others to come to their rescue. In contrast, when wars are expected to be drawn out and costly (when defense has the advantage), leaders believe that they can defend themselves relatively easily, so the dangers of being abandoned by an ally are not as great. This is not to say that reputation is unimportant when defense has the advantage or that it is the most important thing when offense has the advantage, but its importance varies depending on whether leaders believe that states will need to mobilize quickly in the event of war to provide support to allies that have been attacked. During the time period examined here, there was a consistent belief that offense had the advantage (even though the reality is that defense had the advantage).[62] As a result of this belief, reputation should have been relatively important during this time period. But since there is no variation, this is not a factor I can explicitly test within my main case studies.

I can also hold constant system polarity since there is little change during the time period examined. There is some minor movement in terms of the relative capabilities of the great powers, which I discuss in the case studies. But none of the states cease to be great powers, and although Japan only starts to be considered a great power after its victory in the Russo-Japanese War, it was already as powerful as Italy by 1901. According to the Correlates of War capabilities scores, the greatest change occurred between England and the rest of the great powers, with England more powerful than any of the others in 1901, but less powerful than Russia in 1905 and less powerful than Germany in 1908. These capability scores are imperfect, though, because even after its defeat in the Russo-Japanese War, Russia's power

61. For work on the offense-defense balance, see Robert Jervis, "Cooperation under the Security Dilemma," *World Politics* 30, no. 2 (January 1978), 167–214; Stephen Van Evera, "Offense, Defense, and the Causes of War," *International Security* 22, no. 4 (Spring 1998), 5–43; Charles Glaser and Chaim Kaufmann, "What Is the Offense-Defense Balance and Can We Measure It?" *International Security* 22, no. 4 (Spring 1998), 44–82; Stephen Biddle, "Rebuilding the Foundations of Offense-Defense Theory," *Journal of Politics* 63, no. 3 (August 2001), 741–774.

62. Steven Van Evera, "The Cult of the Offensive and the Origins of the First World War," *International Security* 9, no. 1 (Summer 1984), 58–107; Jack Snyder, "Civil-Military Relations and the Cult of the Offensive, 1914 and 1984," *International Security* 9, no. 1 (1984), 108–146; Scott Sagan, "1914 Revisited: Allies, Offense, and Instability," *International Security* 11, no. 2 (Autumn 1986), 151–175.

purportedly increased relative to the other great powers. In 1901 Russia's capabilities score was 0.11, between that of Germany (0.13) and France (0.07); in 1905 it was 0.16, higher than those of Germany and England (both at 0.12). The point is that in this book I only examine the behavior of the great powers in Europe before the First World War and therefore cannot speak to the importance of reputation in other types of systems—bipolar or unipolar—or for smaller powers. I expect medium and small powers to care as much about reputation as great powers—one could even argue that weak states must care more about having reliable allies, since their survival is at greater risk than that of the great powers. It is plausible that reputation also has different levels of importance according to the number of great powers. Whether a great power allies with other great powers or, as in a bipolar system, allies with smaller powers should influence the relative importance of reputation. But, again, because system polarity is unchanging during my cases, I cannot test this possibility.

This book also does not directly deal with the question of whether reputations are assigned to states or to individual leaders. Both have reputations, although this is not something that can be tested here, because there is relatively little change in leadership during the time period examined. With the exception of France, there is little turnover at the very highest level of decision making within each of the great powers.[63] But being able to hold this variable relatively constant is an advantage because it allows me to ignore the issue of whether state or individual reputations matter most, though I do discuss examples in my cases where the role of individual leaders seems to affect state behavior.

The first scope condition that does vary during this time period has to do with crises and expectations of war. Reputation should decline in importance as war is perceived to be more likely, because strategic necessities will outweigh other factors.[64] This means that in crises or when war is expected states are more likely to ally with others that have a strategic position or a lot of military power. This does not mean they will ignore reputation and

63. England's King Edward VII reigned from 1901 to 1910; Germany's Kaiser Wilhelm II, from 1888 to 1918; Russia's Tsar Nicholas II, from 1894 to 1917; Austria-Hungary's Emperor Franz Joseph, from 1848 to 1916; and Italy's King Victor Emmanuel III, from 1896 to 1947. There is turnover at the ministerial levels—Germany had three foreign ministers between 1900 and 1910, England had four prime ministers representing two different political parties, and Italy had seven foreign ministers during that same time period. But a sufficient analysis of reputation at all these various levels is beyond the scope of this book.

64. This claim is consistent with Daryl Press's findings about calculations being a more important determinant of state behavior than past behavior. While Press's argument may be valid, he only examines crises, which is precisely when strategic factors should outweigh reputation. Therefore, while his study provides evidence of the limited value of reputation in crises, it tells us little about the importance of reputation after a crisis or in noncrisis situations. Press, *Calculating Credibility.*

willingly partner with unreliable states but that reputation will be a less important criterion for an ally than capabilities when war appears to be likely. In contrast, when war is considered unlikely, reputation should be relatively more important because states have more to lose if an ally drags them into an unwanted war or if an attempt to deter fails because of an ally that is perceived to be unreliable. During the cold war we might expect allies to care a lot about reputation during periods of détente and care relatively less during periods of heightened tension between the superpowers, when strategic interests become more important. In the four cases examined in this book, reputation should become increasingly less important for Europe's great powers with each successive crisis leading toward the First World War, as strategic interests became more critical. Although Europe's leaders did not know when war would occur, public opinion in 1912 viewed war to be significantly more likely than in 1905,[65] and this will be reflected in the relative importance of reputation.

It is also possible that my argument is most applicable to bilateral alliances, because when two states form an alliance each puts a great deal of trust in the other. As the number of member states increases, the importance of each state's reputation may diminish because trust is more diffused as more states are able to free ride.[66] In bilateral agreements, however, if one state free rides or reneges on its commitment, the alliance becomes less relevant. I do not argue that reputation is irrelevant for multilateral alliances. On the contrary, the reputation of the alliance as a whole may become very important. But an individual state's reliability may have less influence on the formation or structure of a multilateral alliance than it has on bilateral agreements. States with an unreliable ally may also attempt to enlarge the alliance to help offset the ally's reputation by further decreasing its autonomy. Although there were no large multilateral alliances during the pre–First World War era, there were bilateral and trilateral alliances, so this variation provides some information about the connection between reputation and alliance size.

Finally, states that have more opportunities to ally will put greater emphasis on the importance of having a reliable ally, whereas states with few

65. A quick search of articles in the *Times* (London) reveals that the words "war" and "Europe" do not both appear in any article titles between 1904 and 1910, but they appear in the title of five articles between 1911 and 1913. Similarly, the phrase "European war" appears in the text of thirty-three news articles between 1904 and 1907, but shows up in the text of sixty-two articles between 1909 and 1912 (and in the text of thirty-five articles in 1913 alone).

66. This is similar to the arguments made by Mancur Olson and Charles Kindleberger regarding the increased difficulty of providing public goods as the number of actors increases. Mancur Olson, *The Logic of Collective Action: Public Goods and the Theory of Groups*, (Cambridge: Harvard University Press, 1965); Charles Kindleberger, "Dominance and Leadership in the International Economy: Exploitation, Public Goods, and Free Rides," *International Studies Quarterly* 25, no. 2 (June 1981), 242–254.

alliance options will have to make do with any allies they can find, regardless of their reliability. This is the variable with perhaps the greatest degree of differentiation during the period examined. The British always had many potential allies, and therefore they should have put a great deal of emphasis on the reliability of the states with whom they chose to ally. In contrast, Germany and Austria-Hungary had few options other than to remain in the Triple Alliance, and therefore they should have assigned less importance to the reliability of an ally. Or at the very least, states with fewer options should have punished unreliable allies less than states that had many other alliance options.

3

The End of Splendid Isolation

British Pursuit of an Ally, 1901–1905

Associate yourself with men of good quality if you esteem your own reputation; for 'tis better to be alone than in bad company.

George Washington

Important Dates

20 May 1882	Triple Alliance signed (Austria-Hungary, Germany, and Italy)
4 January 1894	Dual Alliance signed (France and Russia)
1 August 1894–17 April 1895	Sino-Japanese War
11 October 1899–31 May 1902	Boer War
16 October 1900	Yangtze agreement signed (England and Germany)
29 October 1900	Japan joins the Yangtze agreement
18 March–19 December 1901	Anglo-German alliance negotiations
6 November 1901–30 January 1902	Anglo-Japanese alliance negotiations
28 June 1902	Triple Alliance renewed
8 February 1904–5 September 1905	Russo-Japanese War
8 April 1904	Anglo-French Entente signed (aka the Entente Cordiale)

21 October 1904	Dogger Bank Incident
12 August 1905	Second Anglo-Japanese Alliance

Key Actors

England

Edward VII	King (1901–1910)
Robert Cecil, the Marquis of Salisbury	Prime Minister (1895–1902)
Henry Lansdowne	Foreign Secretary (1900–1905)
William Selborne	First Lord of the Admiralty (1900–1905)
Joseph Chamberlain	Secretary of State for the Colonies (1895–1903)
Francis Lascelles	Ambassador to Germany (1895–1907)
Claude MacDonald	Envoy/Ambassador to Japan (1900–1912)
Francis Bertie	Assistant Undersecretary of Far Eastern Affairs (1894–1903); Ambassador to Italy (1903–1905)
George Curzon	Viceroy of India (1899–1905)

Germany

Wilhelm II	Kaiser (1888–1918)
Bernard von Bülow	Chancellor (1900–1909)
Hermann von Eckardstein	Ambassador to England (1901–1902)

Japan

Komura Jutaro	Foreign Minister (1901–1905)

Britain's attitude toward the European Continent at the end of the nineteenth century is often described as one of "splendid isolation." This is an unfortunate term because it mischaracterizes British foreign policy during that time. Rather than avoiding involvement in European power politics—

which is how U.S. isolation is frequently described—Britain simply avoided any long-term formal defense commitments, giving it a free hand to switch allegiances and maintain the balance of power on the Continent. However, events toward the end of the nineteenth century contributed to a shift in British thinking. Growing competition for colonies among Europe's great powers brought with it increased threat from foreign navies, particularly France and Russia after their formation of the Dual Alliance on 4 January 1894. In addition, the Boer War (1899–1902)—opposed by much of the rest of Europe—illustrated to many in the British government the limited resources they had available for maintaining their empire and for unilaterally preserving Europe's balance of power.[1]

As a result, for the first half-decade of the 1900s, British alliance decisions significantly diverged from previous policy. Britain initially looked to Germany for increased cooperation, as a direct balance against both France and Russia. However, within a year the British government abandoned its alliance negotiations with Germany and instead turned to Japan as a way to balance against Russia in Asia. England was then nearly dragged into a war when Japan attacked Russia, but the British felt so compelled to honor their agreement that they went beyond the required neutrality. Then, during the Russo-Japanese War, England formed the Entente Cordiale with France, which was at least partly a result of the two states' mutual concern over being dragged into war by their allies. This agreement not only influenced the outcome of the war between Japan and Russia, as well as the First Moroccan Crisis, but it also helped lay the foundation for the division of Europe leading up to the First World War.

In examining Britain's shift from balancer to ally, in this chapter I focus on four separate but related cases, each of which illustrates the importance of a state's reputation for its alliance policies, but in different ways. The first case examines the Anglo-German alliance negotiations, which failed in large part because of Germany's reputation for being unreliable. This not only illustrates the challenge facing unreliable states in search of an ally, but negotiations over the terms of the alliance also provide a useful test of my claims regarding alliance variation.

The second case examines the more successful negotiations between England and Japan. After failing to accept an alliance with Germany, the British instead opted for an agreement with a more reliable Japanese ally, which itself viewed an alliance with England favorably, at least partly because of England's reputation for reliability. The Anglo-Japanese negotiations also test my claims concerning alliance variation.

1. Paul Schroeder, "World War I as Galloping Gurtie: A Reply to Joachim Remak," *Journal of Modern History* 44, no. 3 (September 1972), 324; George Monger, *The End of Isolation: British Foreign Policy, 1900–1907* (London: Thomas Nelson, 1963), 1–20.

British support for their ally during the Russo-Japanese War then provides the remaining two cases in this chapter. The first circumstance is the renewal of the Anglo-Japanese treaty on more favorable terms for the British. The second is the Entente Cordiale signed between England and France. These are two important tests because they look at the behavior of states during a war, whereas the next three chapters focus on crises short of war. In addition, both of these cases further enhance my claims about the relationship between reputation and alliances, and specifically strengthen the hypotheses on alliance variation.

In each of the sections that follow, I discuss the relevant details of each observation, focus on how the main counterarguments attempt to explain not only state behavior but also instances of alliance formation, termination, and variation after the incident, and then illustrate how adding reputation enhances our ability to explain the alliance behavior of states. I then summarize the results at the end of the chapter and discuss the relative merits of each reputation hypothesis compared to the competing theories.

Mercer contends that states frequently act out of concern for their reputation, but he finds that because states do not get credit for a reputation for being reliable they should only act out of strategic interests.[2] Likewise, Daryl Press finds that capabilities are a more valid explanation of state behavior than past actions, at least during crises.[3] I do not disagree with either Mercer or Press and show in my cases that states frequently do act according to their strategic interests. Nevertheless, the purpose of this book is to assess whether those actions affect a state's reliability as an ally. Therefore, in each of the cases I examine the variety of strategic reasons for states behaving the way they do during crises, but then I focus on the consequences of their behavior for their reputation, and thus on the behavior of their allies in response.

Not every case tests all five hypotheses presented in chapter 2; for instance, if no new alliances are sought by any of the actors, then the case does not provide any type of test for the hypotheses on alliance formation. In fact, this chapter provides no real test of the two hypotheses on alliance termination, since no states were completely abandoned by an existing ally. However, this chapter, like all of the empirical chapters, provides a significant number of overall tests to allow for several useful conclusions regarding the relationship between a state's reputation and its alliance options.

2. Jonathan Mercer, *Reputation and International Politics* (Ithaca: Cornell University Press, 1996), 226–227.

3. Daryl Press, *Calculating Credibility: How Leaders Assess Military Threats* (Ithaca: Cornell University Press, 2005).

Anglo-German Alliance Negotiations

On 16 October 1900, England and Germany signed the Yangtze agreement, by which the two governments (joined by Japan later that month) sought to uphold freedom of trade for China, often referred to as the Open Door.[4] The agreement was intended to prevent Russian expansion, but it brought England and Germany closer to what Joseph Chamberlain, the British secretary of state for the colonies at the time, referred to as a "natural alliance."[5] An alliance with Germany was considered natural at least partly because the British did not believe they had many other options.[6] William Selborne, who became First Lord of the Admiralty on 24 October 1900, wrote, "I can see only one possible alternative [to a general suspension of armaments in Europe] and that is a formal alliance with Germany."[7]

The first hint of German interest in an alliance came in a statement by Kaiser Wilhelm II during a January 1901 trip to London to be with Queen Victoria, his dying grandmother.[8] Before returning to Berlin, he told a British audience, "We ought to form an Anglo-German alliance, you to keep the seas while we would be responsible for the land."[9] German public opinion, however, was strongly anti-British, primarily on account of its opposition to the Boer War.[10] For instance, one German newspaper stated, in reference to the kind response given to Wilhelm on his leaving London: "At another time this, perhaps, would awaken a sympathetic echo in Germany, but so long as the *godless and unjust Boer war* continues the wall of division remains between Germany and British public opinion."[11] As a result, Bernhard von Bülow, who was appointed German chancellor on 16 October 1900,[12] made every effort to assure the public that his government was not contemplating an alliance with England.

Despite von Bülow's promises, or perhaps without his knowledge, on 18 March 1901 Baron Hermann von Eckardstein, the German ambassador

4. *Times* (London), 22 October 1900, p. 7, col. A; "The Anglo-German Agreement," *Times* (London), 1 November 1900.

5. William Langer, *The Diplomacy of Imperialism, 1890–1902* (New York: Knopf, 1951), 659; George Gooch, *Before the War: Studies in Diplomacy*, vol. 1, *The Grouping of the Powers* (London: Longmans, Green, 1936), 6; Monger, *End of Isolation*, 14; Paul Kennedy, *The Rise of the Anglo-German Antagonism, 1860–1914* (London: Ashfield, 1980), 230–231; Stephen Lee, *Aspects of British Political History, 1815–1914* (London: Routledge, 1994), 260.

6. As I discuss later in this chapter, the Germans probably believed the same thing.

7. Monger, *End of Isolation*, 12.

8. "Arrival of the German Emperor," *Times* (London), 21 January 1901.

9. Kennedy, *Rise of Anglo-German Antagonism*, 243–244.

10. "Foreign Opinion," *Times* (London), 6 April 1900.

11. Cited in "German Press Anti-British," *New York Times*, 7 February 1901, emphasis added.

12. "Hohenlohe Has Resigned," *New York Times*, 18 October 1900.

in London, unofficially proposed that England and Germany sign a defensive alliance.[13] In principle, many in the British government concurred that an alliance with Germany would be welcome. As a growing commercial power, Germany shared British interests in preserving the Open Door and thus was also concerned about the possibility of Russian expansion into China. In addition, although Germany had already begun to build up its naval power, at that time the German navy posed less of a threat to British interests, particularly in Asia and Africa, than did the combined French and Russian navies. This was especially true given the conclusion of the Franco-Russian alliance, or Dual Alliance, in 1894. An alliance would make the German naval buildup useful to the British rather than a threat,[14] because Germany could balance the French navy in Europe, allowing England to focus more naval power in other parts of the empire.

Notwithstanding the strategic interests in cooperating with Germany, negotiations broke down by the end of 1901,[15] and Germany's reputation had a lot to do with the failure of the negotiations. Instead, the British pursued, and eventually completed, an alliance with Japan. As the following discussion illustrates, although there were strategic benefits to an alliance with Japan, those benefits did not outweigh the possible gains of an alliance with Germany. Only by incorporating reputation can we explain the failure of the Anglo-German negotiations in favor of an alliance with Japan.

Negotiations with Germany

One way to illustrate how including reputation improves on existing alliance theories is to look at whether those theories sufficiently explain British behavior in 1901. There are two primary British decisions to examine here. First, why did the British initially approach Germany? Second, why did the negotiations fail, leading England to ally with Japan instead?

When England first began to search for an ally, it was clearly the most powerful state in Europe. Only the United States was more powerful globally. (Table 3.1 shows the great power rankings in 1901, according to the Correlates of War capabilities score.) Because the United States was unwilling to ally with any European states in the period I examine prior to the

13. There is some debate over which government made the formal alliance proposal first, but credible evidence points to von Eckardstein as having made the first move on behalf of the German government. George Gooch and Harold Temperley, eds., *British Documents on the Origins of the War, 1898–1914*, vol. 2, *The Anglo-Japanese Alliance and the Franco-British Entente* (London: His Majesty's Stationery Office, 1927), no. 77 (18 March 1901), 60–61.

14. Gooch, *Grouping of the Powers*, 9; Monger, *End of Isolation*, 63.

15. Gooch and Temperley, *Anglo-Japanese Alliance and the Franco-British Entente*, no. 94 (19 December 1901), 80–83.

Table 3.1. The great powers in 1901

State	Capabilities score	Alliance (combined score)
United States	0.20	None
England	0.17	None
Germany	0.13	Triple Alliance (0.20)
Russia	0.11	Dual Alliance (0.18)
France	0.07	Dual Alliance (0.18)
Austria-Hungary	0.04	Triple Alliance (0.20)
Italy	0.03	Triple Alliance (0.20)
Japan	0.03	None

First World War, I exclude it from all discussion of the alliance behavior of the great powers in these cases.

In examining the conventional explanations for the British pursuit of an alliance with Germany, only one of the three alliance theories can explain the British choice, but then it cannot explain why the negotiations fell apart. If we focus on capabilities, balance of power theory has difficulty explaining England's decision to abandon isolation and search for an ally in the first place. Because of England's power, an alliance with any other European power would have tipped the balance, but one with Germany would have especially altered the balance of power in Europe, since the Triple Alliance was already more powerful than the Dual Alliance. In fact, the best way for England to maintain the balance of power would have been to remain neutral and preserve its flexibility in the event that one of the existing alliances surpassed the other.

If we add geography and intent to capabilities, Walt's balance of threat theory is more successful at explaining the initial British decision to negotiate with Germany.[16] Germany was a logical partner to balance against the Dual Alliance of France and Russia, which at the time was perceived to be a more dangerous threat to British interests, particularly in Asia and Africa. According to one London *Times* article, "the Dual Alliance is working in every possible direction against British interests. One of its first plans after the alliance was concluded consisted in cutting off British India from its *Hinterland* by establishing communication between the French and Russian possessions in Tongking and Central Asia across Yun-nan and Tibet."[17] By

16. Stephan Walt, *The Origins of Alliances* (Ithaca: Cornell University Press, 1987).

17. "Russia and Tibet," *Times* (London), 29 June 1901, emphasis in original. Tongking refers to the northernmost part of modern Vietnam; Yun-nan refers to the southernmost province in China.

itself, however, balance of threat theory cannot explain why the negotiations were ultimately abandoned in favor of an alliance with Japan. Nor can it explain the nature of the alliance that England and Japan formed, since the agreement failed to address potential threats to British interests anywhere except in Asia.

Some scholars suggest that states ally to control the actions of certain states, in what Paul Schroeder refers to as "managing the threat," or what Patricia Weitsman calls "binding."[18] One can certainly make the argument that this was part of the British thinking in their pursuit of an alliance with Germany. Although, if the British perceived the combined forces of France and Russia to be a greater threat than Germany (greater even than Germany and Austria-Hungary combined), then the theory is unable to explain why England approached Germany first, rather than France or Russia. The British did consider an agreement with Russia, but only after the German negotiations broke down, and any Russian agreement was forgotten once England signed the treaty with Japan. Furthermore, the British only allied with France and Russia once Germany became a perceptibly greater threat in comparison to the other great powers—after Japan defeated Russia, and then as a result of Germany's aggressiveness during the First Moroccan Crisis.[19]

Neither Mercer's argument nor my own hypotheses on reputation apply to the British decision to seek an alliance with Germany. But Mercer's general argument would suggest that British decision makers should not have taken a negative view of past German actions unless those actions were particularly unfavorable to the British. And even then, if allies always have a negative reputation, Germany should not have suffered any negative consequences for its past unreliable behavior. If an alliance were to form regardless of German reliability, and that alliance was not more binding on Germany than on the British, then that would falsify my arguments about both alliance formation and alliance variation. On the other hand, if the British decided against an alliance because of Germany's reputation, then that challenges Mercer's general assertion that leaders should not be concerned about their state's reputation.

Explaining the Failed Negotiations

Although reputation cannot explain everything, it effectively complements the conventional theories of alliance formation and adds to our under-

18. Paul Schroeder, "Alliances, 1815–1945: Weapons of Power and Tools of Management," in *Historical Dimensions of National Security Problems*, ed. Klaus Knorr (Lawrence: University of Kansas Press, 1976), 227–262; Patricia Weitsman, *Dangerous Alliances: Proponents of Peace, Weapons of War* (Stanford: Stanford University Press, 2004).

19. John White, *Transition to Global Rivalry: Alliance Diplomacy and the Quadruple Entente, 1895–1907* (Cambridge: Cambridge University Press, 1995), 226.

standing of alliance behavior by explaining both the decision to avoid allying with unreliable states and the nature of the alliance that does form. Only balance of threat theory is able to explain England's pursuit of an alliance with Germany. Unless British perceptions of threat changed, balance of threat theory cannot by itself explain the failure of the negotiations. Even though the failed negotiations are consistent with balance of power theory and binding theory, because they cannot explain the initial British decision to approach Germany they cannot be considered successful explanations of British behavior. To explain the failure of the negotiations, we must incorporate reputation.

The first question in testing my argument about alliance formation is to determine how the British perceived Germany's reliability; to explain England's decision to not ally with Germany using reputation as a criterion, we must first identify whether or not the British perceived Germany to be unreliable and/or if Germany behaved during the negotiations in a way that suggested it was unreliable. If the British believed that Germany was unreliable, then hypothesis 1 on alliance formation would expect the British to be unwilling to form an alliance, or, at the very least, based on my arguments about alliance variation (hypothesis 5), to demand an agreement that would constrain Germany without decreasing British autonomy.

Initially, the British cabinet was split between those who saw the value of an alliance with Germany and those who favored *rapprochement* with France and Russia. A memorandum circulated by Francis Bertie, assistant undersecretary of far eastern affairs at the time, provides some indication that Germany's past behavior was part of the British calculation during the alliance discussions (regardless of whether or not the British benefitted from those past actions):

> It would be a great relief to be able to feel that we had secured a powerful and *sure* ally for the contingency of an attack on the British Empire . . . but in considering offers of alliance from Germany it is necessary to remember the history of Prussia as regards alliances and the conduct of the Bismarck Government in making a treaty with Russia concerning and behind the back of Austria the ally of Germany. . . . She has beaten and robbed Denmark, and for that purpose she took as partner Austria and then turned round on her confederate and drove her out of Germany.[20]

Obviously Bertie referred to Germany's reputation—even past *Prussian* actions—to make his case that an alliance with Germany would be dangerous because of its history as an unreliable ally. Taking a similar view,

20. Gooch and Temperley, *Anglo-Japanese Alliance and the Franco-British Entente*, no. 91 (9 November 1901), 73–76, emphasis in original.

Britain's prime minister, Robert Gascoyne Cecil, the Marquess of Salisbury, wrote: "She [Germany] will . . . never stand by us against Russia; but is always rather inclined to curry favor with Russia by throwing us over."[21] Lord Salisbury's comment appears in a personal correspondence to Lord George Curzon, who at the time was the viceroy of India but who had been Salisbury's private secretary in 1895. As a result, even if Bertie's argument referred to Germany's reputation for being an unreliable ally simply because of a personal preference for an alliance with some other state, Salisbury's letter to a trusted friend is a credible expression of his concerns about German unreliability, which were clearly shared in the British government.

Germany's behavior just prior to the alliance negotiations provided the British with further evidence of its unreliability. Toward the end of January 1901, Russia received concessions from China that Japan and England both perceived to be in violation of the Yangtze agreement. However, Germany claimed that it did not regard this as a threat to Chinese sovereignty or to the Open Door policy and thus declined to act.[22] In response to Germany's position, critics of an alliance believed that Germany was reluctant to oppose Russia and that it had not provided England and Japan with adequate support even after encouraging Britain to stand up to the Russians.[23] Bertie claimed that "the Germans want to push us into the water and then steal our clothes."[24] As a result, British distrust of Germany increased.

According to hypothesis 1, the British should have abandoned the alliance negotiations right then. That they continued to negotiate an alliance may be a function of the split cabinet, or more likely the strategic belief that Germany was the only possible ally to counter the growing Franco-Russian threat. Although this fails to fully support the first hypothesis on alliance formation, it does not invalidate it, given that the negotiations did eventually break down, and Germany's reputation clearly had a great deal to do with the British decision to consider other options once they became available.

Although an Anglo-German alliance never materialized, it is useful to examine the British position during the negotiations to determine the validity of the hypothesis on alliance variation. According to hypothesis 5, because of Germany's unreliability, we should see the British pushing for high levels of obligation (for Germany to pay some up-front costs) and precision (very clear language) to both constrain German actions and to avoid being

21. Cited in Monger, *End of Isolation*, 17.

22. Monger, *End of Isolation*, 23; Kennedy, *Rise of Anglo-German Antagonism*, 243–244.

23. Monger, *End of Isolation*, 29, 43; J. A. S. Grenville, "Lansdowne's Abortive Project of 12 March 1901 for a Secret Agreement with Germany," *Bulletin of the Institute of Historical Research* 27, no. 76 (November 1954), 213.

24. A note, Bertie to Salisbury, 9 March 1901, Foreign Office 46/545, cited in Grenville, "Lansdowne's Abortive Project of 12 March 1901," 213.

abandoned. Likewise, since the British seemed more concerned with being abandoned by Germany than with being entrapped, I also expect the British would have demanded high levels of delegation (control over the German military, or at least its naval operations).

The negotiations never progressed far enough for either side to address issues of obligation or delegation. However, the British did demand very high levels of precision. Lord Henry Lansdowne, the British foreign secretary, welcomed possible German cooperation in the Far East but was reticent enough about any type of commitment with Germany to be leery of a broad general alliance.[25] On 29 March 1901, Lansdowne wrote a letter to Francis Lascelles, the British ambassador in Berlin, saying that his British colleagues "regard with a certain amount of apprehension the idea of an international arrangement of the somewhat indefinite but very far-reaching character . . . suggested to me. If the matter was to be advanced we ought to endeavor to form *a more precise conception* of the contingencies for which we desired to provide."[26]

In contrast to the British idea of a very narrow, specific agreement exclusive to the Far East, the German offer was for the British to join the Triple Alliance, through which England would be asked to make a commitment not only to Germany but to Austria-Hungary and Italy as well.[27] This proposal created at least two potential problems for the British. First, at that time the articles of the Triple Alliance were secret. (For the text of the treaty, see appendix A.) Therefore, the Germans were asking the British to join an alliance without first knowing all of its terms. The second problem with the German proposal is that such an agreement would not allay British fears of being abandoned by Germany, while additional commitments to Italy and Austria-Hungary would increase British concerns about being dragged into a European conflict.[28] This was particularly true given Austria-Hungary's tense relationship with Russia. The British may have been willing to look past Germany's reputation if an alliance was formed that constrained Germany, thus reducing its ability to abandon England during a crisis. However, adding states to the agreement that were themselves likely to entrap England into an unwanted conflict intensified British fears about any type

25. Monger, *End of Isolation,* 30; Lee, *Aspects of British Political History,* 260.

26. Gooch and Temperley, *Anglo-Japanese Alliance and the Franco-British Entente,* no. 79 (29 March 1901), 62, emphasis added. For the German side, see E. T. S. Dugdale, *German Diplomatic Documents, 1871–1914,* vol. 3, *The Growing Antagonism, 1898–1910* (London: Methuen, 1930), no. 58 (16 May 1901), 145–146.

27. Dugdale, *Growing Antagonism* no. 53 (14 April 1901), 144; Gooch and Temperley, *Anglo-Japanese Alliance and the Franco-British Entente,* no. 86 (29 May 1901), 68, and no. 94 (19 December 1901), 80–83; Monger, *End of Isolation,* 35.

28. F. R. Bridge and Roger Bullen, *The Great Powers and the European States System, 1814–1914* (Harlow, UK: Pearson, 2005), 267.

of alliance with Germany. Nevertheless, the Germans were unwavering in their demands for a "Quadruple Alliance."

Ultimately, British alliance negotiations with Germany fell apart in December 1901 for two main reasons. First, many in the British government did not trust Germany from the beginning, and German inaction during the 1901 China crisis brought the rest of the British government into agreement with that position. Second, Germany asked too high a price for an alliance with England, including a British commitment to the defense of Germany's other allies. Germany's key diplomat in England, von Eckardstein, could also take some of the blame for the collapse of negotiations, because despite his good intentions he was unable to convince the British of Germany's benevolent intentions.

Germany's intransigence seems to have been based largely on its belief that the British had no other possible allies and would eventually realize they needed Germany, at which point the Germans could dictate the terms of the alliance.[29] If true, this is consistent with one of my scope conditions. If a state has several alliance options, it can afford to care about the reliability of its allies. However, if the number of potential allies is low (either because there are few major powers with which to ally or because the state's reputation has fallen, making it a less attractive ally), a state's emphasis on reputation will also decline. This helps explain why England first approached Germany, despite concerns about reputation, but quickly changed course once Japan became available as an alternative great power ally.

Interestingly, even after the collapse of the negotiations, Lansdowne was still willing to consider some type of limited entente with Germany.[30] However, instead of an alliance that would commit England to definite action as the Germans desired, he proposed a set of agreements that would declare common interests in certain areas, such as the Mediterranean or the Persian Gulf.[31] Therefore, the British were still willing to discuss a less-formal type of agreement with Germany, and one that was less binding on England, even though a formal military alliance had become unacceptable because of Germany's lack of reliability.

Anglo-Japanese Alliance Negotiations

After Japan's victory in the Sino-Japanese War (1894–95), Russia, Germany, and France put pressure on Japan to give up its gains from the war (often

29. Dugdale, *Growing Antagonism* 17. 195 (26 November 1901), 151–152; Gooch, *Grouping of the Powers*, 7.

30. Bridge and Bullen, *Great Powers and the European States System*, 267.

31. Monger, *End of Isolation*, 66.

referred to as the "triple intervention").[32] As a result, by the turn of the century the Japanese were primarily concerned about any future conflict with Russia leading to an expanded war against multiple European states, particularly given France's 1894 alliance with Russia. However, the Japanese believed that a British commitment would be enough to deter other states from entering a war against Japan.

Japan initially broached the subject of an agreement on 16 October 1901 while the British were still muddling through alliance negotiations with Germany.[33] As a result of its inability to develop a satisfactory alliance with Germany, the British government decided instead to pursue an alliance with Japan to balance the growing threat to its colonial and naval interests, at least in Asia. On 6 November 1901, still a month before the collapse of talks with Germany, the British gave their draft version of an alliance to the Japanese. Over the next three months, the two sides exchanged drafts, each of which suggests that England was much more comfortable giving up some autonomy to the Japanese than they were to Germany.[34] This may partly be a function of Japan posing less of a direct threat to England than Germany did. But the difference in the two states' reliability also contributed to British decision making.

The final text of the treaty was signed on 30 January 1902 and then laid out before the British Parliament on 11 February 1902. (For the text of the treaty, see appendix B.)[35] The agreement obligated England and Japan only to consult each other in crises and to aid one another in the event that either state was attacked by two other major powers. In a war between Japan and just one European state, Britain merely promised to remain neutral. The treaty also recognized Japan's particular interest in Korea, as well as the allies' mutual interests in China, while no Japanese support was promised for other British interests in Asia, such as those in India.[36]

Explaining the Alliance with Japan

Existing alliance theories have mixed success at explaining the British and Japanese choices leading up to their alliance. On one level, balance of power theory would see the Anglo-Japanese Alliance as a natural balance against

32. Langer, *Diplomacy of Imperialism;* Charles Spinks, "The Background of the Anglo-Japanese Alliance," *Pacific Historical Review* 8, no. 3 (September 1939), 317–339.

33. Ian Nish, *The Anglo-Japanese Alliance: The Diplomacy of Two Island Empires, 1894–1907* (London: Athlone, 1985).

34. For various drafts during the treaty negotiations, see Gooch and Temperley, *Anglo-Japanese Alliance and the Franco-British Entente*, no. 125 (30 January 1902), 114–120.

35. "Great Britain and Japan: Important Agreement," *Times* (London), 12 February 1902.

36. Gooch and Temperley, *Anglo-Japanese Alliance and the Franco-British Entente,* no. 125 (30 January 1902), 114–120.

both the Dual Alliance and the Triple Alliance, since the combined capabilities scores of all three alliances were between 0.18 and 0.20. Yet balance of power theory is problematic for two reasons. First of all, the combined power of the Anglo-Japanese Alliance did not apply to Europe. Therefore, the alliance did not help England balance power at all on the Continent (other than freeing up some of the British navy in Asia to be repositioned elsewhere). Second, the alliance tipped the balance of power in Asia toward Japan, since the combined British and Japanese navies in Asia were vastly superior to Russia's navy.

Balance of threat is a decent fit, since it partly explains England's decision to ally with Japan, but only with respect to Asia. Whereas an alliance with Germany would have helped balance the threat from both France and Russia, the agreement with Japan was aimed almost exclusively at preventing Russia from encroaching further into Asia. To be sure, there were strategic benefits to an alliance with Japan, not the least of which is that England could spend fewer resources in Asia and spend more energy maintaining the balance of power in Europe. But by incorporating concerns of German reliability, and because no other states were perceived to be possible allies, the alliance with Japan becomes even more understandable. Both balancing theories do make more sense by themselves from the Japanese viewpoint, since an alliance with England balanced against both Russia's status as a regional power and the threat that its rising power posed to Japan. Yet, as I show in the next section, the Japanese still paid close attention to England's reputation as a reliable ally even before making the offer of an alliance.

Binding theories also cannot explain the British decision to ally with Japan. Japan posed no real threat to England, nor did the British hold any preconceived notions about being able to control Japan through an alliance. I found no evidence that this was one of the British motivations, particularly since they made minimal attempts to prevent war between Japan and Russia, despite having been asked by the Japanese at the beginning of the alliance negotiations what the British response would be to a war between Japan and Russia. If managing the threat had been the goal, more significant attempts would have been made to ally with France or Russia. Similarly, had Japan been trying to ally for binding purposes, it would have allied with Russia instead of England. Japan did make some attempts to negotiate an agreement with Russia, but these were quickly dropped when an agreement with England became possible.

In what is a very clear example of reputation influencing alliance choices, prior to its initial alliance offer of October 1901 the Japanese government evaluated Britain's history of honoring its commitments. When Komura Jutaro became foreign minister in September 1901—just one month before the Japanese offer of alliance—one of his first acts was to have the foreign ministry research whether Britain had ever violated its obligations under an alliance. The response was that there had been occasions when Britain violated international treaties but it had never abandoned an ally.[37] The degree to which British reputation directly influenced Japanese decision makers is unclear, but the timing strongly suggests that Komura gave his support to an alliance with Great Britain based heavily on British reputation, measured by its consistent support for allies in the past.

On the British side, some cabinet members expressed concern about allying with Japan and being dragged into a war against Russia. Certainly, Lansdowne believed that Japan would be emboldened by an alliance with England and made this very argument in a letter to King Edward VII: "The Anglo-Japanese Alliance . . . although not intended to encourage the Japanese Government to resort to extremities, had, and was sure to have, the effect of making Japan feel that she might try conclusions with her great rival in the Far East, free from all risk of a European coalition such as that which had on a previous occasion deprived her of the fruits of victory."[38] Although this was of real concern and influenced the negotiations, it did not prevent the agreement from being reached. Moreover, there is little evidence that these fears were based on past Japanese behavior. Instead, they were a product of the strategic environment at the time, and therefore they cannot be attributed to reputation. Nevertheless, these concerns were dealt with through stipulations in the treaty that stated that Britain was only obligated to enter a war if Japan faced two or more great power adversaries. Otherwise, Britain was expected only to maintain neutrality.

Design of the Alliance

The Anglo-Japanese Alliance clearly provided strategic advantages to both member states. According to Lord William Selborne, an alliance with Japan would help prevent Russian expansion in the East while simultaneously freeing up British naval vessels for redeployment to more vital areas.[39] Nevertheless, because a German alliance would have had similar strategic benefits, one must evaluate what the British obtained from Japan that they would not have gotten from Germany, namely, a reliable partner. Japan's primary gain from an alliance with Britain was that their combined naval forces would offset the French and Russian fleets in the Far East, particularly since Japanese finances no longer permitted enough naval construction to

37. Nish, *Anglo-Japanese Alliance,* 174–175.

38. Gooch, *Grouping of the Powers,* 75.

39. Memorandum by Lord Selborne, 4 September 1901, FO 46/547, reproduced in Zara Steiner, "Great Britain and the Creation of the Anglo-Japanese Alliance," *Journal of Modern History* 31, no. 1 (March 1959), 29–31. See also Beryl Williams, "The Strategic Background to the Anglo-Russian Entente of August 1907," *Historical Journal* 9, no. 3 (1966), 369; Nish, *Anglo-Japanese Alliance,* 172.

keep up with the competition. The Japanese also feared a Russian incursion into Korea and believed that an alliance with England would deter other European powers from supporting Russia in a future conflict, a belief based largely on England's reliability as an ally.

As I expect, the nature of the agreement is consistent with the hypothesis on alliance variation. Because neither England nor Japan perceived the other to be unreliable, both sides were favorable to an alliance with low levels of obligation, precision, and delegation. Neither state asked the other to pay any up-front costs, and the level of ambiguity in the treaty language clearly satisfied both sides. The negotiations had three contentious points: the geographic scope of the alliance (which I classify as an example of precision), the extent of Japanese interests in Korea (also precision), and combined naval strength in the Far East (delegation). With respect to the two issues of precision, the agreed-on treaty was geographically limited to the Far East, and although it recognized British interests in China, it admitted that Japan was interested "in a peculiar degree" in Korea.

One could certainly argue that on the issue of precision, the Japanese gained a preferable outcome compared to the British, since it did not obligate Japan to support England in the same manner as the British were expected to support Japan. Moreover, Japan's interests in Korea were given more importance than any British interests in the Far East. However, the point here is not that reputation fails to explain things given that the British gave up more than the Japanese. Rather, there are three key points for evaluating the hypothesis on alliance variation.

First, although on these two issues of precision the British may have given up more autonomy than the Japanese, the treaty was extremely vague in every other way, particularly compared to the treaty terms England was willing to offer to Germany. Second, the two states settled the military integration issue by exchanging vague notes (see the end of appendix B) in which they agreed that in time of peace their naval forces "should, so far as possible, act in concert."[40] Again, the vagueness of this language is fitting for an alliance between two reliable states, whereas we would expect an agreement with an unreliable state to be much more binding in its delegation. Moreover, although Japan's reputation was not questioned, the British did fear being dragged into a war with Russia because of the alliance. So the agreement was constructed to merely require British neutrality unless Japan faced two or more great powers. Finally, and perhaps most important for my general argument, the British were willing to give up some sovereignty and sacrifice some of their European interests for an alliance with a reliable Japan, which they were unwilling to do for an unreliable Germany.

40. Gooch and Temperley, *Anglo-Japanese Alliance and the Franco-British Entente,* no. 125 (30 January 1902), 114–120.

A final point about this case is that shortly after completion of the agreement, the Japanese were emboldened to challenge Russia. This was less a result of the alliance itself than it was a result of England's reputation, because Japan counted on its ally's reliability when deciding whether or not to go to war with Russia. The Japanese believed that England would honor its obligation to fight alongside Japan should the French enter the war on Russia's side, and this gave Japan the extra incentive to attack Russia. The best evidence that this was part of Japan's goal in forming an alliance is that, prior to the negotiations, the Japanese asked what the British position would be in a war, requesting merely neutrality.[41] Even though the treaty only called for British neutrality unless Russia was joined by another European power, it meant that if Russia were given assistance, the Japanese believed they would have a strong naval ally. As it turns out, British reliability did deter other great powers from helping Russia, including Russia's Dual Alliance partner, France.

The Russo-Japanese War and the Second Anglo-Japanese Alliance

Russia's expansion into Korea in May 1903,[42] and its failure to withdraw troops from Manchuria in spite of its promises to do so, prompted the Japanese to push for negotiations that would divide the region into spheres of influence, with Russia conceding influence in Korea while Japan agreed to concede influence in Manchuria.[43] The Russian government perceived Japan's proposal to be an ultimatum, and they were unwilling to compromise under such terms. As a result, the Japanese broke off negotiations on 5 February 1904, severed diplomatic relations with Russia the next day, and then attacked the Russian fleet at Port Arthur on 8 February.[44]

According to the terms of the Anglo-Japanese Alliance, Britain was not even required to honor its neutrality commitment, since Japan was, by most accounts, the instigator.[45] But not only did the British maintain their neutrality, they made two significant moves that contributed to Japan's victory.

41. Ibid., no. 105 (16 October 1901), 96–98.

42. "The Manchurian Question: The Russians at Niu-Chwang," *Times* (London), 9 May 1903.

43. Dwight Lee, *Europe's Crucial Years: The Diplomatic Background of World War I, 1902–1914* (Hanover, NH: University Press of New England, 1974), 87; John White, *The Diplomacy of the Russo-Japanese War* (Princeton: Princeton University Press, 1964), 95–111.

44. "Russia and Japan: Negotiations Broken Off, Ministers Recalled," *Times* (London), 8 February 1904; "War Begun: Russian Warships Torpedoed, Night Attack on Port Arthur," *Times* (London), 10 February 1904.

45. "The War: The Attack on Port Arthur, Further Russian Losses," *Times* (London), 11 February 1904.

The British put pressure on Turkey to honor existing treaties and prevent Russia's Black Sea fleet from passing through the Dardanelles Strait to reinforce its Far East fleet.[46] England also denied Russian ships transit through the Suez Canal and refused coaling facilities to ships of the Russian Baltic fleet on the grounds that neutral states could not supply belligerent vessels.[47] As a result, England denied Russia the ability to direct its full naval power against Japan, effectively contributing to a Japanese victory.

The closest the British came to being dragged into the war was during the Dogger Bank Incident, in which on 21 October 1904, the Russian Baltic fleet opened fire on a group of British fishing vessels, claiming afterward that they believed the ships to be Japanese torpedo boats.[48] In response, the British demanded an apology, full compensation for those affected, and an investigation into the incident. The Russian government accepted all of these demands,[49] but only after several British naval vessels shadowed the Russian fleet and blockaded it in the Spanish port at Vigo.[50] Notably, this move also contributed to Japanese perceptions of British reliability as an ally, even though the Russian fleet would not have arrived in time to assist in the war even without the British blockade.

Britain's support for Japan during the war, through its "benevolent neutrality," prompted the Japanese to ask for a treaty renewal in 1905 (a full two years before the end of the first alliance), in which they acceded to an agreement with an expanded commitment to England. The second alliance, signed on 12 August 1905, not only extended the duration of the agreement for ten years but also enlarged the geographic scope of the alliance to include India and "countries east of it." (See appendix D for the full text of the second treaty.)[51] The new alliance called for military support in the event that either ally was attacked *by a single state*, a significant revision of the 1902 treaty that I suggest was a response to enhanced British reputation. Given Japan's likely defeat of Russia, and the growing naval tension

46. The Treaty of the Dardanelles, signed between the United Kingdom and the Ottoman Empire on January 5, 1809 to end the Anglo-Turkish War, confirmed the principle that no state's warships would be allowed to enter the Dardanelles and the Bosporus straits. The other major powers later agreed to this principle during the London Straits Convention of 1841. C. G. Fenwick, "The New Status of the Dardanelles," *The American Journal of International Law* 30, no. 4 (October 1936), 701.

47. Monger, *End of Isolation,* 154; Nish, *Anglo-Japanese Alliance,* 289.

48. Richard Connaughton, *The War of the Rising Sun and Tumbling Bear: A Military History of the Russo-Japanese War, 1904–5* (London: Routledge, 1991), 245–246. This incident is also sometimes referred to as the North Sea Incident, the Russian Outrage, and the Incident of Hull.

49. J. G. Merills, *International Dispute Settlement* (Cambridge: Cambridge University Press, 1999).

50. Connaughton, *War of the Rising Sun,* 248–250.

51. "Great Britain and Japan: The New Treaty of Alliance," *Times* (London), 1 September 1905.

between England and Germany, this stipulation was much more strategically beneficial to the British. In addition, initial plans for secret notes to be exchanged concerning British naval and Japanese army obligations were cancelled. Instead, an article was drafted calling for consultation from time to time.[52]

Explaining the Renewal of the Alliance

Only one of the three theories on alliance behavior can explain why the alliance was renewed. If the alliance was meant to balance power in Europe, then it follows that it would be renewed. However, the primary purpose was to balance power against Russia in Asia, and given that the war weakened Russia, balance of power theory should predict that the alliance would fall apart, or at least not be renewed early.

Balance of threat theory has a better explanation, though its results are still incomplete. On the positive side, Russia was still considered a threat in Asia, despite losing the war. Therefore, it made sense for both England and Japan to renew the alliance. It also explains the change to the alliance in which the allies would defend each other against a single state, since members of the British and Japanese government were concerned that Russia might attack Japan in the future out of revenge. So this change to the agreement was an attempt to deter the still-existent Russian threat. The problem with the theory is that the alliance provided England with no added security in Europe, and if the British were concerned about balancing threat, Germany was quickly becoming a greater threat than Russia (and by 1905 was more powerful than England according to the Correlates of War capabilities scores). That England had also signed an agreement with France (discussed in the next section) suggests that the balance of threat theory has some overall validity in explaining British and Japanese alliance choices. It just cannot specifically explain the renewal of the Anglo-Japanese Alliance.

Binding theory is the most problematic of the three because England had even less need to manage Japan's behavior in 1905 than it had in 1902, when the British feared being drawn into a war by Japan. As with balance of threat, this case does not weaken the theory per se, it simply is not a case that fits the theory. Nor can it explain why the alliance transformed the way that it did.

There were two other strategic reasons for the early renewal of the treaty that do not easily fit within the existing alliance theories. Japan's victory over Russia made certain aspects of the original alliance less relevant—specifically, the mutual recognition of Korea's independence laid out in

52. Nish, *Anglo-Japanese Alliance*, 325.

Article I became outdated given Russia's likely decline in power after the war.[53] Both parties also hoped that a renewed alliance would increase Russia's willingness to compromise during the peace talks.[54] Despite these valid reasons for reviewing the alliance, none of the above explanations tell us why the alliance was changed, seemingly to the benefit of the British.

Mercer does not address the Russo-Japanese War in his book, but based on his claims we should not see any change to the Anglo-Japanese Alliance as a result of British actions. Since British behavior during the war was positive for the Japanese, Mercer would expect those actions to be explained away as a function of situation and self-interest rather than as a product of British reputation. If instead the British benefitted because of their support for Japan, either in their alliance with Japan or in their pursuit of other alliances, then this case poses a challenge for Mercer's argument.

Consequences of British Reliability

Support for my general argument about reputation and a state's alliance autonomy is illustrated by the effect that British actions during the Russo-Japanese War had on both its ally, Japan, and on its adversary, France. England's "benevolent neutrality" not only contributed to Japan's success in the war (and as a result its elevation to great power status) but, if my claims are correct, it should have enhanced the Japanese government's perception of British reliability. According to Ian Nish, British popularity rose among the Japanese people as a result of the war, and "when the China squadron of the Royal Navy visited Japanese ports in October to celebrate Japan's victory, [Claude] MacDonald [head of the British legation in Tokyo] felt that Britain's reputation was at its highest point."[55] If true, then the Japanese should have been willing to give up more autonomy to the British without demanding any additional constraints on Britain's autonomy. Although this case primarily tests the hypothesis on alliance variation (hypothesis 5), it is an important test, because if the alliance improved for the British simply because they honored their promise to remain neutral, then that heavily strengthens the argument about a state's reliability contributing to the nature of its alliances. In addition, although the first two cases in this

53. Williams, "Strategic Background to the Anglo-Russian Entente," 363; Ira Klein, "The Anglo-Russian Convention and the Problem of Central Asia, 1970–1914," *Journal of British Studies* 11, no. 1 (November 1971), 138.

54. This might suggest a belief by the British and Japanese that an alliance of reliable allies enhances deterrence. Although this topic is not directly addressed in this book, the notion surfaces again in the next chapter and I discuss its implications in the conclusion.

55. Ian Nish, "British Legations in Tokyo and Beijing during the Russo-Japanese War, 1904–1905," in *Diplomats at War: British and Commonwealth Diplomacy in Wartime*, ed. Christopher Baxter and Andrew Stewart (Leiden, NL: Martinus Nijhoff, 2008), 40.

chapter examined the nature of alliances that formed, this case is about the transformation of an existing alliance as a result of an improved reputation.

Another issue related to reputation is whether British perceptions of Japan changed. That Japan did engage in war shortly after concluding the alliance should have increased British concerns about Japan's reliability—specifically for entrapment. The British were not dragged into a war as many feared would happen. However, this was probably more a function of Britain's reliability deterring other European states from joining Russia than anything the Japanese did to avoid dragging England into war. One could also argue, though, that because the outcome of the Russo-Japanese War was favorable to the British, they would not see Japan as any less reliable as an ally. Mercer is the one who suggests that outcomes influence whether states attribute behavior to situation or character. In cases where the outcome is perceived to be favorable, state behavior should be attributed to situation. Not only did Japan's victory reduce the Russian threat against British interests in Asia but it also reduced the overall naval threat from the combined Franco-Russian fleets. Moreover, the new entente with France, signed during the war, further eased British concerns about being isolated from the continental alliance system.

Not only do the terms of the new agreement support hypothesis 5 but I contend that it also lends some support to my arguments about alliance formation and termination. Hypothesis 2 suggests that reliable states will ally with one another. Clearly the British proved themselves to be reliable. I find no evidence that Japanese reliability declined, but I do consider the possibility that British fears of entrapment grew, so I give this argument mixed results. Similarly, hypothesis 3 suggests that if Japan's reliability declined then that would endanger the alliance. Although that did not happen, because the British were not dragged into war, and since I found no evidence that British perceptions of Japanese reliability declined, I give that argument mixed results for the Japanese portion of the case. On the other hand, because British reliability improved, the renewal of the alliance supports the hypothesis, at least with respect to the British portion of the case.

Mercer only briefly touches on the Dogger Bank Incident, and only as it related to German perceptions of British resolve, which he argues did not improve as a result of the incident.[56] But in light of British animosity toward Russia, the incident made its willingness to support Japan even more evident. Despite having the potential for a serious conflict between England and Russia, I found no evidence that the British blamed Japan for the Dogger Bank Incident, so this should not have diminished British perceptions of Japan's reliability as an ally. Therefore, not only do British perceptions of

56. Mercer, *Reputation and International Politics*, 102.

Japan's reliability not appear to have suffered but England was willing to renew the alliance, especially since they benefitted from the changes made to the agreement.

Although both states were willing to bind themselves more closely together, both were also still satisfied with vague language, for example, concerning British naval assistance and a general Japanese obligation to assist British interests in India (delegation). In examining the renewed alliance, it is clear that both states retained low levels of obligation. As with the original alliance no up-front costs were required of either party. What changed, mostly favoring the British but not detrimental to the Japanese, were precision and delegation. Given that Japan's reliability should not have declined, while British reliability should have improved, these changes are consistent with my hypothesis on alliance variation.

The Entente Cordiale

Not only did British actions in support of its ally contribute to a favorable renewal of the Anglo-Japanese Alliance but British reliability also compelled the French to sign an agreement with England rather than risk having to support its Russian ally in a war against England and Japan.[57] As a result, on 8 April 1904, England agreed to ensure French rights over Morocco in return for France's acceptance of British control over Egypt.[58] This agreement on Morocco and Egypt was one of the three components that in combination made up the Entente Cordiale. (For the full text of the agreement, see appendix C.)

The Entente Cordiale was not a defensive alliance in the same fashion as either the Dual Alliance or the Anglo-Japanese Alliance. It was more of an agreement to settle several controversial commercial matters between the two countries, and rather than a pledge of assistance it simply helped end antagonism between the two states. For the British in particular this was not a general commitment that tied British and French defenses together. However, this case still provides useful tests of the hypotheses on alliance formation and variation because of the manner in which the agreement transformed over time. Plus, once England and France signed the Entente, it became a part of the British strategic interest to support France, particularly over Morocco, further enhancing the British reputation for reliability. The Entente also provided the foundation for the Triple Entente with

57. "The Anglo-French Agreement: Terms of Settlement," *Times* (London), 9 April 1904.

58. Gooch and Temperley, *Anglo-Japanese Alliance and the Franco-British Entente*, no. 417 (8 April 1904), 373–398, esp. 385–395; George Manhart, *Alliance and Entente, 1871–1914* (New York: F. S. Crofts & Company, 1932), 38–41.

Russia, effectively driving Europe's great powers into two separate camps prior to the First World War.

Explaining the Entente with France

Existing theories of alliance formation are able to explain why England and France signed an agreement, but they have trouble explaining the particular timing of the agreement, as well as its design. Balance of power theory does a decent job of explaining the Entente Cordiale during the Russo-Japanese War (particularly with the growing recognition that Russia would be weakened by losing the war). A less-powerful Russia would tip Europe's balance of power in favor of the Triple Alliance, and the British decision to side with France was consistent with long-held British policies of ensuring the balance of power on the Continent. On the other hand, given England's alliance with Japan, and Japan's rising status as a major power, an agreement with France went well beyond preserving the balance.

Balance of threat theory is problematic in several ways. Even if Germany was perceived to be a common threat to both England and France, it was still less powerful than England in 1904. (Germany did not become more powerful than England until 1905.) Therefore, while the theory explains the Entente, the timing is a problem for the theory. In addition, the nature of the agreement, which focused on solving commercial issues between England and France, provided no indication that it was specifically directed at Germany (even if the German government seemed to believe it was the primary target).

Binding theories also explain the decision of both states to ally with each other. Both England and France were concerned with being dragged into a war because of their existing alliances, and the agreement provided a way to avoid that possibility. The timing of the agreement is obvious, as it was signed while the Russo-Japanese War was underway. But the fact that the agreement never explicitly addressed military issues is somewhat problematic if its purpose was to avoid war by managing each other's behavior. This became less of an issue as the Entente matured and the two states continuously met to discuss how their navies would cooperate to defend France's coastline. But the initial agreement did not guarantee such military integration.

Mercer's theory also has some trouble explaining the Entente Cordiale, partly due to the problem of conflating resolve and reliability. On the one hand, both England and France were able to stay out of the war, which each would view as positive, since entrapment would have likely meant a general European war if everyone honored their treaty commitments. So, Mercer would not expect either England or France to receive a more reliable reputation, meaning that no agreement between the two can be explained at that time other than through strategic interests.

On the other hand, Mercer contends that states always view their enemies as having resolve. The French might have correctly perceived England to be resolute even before they supported Japan. And since British support was a negative for France and Russia, their perceptions of British reputation should have increased, making an alliance with England more likely. But, even then, Mercer cannot explain the timing of the Entente, given that British behavior should have merely confirmed its reliability for the French if adversaries are always thought to have a strong reputation. As such, it is difficult to even identify what Mercer's argument would be from the French perspective.

Critical for understanding the timing of the agreement—just two months after the start of the Russo-Japanese War—is that both states saw the other as willing to support their ally if necessary (if a third state joined the conflict). Tension between France and England had already been in decline, and even though the French offer of entente was based on their strategic interest in avoiding war, French fears of being dragged into a war were heavily based on the belief that England would honor its obligation to defend Japan if the terms of the Anglo-Japanese treaty called for it to do so. Had British reliability been lower, the Entente would not have formed because British promises to support Japan would have been less believable and France would have been less concerned about having to go to war with the British.

Mercer's argument is that because French behavior produced an outcome favorable to the British, the British should not have seen them as any more or less reliable. In contrast, I suggest that the French decision to not fight with Russia could have negatively influenced British perceptions of French reliability. France was under no real obligation to fight with Russia since the targets of the Dual Alliance were England and Germany. So it is possible that French behavior did not alter British perceptions of French reliability. Yet Russia's perceptions of its ally were negatively affected, which I examine in chapter 4.

Even if the British did not lower their perceptions of French reliability, the British clearly did much more to support Japan then the French did to support Russia. As a result, if my claims are valid, then the British should have demanded more from the French then they were willing to give up. This perhaps explains British reluctance to sign an agreement requiring any more obligation than an entente, even while the French were willing to discuss a more formal alliance that would have been more binding on France.

There is very little obligation, precision, or delegation apparent in the Entente Cordiale, other than the willingness of both parties to protect each other's rights in their respective colonies. Nevertheless, the British viewed this commitment to French control in Morocco as complete, and it compelled them to fully support France in the tensions that arose with Germany in 1905. Chapter 4 shows how British support not only helped France emerge from the First Moroccan Crisis successfully but it also led to French offers for a more beneficial defense alliance, as well as Russia's willingness to negotiate an agreement with England, resulting in the Triple Entente.

This chapter included four separate observations: the failed Anglo-German alliance negotiations, the successful Anglo-Japanese alliance negotiations, the renewal of the Anglo-Japanese Alliance during the Russo-Japanese War, and the creation of the Entente Cordiale. Dividing this chapter in this way illustrates how reputation influenced several aspects of Britain's move away from splendid isolation at the beginning of the twentieth century. Reputation does not always provide a better explanation for state behavior than strategic interests. For example, reputation cannot explain the British government's initial interest in a German alliance. But by examining Europe's great power alliance choices from 1900 to 1905, I find significant support for the argument that a state's reputation for reliability influences the alliance decisions of other states and that incorporating reputation often improves on existing theories of alliance behavior. (Table 3.2 summarizes the findings from this chapter.) Reputation also is frequently the only explanation for the design of the alliances that form or for explaining the transformation of existing alliances.

This time period is a fairly difficult test of reputation because the British decision to abandon splendid isolation was predicated on the recognition that they faced a growing threat to their naval dominance and colonial interests. Therefore, because of the strategic importance of alliances during this period, reputation might have been outweighed by other factors such as power, interests, and geography.

This is also a critical time in history. If Britain and Germany had successfully negotiated an alliance, Europe would have looked very different both before and after the First World War. In addition, the Anglo-Japanese Alliance (combined with Japan's victory over Russia) elevated Japan to great power status. Therefore, Germany's poor reputation not only reduced its chances of forming an alliance with Britain and forced it to depend on less-reliable allies, but it also had important implications for all of Europe and Asia.

Although existing theories are able to explain some of the alliance decisions discussed in this chapter, reputation played a significant part in the British decision to abandon alliance negotiations with Germany, in Japan's decision to pursue an alliance with Britain, in the renewal of the Anglo-Japanese Alliance, and in the development of the Entente Cordiale between England and France. Of the three existing alliance theories I examine,

Table 3.2. Review of chapter findings

Observation	Anglo-German negotiations		Anglo-Japanese Alliance		Second Anglo-Japanese Alliance		Entente Cordiale	
	England[a] (up)	**Germany[a] (down)**	**England[a] (up)**	**Japan[a] (up)**	**England[a] (up)**	**Japan[a] (mixed)**	**England[a] (up)**	**France[a] (mixed)**
H1: alliance formation	+	+	+	+	N/A	N/A	+	0
H2: similar reliability	+	+	+	+	0	0	0	0
H3: lose abandoned ally	N/A	N/A	N/A	N/A	+	0	N/A	N/A
H4: lose other allies	N/A	N/A	N/A	N/A	N/A	N/A	N/A	N/A
H5: alliance variation	+	+	+	+	+	+	+	+

Note: N/A = not applicable to case; – = no support; 0 = mixed findings; + = strong support
[a] State (reliability level)

balance of threat theory appears to provide the best set of overall explanations for state behavior, although even it has trouble with many of the alliance choices in this chapter, such as the British decision to ally with Japan instead of Germany in 1901, as well as the timing of the Entente Cordiale.

Mercer's argument also fails to explain many of the cases in this chapter, particularly where England benefitted in tangible ways from its reputation, both in finding other reliable allies and in preserving its autonomy within its alliances. The Entente Cordiale case also points out a problem with Mercer's argument about resolve when we try to apply it to reliability, since supporting an ally should solidify a state's positive reputation in the eyes of an adversary but at the same time can produce a negative outcome that should make an agreement with that adversary less likely.

In contrast, my hypotheses on alliance formation and variation are consistently supported throughout the chapter. The first case examined the British decision to abandon splendid isolation. Despite England's growing desire for an ally and its willingness to consider an agreement with Germany, the British were unwilling to conclude such an alliance, partly because of Germany's reputation for being unreliable, but also because of Germany's failure to defend the Yangtze agreement during the negotiations. Even though Germany's unreliability did not initially prevent the British from negotiating an alliance, given the threat posed to England from France and Russia and the limited number of available allies, reputation did contribute to British demands for high levels of precision. The British wanted the agreement to clearly spell out the obligations of the two parties and were unwilling to join a more general alliance that could conceivably expand the scope of England's commitment. Ultimately, England withdrew from the negotiations in favor of an ally that was perceived to be more reliable. Germany then had to be satisfied with an alliance that included Austria-Hungary, a state that most observers believed was ready for implosion, and Italy, which had already begun to move away from the Triple Alliance and toward France.

Like the first case in this chapter, the Anglo-Japanese Alliance tests the hypotheses on alliance formation and alliance design. Although both England and Japan had strategic reasons for signing an agreement, Japanese decision makers clearly considered British reliability prior to their offer of alliance. Had British reliability been lower, those same strategic interests might have been outweighed by the costs of either being dragged into war or of being abandoned. But, because the British had such a reliable reputation, the new Japanese foreign minister gave his support to an alliance. Moreover, there is no indication that the British saw Japan as an unreliable ally. Had the British perceived Japan to be less reliable, an alliance would have been more difficult to form (or the British might have demanded an agreement that was more constraining on the Japanese). Alternatively, the

British might have reconsidered the alliance with Germany, or even returned to a policy of splendid isolation. The Japanese, in turn, would have been forced to go alone or try to ally with Russia to manage the threat. As a result, this case supports both hypotheses on alliance formation: reliable states have an easier time finding allies and reliable states tend to ally with one another. The terms of the Anglo-Japanese treaty also support hypothesis 5, which suggests that an agreement between reliable states will contain low levels of obligation, precision, and delegation. Both states were willing to form an alliance that allowed each to retain a great deal of autonomy through a treaty with no up-front costs, vague language on most points, and no delegation of military authority.

The Russo-Japanese War also provides an important test of hypothesis 5 because it is one of two instances I examine in which a state's reliability as an ally is tested by war (the other being the Dual Alliance). Although British willingness to go to war was never tested, since the treaty required simple neutrality as long as Japan only faced Russia, England's actions clearly assisted Japan in its victory over Russia. Its "benevolent neutrality" contributed to changes in the alliance that were favorable to England. The hypothesis on alliance variation would expect Japan to give up more autonomy while demanding less of England. And, as expected, the scope of the alliance expanded to include areas of particular interest to England, and the terms of the alliance changed so that support was expected when an ally faced just one state in war (a condition more likely to entrap Japan than to drag England into war, even though the alliance was still restricted geographically to Asia).

Britain's reliability not only helped deter France from entering the war on Russia's side against Japan but it also helped lead to an entente between the French and British. The final case of this chapter provided an interesting test of reputation, which not only helps explain why France and England signed an agreement but also gives a plausible explanation for the timing of the agreement—out of concern that England would support Japan in war against France's Russian ally. Although the agreement was not a military alliance in the strictest sense, it does strengthen the hypotheses on alliances formation, because British reliability increased the likelihood of the agreement. The French clearly believed that England would honor its commitment to Japan and were unwilling to support Russia if it meant risking war with England.

Where my argument is weakest is if we accept that French reliability did not improve because of its lack of support for Russia against Japan. Then the alliance formation results are mixed since France was able to form an alliance with a reliable England. But this also explains why the initial agreement between England and France was an informal entente rather than a military alliance that obligated either side to take any military actions. As a result, I give these hypotheses mixed results for both observations, but England's ability to form an agreement with a previous adversary, largely because France wanted to avoid war, is a strong case for reputation influencing state behavior generally.

One important note needs to be made here. Given the strong correlation between the findings from this chapter that support my hypotheses and the role of England in all four observations, it is conceivable that the British place a uniquely high value on reputation compared to other countries. Mercer alludes to the possibility that there are cultural differences regarding the importance of reputation.[59] If true, then I expect the remaining three chapters to exhibit the same observable trend—cases that include England will provide greater support for my hypotheses than those that do not. This would neither strengthen nor weaken my argument but would add another layer to the puzzle of when a state's reputation matters, particularly if the result is that reputation matters more when dealing with certain states or cultures.

In the next chapter I examine the First Moroccan Crisis and the effect that state behavior had on alliance decisions in the aftermath of the crisis. Unlike this chapter, chapter 4 considers only one case, but each of the allies involved in the crisis provides several observable tests of my hypotheses, which makes for important comparisons on how the level of one state's support for an ally affects the relationship between the states.

59. Mercer, *Reputation and International Politics,* 222–224.

4

The First Moroccan Crisis

Testing the Anglo-French Entente, 1904–1907

The reputation of a thousand years may be determined by the conduct of one hour.

JAPANESE PROVERB

Important Dates

8 April 1904	Entente Cordiale (Anglo-French Entente) signed
27 October 1904–10 February 1905	Russo-German alliance negotiations
31 March 1905–7 April 1906	First Moroccan Crisis
30 April 1905	Anglo-French military conversations begin
6 June 1905	Dismissal of French foreign minister Théophile Delcassé
23–24 July 1905	Treaty of Björko negotiations (Germany and Russia)
16 January–7 April 1906	Algeciras conference
31 January 1906	Anglo-French joint military planning authorized by British government
8 July 1907	Triple Alliance renewed (tacitly)
31 August 1907	Anglo-Russian entente/Triple Entente signed

Key Actors

Austria-Hungary

Agenor Goluchowski	Minister of Foreign Affairs (1895–1906)
Aloys von Aehrenthal	Minister of Foreign Affairs (1906–1912)
Moritz von Auffenberg	Army General (1910–1911); Minister of War (1911–1912)
Ladislaus von Szögyény-Marich	Ambassador to Germany (1892–1914)

England

Edward VII	King (1901–1910)
Henry Lansdowne	Foreign Secretary (1900–1905)
Edward Grey	Foreign Secretary (1905–1916)
Francis Bertie	Ambassador to Italy (1903–1905); Ambassador to France (1905–1918)

France

Maurice Rouvier	Prime Minister and Foreign Minister (1905–1906)
Émile Loubet	President (1899–1906)
Théophile Delcassé	Foreign Minister (1898–1905)
Stephen Pichon	Foreign Minister (1906–1909)
Paul Cambon	Ambassador to England (1898–1920)
André Tardieu	Foreign Affairs Editor, *Le Temps* (1905–1914)

Germany

Wilhelm II	Kaiser (1888–1918)
Bernard von Bülow	Chancellor (1900–1909)
Heinrich von Tschirschky	Foreign Secretary (1906–1907)

Friedrich von Holstein	Foreign Office Political Counselor (1878–1906)
Anton Monts	Ambassador to Italy (1902–1905)

Russia

Nicholas II	Tsar (1894–1917)
Sergei Witte	Prime Minister (1905–1906)
Vladimir Lamsdorf	Minister of Foreign Affairs (1900–1906)
Alexander Nelidov	Ambassador to France (1903–1910)

France signed an entente with England on 8 April 1904 to increase French control over Morocco. Between 1900 and 1904, the French negotiated similar agreements with Italy and Spain.[1] For example, France agreed to accept Italian rights in Tripoli in exchange for Italy accepting French control over Morocco (and an Italian promise that the Triple Alliance did not pose a threat to France). However, France failed to negotiate any type of settlement with Germany, believing that German interests in Morocco were minimal, and because the French foreign minister refused to deal with the Germans.[2] The German government viewed this as an affront to its status as a major power and demanded some form of compensation for French control of Morocco.

To emphasize German interests in Morocco, Kaiser Wilhelm II sailed to Tangier.[3] When he arrived on 31 March 1905, he gave a speech regarding the autonomy of the sultan: "The object of my visit to Tangier is to make it known that I am determined to do all that is in my power to safeguard efficaciously the interests of Germany in Morocco, for I look upon the Sultan as an absolutely independent sovereign."[4] Germany also demanded the resignation of France's foreign minister, Théophile Delcassé, the man who largely orchestrated France's Moroccan policy and who was widely

1. Cedric Lowe and Michael Dockrill, *The Mirage of Power: British Foreign Policy, 1914–22* (London: Routledge & Kegan Paul, 1972), 7–9; Eugene Anderson, *The First Moroccan Crisis, 1904–1906* (Chicago: University of Chicago Press, 1930), 81–109.

2. Jonathan Mercer, *Reputation and International Politics* (Ithaca: Cornell University Press, 1996), 76.

3. "The Emperor William's Visit to Tangier: German Semi-Official Statement," *Times* (London), 23 March 1905.

4. Cited in Bernadotte Schmitt, *England and Germany, 1740–1914* (New York: Howard Fertig, 1967), 227. See also Dwight Lee, *Europe's Crucial Years: The Diplomatic Background of World War I, 1902–1914* (Hanover, NH: University Press of New England, 1974), 114–115; Joanne Mortimer, "Commercial Interests and German Diplomacy in the Agadir Crisis," *Historical Journal* 10, no. 4 (1967), 440.

perceived to be hostile toward Germany. Maurice Rouvier, the French prime minister, responded by forcing Delcassé's resignation on 6 June 1905.[5]

Despite Delcassé's resignation, the Germans pressed for an international conference,[6] believing that England and the United States would oppose French control of Morocco in favor of the Open Door, just as they had opposed Russian expansion into China. The conference was held in Algeciras, Spain, from 16 January to 7 April 1906.[7] Thirteen states participated, including the six European great powers, Belgium, Morocco, the Netherlands, Portugal, Spain, Sweden, and the United States. In the end, only Austria-Hungary and Morocco sided with Germany, and, although the conference confirmed Morocco's independence, it reserved for France a privileged position there. Most observers perceived this to be a German defeat, even though the Germans spun the result as a victory for the Open Door and for their interests in Morocco.[8]

In this chapter I discuss how Europe's great powers reacted to the crisis and whether their behavior at the Algeciras conference affected their relationships with other states. In particular, I examine whether reputation accurately explains changes to these relationships, based on the different levels of support that France and Germany received from their allies. France received support at the conference from both England and Russia, but Russia simultaneously negotiated a treaty with Germany during the crisis. As a result, although perceptions of British reliability should have risen, perceptions of Russian reliability should have declined, or at least not risen as much as those of the British. Even though both allies appear to have lost some autonomy after the crisis, the British were able to preserve much more freedom of action than the Russians. In addition, British support for France helped change Russia's opinion of England, opening up the possibility for an Anglo-Russian entente.[9]

There is an even more observable difference in the level of support Germany received from its two allies, and therefore in how relations with those allies changed. Although Germany received strong support from Austria-Hungary, Italy sided with France at Algeciras. As a result, few changes occurred between Austria-Hungary and Germany, whereas Italy was more closely bound to the Triple Alliance in an effort to offset its disloyalty.

5. "M. Delcasse's Resignation," *Times* (London), 9 June 1905.

6. "The Proposed Morocco Conference: Germany and the Anglo-French Entente," *Times* (London), 19 June 1905.

7. "The Morocco Question: Meeting of the Algeciras Conference," *Times* (London), 17 January 1906.

8. "The Morocco Conference in the Reichstag: Speech by the Chancellor," *Times* (London), 6 April 1906; "Germany and the Powers," *Times* (London), 16 April 1906.

9. G. Gooch and Harold Temperley, eds., *British Documents on the Origins of the War, 1898–1914*, vol. 4, *The Anglo-Russian Rapprochement, 1903–7* (London: His Majesty's Stationery Office, 1929), no. 191 (6 September 1905), 198–199.

I begin each section with a discussion of how the state behaved during the crisis and what alliance changes occurred as a result. I then explore some of the possible explanations for those changes, including strategic interests and Mercer's arguments about states not being able to change their reputations. I then assess the value of my hypotheses on reliability. Ultimately, this chapter provides important tests of all five hypotheses. Although results are mixed, the overall findings support my general claim about a state's reliability affecting its alliance autonomy, and they improve on the ability of our existing theories to explain alliance choices.

England

Although Britain and France were almost at war at the turn of the century because of colonial aspirations in Africa, they signed an entente early in the Russo-Japanese War. This primarily commercial agreement was largely the result of French concerns about having to support Russia in a war against both England and Japan. Despite the agreement being little more than an expression of common economic interests, when Germany threatened France over Morocco, the British felt obligated to support the French during the crisis because the Entente Cordiale specifically recognized French interests in Morocco.[10] This is not to suggest a lack of strategic interest in England's support of France, merely that the entente itself had become one of England's strategic interests. In fact, the foreign secretary Edward Grey believed it was England's moral duty to support France.[11]

It is also likely that the French expected to receive British support. Because of the British reputation for reliability, enhanced by its benevolent neutrality toward Japan in the Russo-Japanese War, France believed that England would uphold the Entente, if not for its own commercial interests, then for the sake of its reputation.[12] It is also relevant to point out that the Germans believed France's agreement with England emboldened the French to stand up to Germany over the situation in Morocco.[13] In his own writings, Germany's chancellor, Bernard von Bülow, suggested that the entente with England gave France the courage to pursue a protectorate over Morocco,[14] much as the alliance with England emboldened Japan to challenge Russia in 1904.

10. "The Morocco Question: Germany and the Anglo-French Entente," *Times* (London), 5 April 1905.

11. "The Morocco Conference: A German White-Book," *Times* (London), 6 January 1906; "Morocco Conference: Aims of the Powers," *Times* (London), 8 January 1906.

12. "The King's Visit to Paris: Meeting with M. Loubet," *Times* (London), 1 May 1905; "Anglo-French Relations," *Times* (London), 17 June 1905.

13. Mercer, *Reputation and International Politics*, 94.

14. Bernhard von Bülow, *Imperial Germany*, trans. Marie Lewenz (Westport, CT: Greenwood Press, 1979 [1914]), 95.

In one sense, supporting France over Morocco was an unusual position for England, given that just one year earlier it had supported Japan against Russia, largely in defense of the Open Door in China. As a result, because of Britain's history of protecting the Open Door, they might have opposed French control of Morocco for commercial reasons, which was the German expectation (and suggests an entirely different reputation that influenced the German decision to challenge France, not because of England's lack of reliability as an ally but because the Germans believed England would continue to support the Open Door as it always had).

Given Germany's earlier unwillingness in 1901 to defend the Open Door in China, German claims of wanting to protect the Open Door in Morocco rang disingenuous. Instead, Francis Bertie, who helped thwart the Anglo-German negotiations in 1901 and who was now the British ambassador in Paris, handed Delcassé a note on 25 April 1905 in which the British government assured France of all possible support in handling the German request for a Moroccan port.[15] According to the American historian and diplomat L. W. Fuller, King Edward VII clearly gave France carte blanche with reference to Morocco.[16] Sidney Lee, an English biographer and critic, provides evidence of this in a statement Edward made to Paul Cambon, the French ambassador in London: "Tell us what you wish on each point, and we will support you without restriction or reserves."[17]

There are two apparent results of Algeciras for England. One was an increased opportunity for expanding the Entente Cordiale to include Russia. The second was that the conversations that had taken place unofficially between French and British military staffs prior to the crisis were officially authorized to continue in 1906 at the beginning of the Algeciras conference. Although strategic reasons are behind these results, the transformation of England's relations with both France and Russia, and the timing of these changes, is best explained by reputation.

Explaining British Behavior

Perceptions of the balance of power in 1905 were likely to be that the balance had tipped in favor of the Triple Alliance because of Russia's defeat in war with Japan. Yet if I remain consistent in my use of the Correlates of War

15. Gooch and Temperley, *British Documents on the Origins of the War,* vol. 3, *The Testing of the Entente, 1904–6* (London: His Majesty's Stationery Office, 1928), no. 93 (25 April 1905), 74–75; John White, *Transition to Global Rivalry: Alliance Diplomacy and the Quadruple Entente, 1895–1907* (Cambridge: Cambridge University Press, 1995), 168; George Manhart, *Alliance and Entente, 1871–1914* (New York: F. S. Crofts & Company, 1932), 46; P. M. H. Bell, *France and Britain, 1900–1940: Entente and Estrangement* (London: Longman, 1996), 35.

16. L. W. Fuller, *The Effect of the First Moroccan Crisis on Anglo-German Relations* (Colorado Springs: Colorado College Publication, 1932), 25.

17. Sidney Lee, *King Edward VII,* vol. 2 (New York: Macmillan, 1927), 361.

Table 4.1. The great powers during the First Moroccan Crisis (1905)

State	Capabilities score	Alliance (combined score)	Behavior
Russia	0.16	Dual Alliance (0.23)	Supported France; Negotiated Björko Treaty
England	0.12	Entente Cordiale (0.18)	Strongly supported France
Germany	0.12	Triple Alliance (0.19)	Primary belligerent; negotiated Björko Treaty
France	0.06	Dual Alliance (0.23) Entente Cordiale (0.18)	Primary belligerent
Austria-Hungary	0.04	Triple Alliance (0.19)	Strongly supported Germany
Italy	0.03	Triple Alliance (0.19)	Supported France

capabilities scores, balance of power theory is problematic in explaining British behavior, because, despite Russia's loss to Japan, combined Franco-Russian power (0.23) was still greater than the combined power of the Triple Alliance (0.19) (Table 4.1 illustrates the relative power of each state, the existing agreements between the great powers, and the behavior of the states during the crisis.) As a result, balance of power theory cannot explain why England would support France, much less why the British would be interested in expanding the Entente Cordiale to include Russia.

There is better support for balance of threat theory. Just three year earlier, rising Franco-Russian naval power was perceived to be the greatest threat to British security, but by 1905 German naval growth was a greater threat than either French dominance in Morocco or the now-defeated Russian military.[18] In addition, by challenging France over Morocco, the Germans proved themselves, at least to the British, to pose a greater threat to the status quo than either Russia or France. Germany would be an even bigger problem for England if it was successful at gaining a port in Morocco. Therefore, balance of threat theory can explain England's willingness to support France against Germany. Yet, what is still lacking is an explanation for the specific agreements that England made with the Dual Alliance states, as well as explaining the way in which the Entente Cordiale transformed after the crisis.

As this and future cases all show, a persistent problem with binding theory is that although it may explain certain alliance choices, it often cannot explain why a state chooses to bind one state rather than another. Binding theories are easier to evaluate if we focus on a narrow interpretation in

18. Paul Kennedy, *The Rise of the Anglo-German Antagonism, 1860–1914* (London: Ashfield, 1980), esp. 266–267; White, *Transition to Global Rivalry*, 226.

which states ally specifically to bind an adversary and thus limit the likelihood of war with that state. However, even if the British were interested in binding an adversary, an alliance with Germany would make more sense by 1905 than supporting France.

The British also had a commercial reason for supporting France. If France were compelled to give up its rights to Morocco, its quid pro quo with England over Egypt might become nullified as well. Some evidence suggests that Britain's support for France at Algeciras was partly based on a British belief that doing so was necessary to improve its relations with Russia. According to a memorandum by Foreign Minister Edward Grey, if Britain stayed out of a Franco-German war, "there would . . . be a general feeling in every country that we had behaved meanly and left France in the lurch. The United States would despise us, *Russia would not think it worthwhile to make a friendly arrangement with us about Asia,* Japan would prepare to re-insure herself elsewhere, [and] we should be left *without the power of making a friend.*"[19].

Clearly, Grey believed that abandoning Britain's commitment to France not only would prevent an alliance with Russia but could also cause current allies, such as Japan, to look elsewhere for a reliable partner. One leader's opinion is not evidence that reputation affects alliances, but if British beliefs about reputation were as strong as indicated, then at the very least it influenced British behavior. Although this and balance of threat theory adequately explain why England sided with France and Russia against Germany, it cannot explain why the Anglo-French agreement transformed in the manner it did nor the timing of the Anglo-Russian agreement. For that, it is necessary to incorporate reputation.

Consequences of British Reliability

The British clearly supported France, and did so at least partly out of a sense of obligation. The main question is whether we can adequately explain the results of that support using strategic interests. It is important to reiterate that I do not discount strategic interests as an explanation for state behavior, especially in deciding whether or not to support an ally. I do not expect states to always care about their reputation when making decisions. My concern is whether their behavior has reputational consequences that influence the alliance choices of other states.

My basic assertion about the connection between reputation and alliance choices is that as one state's reliability rises, it will be able to preserve its

19. Gooch and Temperley, *Testing of the Entente,* no. 299 (20 February 1906), 266–267, emphasis added; see also Keith Wilson, *The Policy of the Entente: Essays on the Determinants of British Foreign Policy, 1904–1914* (Cambridge: Cambridge University Press, 1984), 74–75.

autonomy while its allies will give up more of their autonomy. As a state's reliability declines, it will preserve less autonomy while its allies will demand to keep more of their own. For this case, I expect the British to be able to form new alliances if they desire to do so and not to lose any existing allies. British allies should also demand less obligation, precision, and delegation of England while expressing a willingness to expand their own commitments.

Mercer contends throughout his book that states always perceive their allies to be irresolute.[20] Because England supported France at Algeciras, and because the outcome of the conference was positive for France, Mercer would expect France to explain away British and Russian support as being a product of strategic interests rather than reliability.[21] As a result, Mercer would not expect any change in Anglo-French relations. This is a difficult argument to challenge, because England had strategic reasons for supporting France over Morocco. If he is correct, then France should not have given England any credit for its support, nor should the French have expected British support during the next crisis. In contrast, I contend that French perceptions of British reliability were already high enough to bring about the entente in 1904. Therefore, any positive change to the relationship that occurred after the crisis is noteworthy and would challenge Mercer's argument.

For one thing, on seeing that England would support France at the Algeciras conference, the Germans approached England with another offer of alliance. Once again, though, the British were unwilling to discuss such formal commitments with Germany and instead preferred, after the conference, to purse an agreement with Russia over Persia and Afghanistan.

Curiously, only two weeks after the Algeciras Act was signed, Russia and France agreed to drop the clauses in the Dual Alliance providing for military cooperation against Great Britain. André Tardieu, foreign affairs editor of *Le Temps* at the time and who later served as France's prime minister, provides evidence that British support for France did increase the chances of an Anglo-Russian entente. He wrote in 1908:

> During the negotiations that followed the crisis, before, at and after Algeciras, Great Britain supported us with a loyal energy to which the French owe grateful homage. The weight of English approval which our proposals constantly met with throughout, contributed to insure their success. And this visible unity has exercised an attraction so great that, in the next year, following the example of France, Russia concluded with Great Britain a pact of reconciliation.[22]

20. For example, Mercer, *Reputation and International Politics*, 153.
21. Ibid., 105–106.
22. André Tardieu, *France and the Alliances: The Struggle for the Balance of Power* (New York: Macmillan, 1908), 70–71.

Even before the Algeciras conference ended, Vladimir Lamsdorf, the Russian minister of foreign affairs, invited the British to resume talks on an Anglo-Russian agreement.[23] Then, on 31 August 1907, Britain and Russia signed an agreement effectively creating the Triple Entente. (See appendix E for the text of the part of the agreement pertaining to Persia.)[24] Therefore, this case provides decent support for the argument that reliability improves a state's chances of forming an alliance. As with all of Britain's agreements, strategic interests were involved in the decision to ally with Russia. However, timing suggests that the agreement became more likely once England showed its reliability to France during the crisis.

Just as British reliability toward its Japanese ally created an incentive for France to come to an agreement with England rather than risk a war, British support for France also created an opportunity for the Russians to sign an entente to avoid being outmatched by the Central Powers of the Triple Alliance—Germany, Austria-Hungary, and Italy. This supports hypothesis 1 and gives mixed support to hypothesis 2. As I discuss in the next section, Russia's reputation should have been mixed after the conference. In this case, England is a more reliable ally than Russia. Yet the British clearly preferred an agreement with Russia over one with Germany, and the differences in their reputations may be one factor.

This case also supports my arguments on alliance termination and variation. British support for France had positive effects both on French perceptions of England and on the perceptions of England's other ally, Japan. Because of British support, hypothesis 5 expects France would give up more autonomy and not demand that England give up more. After the conference, Britain and France continued to engage in joint military planning. Conversations existed between the French and British military staffs early on in the First Moroccan Crisis, and informal discussion continued during 1905. However, these were authorized only by the French premier, and they were regarded as unofficial by England until 31 January 1906, when Lord Richard Haldane, the new British minister of war, authorized their continuation after the beginning of the conference.[25] The American historian John White claims that as a result of the conference, "the Entente passed from a static to a dynamic state."[26] These talks might suggest that even though England's formal commitment to France did not change, and both obligation

23. White, *Transition to Global Rivalry,* 308–313.

24. Gordon Martel, *The Origins of the First World War* (London: Longman, 1996), 65; White, *Transition to Global Rivalry,* 308–313. For the full text of the treaty, see Gooch and Temperley, *Anglo-Russian Rapprochement,* appendix 1, 618–620.

25. John Coogan and Peter Coogan, "The British Cabinet and the Anglo-French Staff Talks, 1905–1914: Who Knew What and When Did He Know It?" *Journal of British Studies* 24, no. 1 (January 1985), 110; Bell, *France and Britain, 1900–1940,* 46.

26. White, *Transition to Global Rivalry,* 203.

and precision remained vague within the Entente, British autonomy declined, if only through higher levels of delegation.

Although this initially appears to be a problem for my argument, there are several reasons why this does not disconfirm hypothesis 5. First, Grey suggests that the talks were necessary to *ensure* British autonomy. Given the widespread belief that a general war would be over quickly,[27] Grey recognized that the only way England would be able to offer assistance to France was if plans were already prepared. The talks in no way required the British to participate in a war but ensured that they would be able to do so if they chose.[28] In addition, the British military was already examining plans for a continental war, and any strategy to assist France would require detailed information about France's own plans.[29] Therefore, rather than reduce British autonomy, the talks increased British options for responding to a general war.

The talks were also authorized secretly, so that the prime minister was not informed until after the fact, and the rest of the cabinet was not made aware of their existence until 1911.[30] More supportive of my argument is that the talks—combined with a series of agreements between Britain, France, and Spain in May 1907—created higher levels of delegation for France than for the British. This occurred primarily through agreements by which the French fleet would be concentrated in the Mediterranean, leaving France's Atlantic coast heavily dependent on the British navy for protection.[31] These agreements also freed up the British Mediterranean fleet for operations elsewhere, further increasing British autonomy. As the British historian Frank McDonough states, "the clear aim of these military talks was for Britain and France to co-ordinate plans and strategy in the event of war with Germany but without an agreement which was binding on Britain."[32] It is unlikely France would have left itself vulnerable unless it expected British support. Thus, despite the lack of any clear British commitment to France,

27. Stephen Van Evera, "The Cult of the Offensive and the Origins of the First World War," *International Security* 9, no. 1 (Summer 1984), 58–107; Jack Snyder, "Civil-Military Relations and the Cult of the Offensive, 1914 and 1984," *International Security* 9, no. 1 (Summer 1984), 108–146; Scott Sagan, "1914 Revisited: Allies, Offense, and Instability," *International Security* 11, no. 2 (Autumn 1986), 151–175.

28. George Monger, *The End of Isolation: British Foreign Policy, 1900–1907* (London: Thomas Nelson, 1963), 236–256, 268–274; A. J. P. Taylor, *The Struggle for Mastery in Europe, 1848–1918* (Oxford: Clarendon Press, 1954), 437–438; Fritz Fischer, *War of Illusions: German Policies from 1911 to 1914* (New York: Norton, 1975), 423; Samuel Williamson, *The Politics of Grand Strategy: Britain and France Prepare for War, 1904–1914* (Cambridge: Harvard University Press, 1969), 81–88.

29. Thomas Otte, "The Elusive Balance: British Foreign Policy and the French Entente before the First World War," in *Anglo-French Relations in the Twentieth Century: Rivalry and Cooperation*, ed. Alan Sharp and Glyn Stone (London: Routledge, 2000), 20.

30. Ibid.

31. Lee, *Europe's Crucial Years*, 165–168.

32. Frank McDonough, "The Conservative Party and the Anglo-French Entente, 1905–1914," in Sharp and Stone, *Anglo-French Relations in the Twentieth Century*, 40.

past British behavior led the French to believe the British would, at minimum, prevent the German fleet from threatening France.

Even if British autonomy dropped as a result of the talks, these changes were much less binding on England than the changes France demanded of Russia after the crisis. I explore Franco-Russian relations in the next section, but this relative level of autonomy retained by England over Russia correlates nicely with the level of support France received from each ally and fits my general argument about reputation and alliance autonomy.

The British also preserved more freedom of action than they would have had they abandoned France at Algeciras. Failing to support France might have destroyed the Anglo-French Entente (hypothesis 3). At the very least, it would have made an Anglo-Russian entente less likely (hypothesis 1), would have alarmed the Japanese (hypothesis 4), and would have emboldened Germany even more. According to Fuller, Grey did not believe England should stay aloof: "We could not stay out of a war without losing our good name and our friends and wrecking our policy and position in the world." Hardinge also believed that if England abandoned France, an alliance between France, Germany, and Russia would follow, leaving England isolated.[33] I obviously cannot test these claims, but they are supported by the more binding changes that occurred within the Dual Alliance and suggest that the decline in British autonomy was less than it would have been had the British not been so reliable.

British Perceptions of French Reliability

Although I am primarily concerned with the effects of British and Russian support on their relations with France, it is also useful to examine how the crisis affected British perceptions of French reliability. Because France almost dragged England into conflict with Germany, the British should have preferred to maintain low levels of obligation, precision, and delegation. One of the key arguments Mercer makes during his chapter on the First Moroccan Crisis focuses on France's bowing to German pressure and dismissing Delcassé. Although this incident does not directly relate to a state's reliability as an ally, Mercer cites it as an important event that signaled a lack of French resolve.[34] The British historian A. J. P. Taylor supports Mercer's argument, suggesting that the British blamed Delcassé's dismissal on "French feebleness" and that Lansdowne concluded that the French were useless as a partner.[35] The problem with Mercer's argument is that he makes faulty claims by conflating credibility and reliability. He suggests that the

33. Fuller, *Effect of the First Moroccan Crisis,* 30; Taylor, *Struggle for Mastery in Europe,* 437.
34. Mercer, *Reputation and International Politics,* 80–81.
35. Taylor, *Struggle for Mastery in Europe,* 434.

British would not view the French as reliable allies in the future, since their resolve at Algeciras was explained through situation rather than disposition.[36] However, as I have suggested several times, resolve and reliability are two different reputations, and since France was one of the primary belligerents at Algeciras, its *resolve* was tested, whereas British and Russian *reliability* were tested. Instead, the British had mixed perceptions about this event, with some members of the British government viewing this move more favorably than Mercer and Taylor suggest.

Since the resignation was perceived to decrease French hostility toward Germany, some considered it reduced the likelihood that England would be dragged into a war against the Triple Alliance as a result of its commitment to France. In other words, even if Mercer is correct that French resolve was damaged by this affair, France's reliability as an ally improved by reducing the chance it would drag its allies into an unwanted war. Francis Bertie provides some evidence of this perspective in his suggestion that Delcassé's fall was brought about by his failure to disclose his plans about Morocco as well as to carry out cabinet decisions. In a letter to Lansdowne on 15 June 1905, Bertie wrote, "[Delcassé's removal] has the appearance of being a sacrifice to a German menace, but it is not entirely so."[37] The British ambassador's view of the situation was that a change in foreign ministers was less about a lack of French resolve than simply the need to improve French policy toward Germany so as to avoid war.[38]

According to Edward McCullough, few in France approved of Delcassé's decision to exclude Germany from the earlier discussions on Morocco, and this was illustrated in earlier attempts by Prime Minister Rouvier to remove the foreign minister. In addition, many international newspapers condemned Delcassé's policies and then expressed satisfaction at his resignation.[39] McCullough also suggests that rather than bowing to German pressure, Rouvier believed that removing Delcassé would encourage Germany to drop its demands for an international conference on Morocco and come to a direct agreement with France.[40] Therefore, the removal of the foreign minister may appear to have been about appeasement out of a position of weakness, but it was carried out in the belief that it would be more

36. Mercer, *Reputation and International Politics,* 111.

37. Letter from Bertie to Lansdowne, 15 June 1905, FO 800/127.

38. Eugene Anderson points out numerous reasons for Delcassé's resignation. Anderson, *First Moroccan Crisis,* 284.

39. "Special Cable to the New York Times," *New York Times,* 7 June 1905; "M. Delcassé's Resignation," *Baltimore American,* 8 June 1905; "Delcassé's Resignation," *Dallas Morning News,* 8 June 1905; "The Eclipse of Delcassé," *Boston Journal,* 7 June 1905.

40. Edward McCullough, *How the First World War Began: The Triple Entente and the Coming of the Great War, 1914–1918* (Montreal: Black Rose Books, 1999), 91–92.

beneficial to France than placing the decision in the hands of the international community, particularly given the record of England and the United States in supporting the Open Door. As such, if this action helped avoid war or a risky decision over Morocco's future, then it follows that the British government's perception of French reliability would not have suffered as much as German perception of French resolve.

At the same time, since British perception of French reliability would have declined some as a result of the crisis itself (given that England was dragged into a conflict with Germany on account of the Entente), it makes sense that England would have desired to retain its autonomy while expecting France to give up some of its autonomy. In support of these expectations, is the situation that after the crisis the French did want to move toward a defense pact while the British were unwilling to tie their hands to a formal agreement.[41]

But entrapment was not the only British concern. In discussing how the French did not give the British credit for resolve after the conference, Mercer highlights British fears that France might negotiate with Germany if they doubted British loyalty.[42] However, this reveals more about British perceptions of French reliability than they reveal about French perceptions of England's reputation. The British historian Thomas Otte contends that "the success at Algeciras . . . had by no means laid to rest the traditional fear of French instability and unreliability. It was generally assumed, despite evidence to the contrary, that the French were prone to panic under pressure."[43] Although this particular quote supports Mercer's general argument that the British would have seen France as unreliable no matter what actions they took, his emphasis on the resignation of Delcassé is less important for understanding France's reputation for unreliability than its consistent history of providing only limited support to its allies, such as during the Russo-Japanese War. Likewise, Bertie argued that the British had to walk a fine line between driving the French to ally with Germany and pushing France to challenge Germany.[44] What this means is that too little British support would have led the French to realign with Germany (hypothesis 3), whereas too much support might have led France to challenge Germany to the point of dragging all of Europe into war.

41. Gooch and Temperley, *Testing of the Entente*, no. 391 (2 April 1906), 329; no. 395 (4 April 1906), 330–331; no. 439 (18 September 1906), 389–390; no. 442 (8 November 1906), 393–394.

42. Mercer, *Reputation and International Politics*, 104–105.

43. Otte, "The Elusive Balance," in Sharp and Stone, *Anglo-French Relations in the Twentieth Century*, 21.

44. Ibid., 17.

Russia

England gave France total support throughout the crisis, even going beyond the requirements of its entente. In contrast, although Russia ultimately supported France, the Russian tsar simultaneously negotiated a treaty with the German kaiser while the Algeciras conference was underway.[45] Therefore, given that Russia's support was mixed, it is difficult to make specific claims about the resulting changes to the Franco-Russian relationship. However, because of the different levels of support provided by France's allies during the crisis, if reputation matters we should expect Russian reliability to rise less than British reliability and anticipate that this difference will be reflected in changes to France's alliances that are more binding on Russia than they are on England.

The Dual Alliance between Russia and France formed on 4 January 1894, but the partnership was strained even before the First Moroccan Crisis. In December 1903, Ambassador Paul Cambon advocated a repudiation of the alliance, even though he understood that this might push Russia toward Germany.[46] In addition, France did not support Russia during the Russo-Japanese War. Although not strictly a violation of the alliance, since assistance was only required in the event of an attack by Germany or Austria-Hungary, France's lack of support lowered Russian perceptions of French reliability, particularly in light of British actions to assist Japan. Within two months of the outbreak of the war, the French signed an entente with England, effectively allowing France to stay out of the war. Therefore, between France's lack of support in the war and its entente with England, Russian perceptions of French reliability dropped considerably. According to von Bülow, Germany's attitude during the Russo-Japanese War was "even a shade more kindly [toward Russia] than that of France."[47] After the Dogger Bank Incident, and once it was evident that Russia was going to be defeated by Japan, Tsar Nicholas began searching for a chance to seek revenge for France's disloyalty.

Unlike France during Russia's war with Japan, Russia was obligated to support France over Morocco, since the crisis was initiated by Germany. André Tardieu suggested that Russian "fidelity to the French Alliance was evinced in the most energetic way during the conference at Algeciras."[48] However, Russia's behavior during the crisis is more complicated than that. Although the Russians did support France at the conference itself,

45. "Emperor's Consult in Early Morning," *New York Times*, 25 July 1905.

46. Paul Cambon, *Correspondence, 1870–1924*, vol. 2 (Paris: B. Graset, 1946), 26 December 1903, 102; Taylor, *Struggle for Mastery in Europe*, 419.

47. Bülow, *Imperial Germany*, 81.

48. Tardieu, *France and the Alliances*, 27.

on 24 July 1905, at the height of the crisis, Tsar Nicholas met with Kaiser Wilhelm II at Primorsk, Russia (on the Baltic Sea in the Gulf of Finland) to discuss the terms of a defense treaty (known as the Björko Treaty for the Swedish name of the town).[49] Ultimately, Russia did support France at the Algeciras conference, and according to White, this support was constant throughout the conference.[50]

Two important changes were made to Franco-Russian relations in response to Russia's behavior. According to Eugene Anderson, "on January 21, 1906 [five days after the Algeciras conference began], the Tsar wrote to William II that in keeping with 'the real sense of our Björko Treaty,' he had accepted a proposal of [French] President Loubet's to attach a French general to his person."[51] In addition, on 21 April 1906, just two weeks after the Algeciras conference concluded, the Russian and French Chiefs of General Staff met to develop a military protocol in Paris. According to White, "this reaffirmed the basic purpose of the 1892 accord as that of mutual protection against aggression by Germany."[52]

Explaining Russian Behavior

The Björko Treaty is an interesting component of the case that Mercer simply glosses over,[53] but it is necessary for understanding the effect of reputation on Franco-Russian relations. For one thing, Tsar Nicholas was angered at British "neutrality" and French inaction during the Russo-Japanese War,[54] and he was initially open to an agreement with Germany. Earlier Russo-German negotiations (from October 1904 to February 1905) ended because the Russians refused to ally with Germany without prior French approval. However, by July 1905, the tsar's attitude toward his French ally changed, and because he at least partly blamed Russia's impending defeat to Japan on French inaction, the tsar felt compelled to look for other possible allies. Therefore, although the Russians did not abandon France, this incident fits nicely with hypothesis 3 about unreliable states having trouble keeping their allies. France's perceived lack of reliability nearly pushed Russia to join with Germany, which would have isolated the French and made them even more dependent on the British.

49. Sidney Fay, "The Kaiser's Secret Negotiations with the Tsar, 1904–1905," *American Historical Review* 24, no. 1 (October 1918), 48–72; Fischer, *War of Illusions,* 51; Taylor, *Struggle for Mastery in Europe,* 432.

50. White, *Transition to Global Rivalry,* 191.

51. Anderson, *First Moroccan Crisis,* 304–305.

52. White, *Transition to Global Rivalry,* 185.

53. Mercer, *Reputation and International Politics,* 92.

54. Anderson, *First Moroccan Crisis,* 282.

The treaty negotiated at Björko posed a minimal threat to France and England.[55] However, when word of the meeting leaked, the French and British governments both became uneasy. Even though Vladimir Lamsdorf, Russia's minister of foreign affairs, ultimately convinced the tsar to drop the alliance with Germany, the incident increased French distrust of its Russian ally. It is noteworthy that rather than suggest that the agreement with Germany would hurt Russia's relations with France, to convince the tsar that the alliance might drag Russia into an Anglo-German war Lamsdorf referred to Germany's prior behavior as an unreliable ally.[56]

France's prime minister, Maurice Rouvier, also cited Germany's lack of reliability to convince Alexander Nelidov, the Russian ambassador in Paris, that the French would never accept an alliance between themselves, Russia, and Germany. He claimed that "the nation would not tolerate a closer rapprochement with Germany. It cannot forget what it has suffered from her, of which suffering it has just been reminded in a careless and purposeless way."[57] Thus, even though a possible Russo-German alliance is slightly tangential to this case, it provides further support for my argument about how reputation affects the willingness and ability of states to form alliances, because despite Russia's desire to find another ally in principle, neither France nor Russia was willing to ally with Germany, at least partly because of its reputation.

Although Russia did support France at the Algeciras conference, this did not translate into increased reliability, given the willingness of the tsar to negotiate with Germany during the earlier part of the crisis. In contrast, even though the British had strategic reasons for supporting France, their commitment to France was unwavering. As a result, I expect the French to have perceived a decline in Russia's reliability relative to British reliability, resulting in observable changes to the Franco-Russian alliance that are more binding than the changes to the Anglo-French relationship discussed above.

Existing alliance theories can either explain Russia's support for France or its willingness to negotiate a separate treaty with Germany. None of them, by themselves, are able to adequately explain both Russian actions. Balance of power theory even has trouble explaining both Russian choices. In 1905, at the time of the Björko Treaty, combined Russian and German power alone was greater than that of all the other great powers combined. If Germany's desire for an alliance with Russia and either France or Austria-

55. Article I was a promise to aid each other in the event of one being attacked by a European power, and Article IV even called for France to be invited into the accord. Sidney Fay, "The Kaiser's Secret Negotiations with the Tsar, 1904–1905," *American Historical Review* 24, no. 1 (October 1918), 67–68. See also Beryl Williams, "The Strategic Background to the Anglo-Russian Entente of August 1907," *Historical Journal* 9, no. 3 (1966), 371.

56. Anderson, *First Moroccan Crisis*, 297–298.

57. Cited in ibid., 302.

Hungary had come to pass it would have significantly altered the balance of power in Europe. Likewise, by the time of the Algeciras conference, Russia supporting France was clearly an example of bandwagoning, since all the parties to the conference supported France except Austria-Hungary. And because the Entente Cordiale effectively balanced the power of the Triple Alliance by itself, whichever side Russia took was a problem for balancing.

Regardless of the balance of power, Germany was perceived by most states to be the greatest threat (Austria-Hungary was a close second for Russia). Therefore, Russian support for France during the conference fits balance of threat theory. Yet this theory cannot explain the tsar's willingness to risk the Dual Alliance by signing a treaty with Germany. Binding theory provides a more useful explanation for the Björko Treaty, as an example of Russia attempting to ally with an adversary in order to have greater influence on German behavior. But the theory falls short given that the treaty was dropped in favor of preserving French good will. Adding reputation helps us explain not only why the Björko Treaty was dropped in favor of support for France but also why Franco-Russian relations changed more than Anglo-French relations after the crisis.

Consequences of Russian Behavior

The conventional view of the First Moroccan Crisis was that German actions, intended to drive a wedge between France and its allies, instead brought France, Russia, and England into a more intimate relationship. Although this may be true, I contend that France and Russia drew closer not only out of concern for the growing German threat but also because of declining perceptions of each other's reliability. I also suggest that the increased delegation between Britain and France was surpassed by the degree with which France attempted to bind Russia after the crisis.

Because Mercer argues that states always perceive their allies to have a negative reputation, France should not have been surprised by the limited Russian support and should not have considered withdrawing from the alliance nor demanded a more binding agreement. Therefore, any changes to the Dual Alliance challenge Mercer's arguments on this and support my hypotheses on alliance variation, particularly, if, as I suggest, Russia suffered more for its mixed support than England did for its full support.

Russia's support for France was clearly strategic, based on a desire to gain access to the straits and its need for French financial assistance rather than any sense of obligation to an ally.[58] That does not mean that French (and even British) perceptions of Russian reliability would not change. The

58. Mercer, *Reputation and International Politics*, 106.

evidence suggests that Russia's mixed support for France during the crisis resulted in more binding changes than those that were made between England and France.

The changes made in the Franco-Russian relationship—especially Russia's willingness to accept a French general as an adviser to the Russian government[59]—show not only that France requested a higher level of military integration with Russia but also that Russia was willing to give up some of its autonomy to preserve the alliance with France. For the French, this increased delegation was intended to make it more difficult for Russia to abandon France in the next crisis, or in a war. In addition, the meeting between the Russian and French General Staffs was clearly meant to send a signal to the Germans about the strength of the Franco-Russian relationship; but perhaps more important was the assurance that it provided to France about Russian reliability. In contrast, the British merely participated in military conversations with the French, which the British even viewed as *increasing* their freedom of action, since it provided a greater possibility of fighting with France if the British chose to do so.

Taking a step back, I suggest that Russia's actions, even though they affected French perceptions of Russian reliability, were also a consequence of past French behavior, particularly France's inaction during the Russo-Japanese War.[60] That Russia initially entered into negotiations for an alliance with Germany in October 1904 supports this argument, even though these negotiations ended without an agreement because the Russians were unwilling at that time to ally with Germany without French approval.[61] Not only did the Russians consider another agreement with Germany while Germany initiated a crisis with France but the lukewarm support that Russia gave to France also contributed to a greater level of Russian delegation within the context of the Dual Alliance, especially in comparison to the lack of change in Anglo-French relations.

The final element of the Russian portion of the story has to do with the creation of the 1907 entente between Russia and England. Recall from the previous section my claim that British reputation helps explain Russia's willingness to sign an entente. Yet hypothesis 2 cannot fully explain

59. Anderson, *First Moroccan Crisis*, 304–305.

60. Jonathan Steinberg discusses German support for Russia during the Russo-Japanese War, while Julian Corbett compares German support to French neutrality during the war. Jonathan Steinberg, "Germany and the Russo-Japanese War," *American Historical Review* 75, no. 7 (December 1970), 1965–1986; Julian Corbett, *Maritime Operations in the Russo-Japanese War, 1904–1905* (Annapolis, MD: Naval Institute Press, 1994). Also see "Russia and Germany: A Far Eastern Understanding," *New York Times*, 14 September 1904.

61. Count Sergei Witte was the Russian prime minister and the person chiefly responsible for preventing the treaty's completion. According to his account, the agreement was aimed at France. "Says Czar Was a Traitor," *New York Times*, 19 May 1917.

England's willingness to sign the entente, particularly given Russia's mixed reputation during the 1905 crisis. One must accept the possibility that British interests simply outweighed reputation since the benefits of resolving the issues in Asia may have outweighed British concerns about Russian reliability. And, as Eugene Anderson writes, "mistrust of the Central Power [Germany] was an important inducement for Great Britain and France to complete the Entente Cordiale by an entente between Great Britain and Russia."[62] Not only did Germany's growing naval power threaten England but its aggressive behavior over the situation in Morocco signaled its intentions. Therefore, balance of threat theory can explain the new entente. In addition, even if Russian reliability declined relative to the British, Russia did ultimately support France during the all-important conference at Algeciras, which may have been enough to convince England that it was worthwhile to pursue an entente that preserved British autonomy.

Even if Russian behavior did not prevent England and Russia from signing an entente of their own in 1907, the British were unwilling to accept anything more than an entente. According to Gordon Martel, the agreement between England and Russia "provided for no political action, no military planning, and suggested no possible contingencies that might lead the two powers to consult on these matters in the future."[63] The entente contained no obligation or delegation, and although it was very precise about providing only for the resolution of tension between England and Russia in Persia, Tibet, and Afghanistan, it was vague about the commitments made by either state to protect each other's interests.

As with the British case, although strategic factors are an important explanation for some of the alliance choices during the crisis—particularly given the growth of Germany as a threat—without reputation we cannot explain the way in which France's relationship with Russia grew more binding, especially relative to Anglo-French relations, nor can we explain England's disinterest in binding itself to either France or Russia in spite of the growing German threat. This suggests that a state's reputation is an important element of its autonomy even when strategic interests are also a key factor in a state's behavior.

Austria-Hungary

Austria-Hungary, Germany, and Italy joined as allies with the creation of the Triple Alliance on 20 May 1882. Although the terms of the Alliance were secret, it was believed to be primarily directed at Russia, with France as a

62. Anderson, *First Moroccan Crisis,* 404.
63. Gordon Martel, *Origins of the First World War* (London: Longman, 1996), 67.

secondary target, at least for Germany. Despite the existence of the Alliance, Austria-Hungary was the only state, other than Morocco, to vote with Germany at Algeciras.[64] After the crisis, Germany sent a telegram thanking the Austro-Hungarian government for its support in the crisis and for always supporting Germany. Dubbed the "seconding telegram," its language was taken by many Austrians as an affront to the power of the Austro-Hungarian Empire.[65]

In spite of the tension between Germany and Austria-Hungary, and Italy's failure to support Germany at Algeciras (discussed in the next section), the Triple Alliance was tacitly renewed on 8 July 1907, when none of the signatories to the treaty expressed an interest in withdrawing from the agreement one year before the 1908 deadline of the treaty.[66] The question is whether any changes occurred in the relationship between Austria-Hungary and Germany as a result of the crisis.

No official changes were made to the Triple Alliance itself. However, Germany's treatment of its allies after the crisis reflects the different levels of support it received during the conference. Although there was an increase in military coordination between Austria-Hungary and Germany, the changes to Austria-Hungary's autonomy are significantly less binding than those placed on Italy after it failed to support Germany at the conference.

Explaining Austrian Support

Mercer largely dismisses the role that Austria-Hungary played during the First Moroccan Crisis, primarily because of the domestic problems facing the empire. He suggests that it did not pay attention to Delcassé's resignation and remained relatively passive during the conference.[67] Although Austria-Hungary was considered the "sick man of Europe" and suffered from serious domestic problems, any analysis of an ally's reputation should take into account such issues, because if a state cannot possibly aid its partners, then that will undoubtedly influence its allies' actions or the nature of the alliance. And Germany's interest in an agreement with Russia probably reflects the situation in Austria-Hungary as much as it is a response to its prior behavior as an ally.

64. "Germany Almost Friendless: Conference Has Shown that She Can Rely Only on Austria," *New York Times* 1 April 1906, 4. Morocco primarily sided with Germany because it wanted more autonomy than it would have as a French protectorate.

65. "The Kaiser and the Morocco Conference: Telegram to Count Goluchowski," *Times* (London), 14 April 1906; "The Kaiser's Telegram," *Times* (London), 16 April 1906.

66. "The Triple Alliance," *Times* (London), 15 July 1907.

67. Mercer, *Reputation and International Politics*, 86–88, 97–98.

There were several strategic reasons for Austria-Hungary to support Germany at the Algeciras conference. Among the alliance theories I examine, balance of power theory is the best explanation for Austro-Hungarian behavior at the conference. Balance of power theory suggests that it was necessary for Austria-Hungary to support Germany, particularly since Germany was so overwhelmed at Algeciras.

In the context of Austria-Hungary's behavior at the conference, balance of threat theory cannot explain this case, because there is no indication that Austria-Hungary saw France as a threat to its interests. Germany and Austria-Hungary both perceived Russia to be a threat, and there is some indication (discussed in greater detail in chapter 5) that Austria-Hungary saw its Italian ally as the greatest threat to its own interests. Therefore, the theory cannot explain why Austria-Hungary voted against France. Likewise, since Austria-Hungary did not see Germany as a threat, binding theory cannot explain its support for Germany.

Another important factor is that Austria-Hungary did not have many other potential allies, so even its attempt to play the loyal ally can be seen as a strategic interest, since failing to support Germany might have left Austria-Hungary alone, especially if my hypothesis 3 on alliance termination is valid.

According to Mercer's general argument, because Austria-Hungary's behavior was favorable to Germany, the Germans would explain its support as a function of strategic interests, and therefore would not see Austria-Hungary as any more reliable of an ally, particularly since the outcome of the Algeciras conference was negative.[68] If true, then Austria-Hungary should not have benefitted from its support of Germany, and there should be no changes to the alliance.

Consequences of Austrian Behavior

Based on Austria-Hungary's support for its ally, I hypothesize that it would be able to form new alliances, not lose any existing allies, and preserve its current levels of obligation, precision, and delegation within its existing alliances. Because Austria-Hungary did not attempt to form any new alliances, I can make no claims about its ability to do so. But the renewal of the Triple Alliance is related to my hypotheses on alliance termination, because a state that supports its ally should be able to renew its alliances, just as Britain was able to do with Japan in 1905. There are also strategic reasons for the renewal of the Triple Alliance.

From the German perspective, renewing the alliance with Austria-Hungary fits both balancing theories, since the balance of power required the preservation of the Triple Alliance and Germany perceived France and

68. Ibid., 91.

Russia to be threats to its interests. Binding theory does not explain Germany's interests in renewing the alliance, though it may explain Germany's willingness to negotiate the agreement with Russia at Björko.

For Austria-Hungary, balance of power theory can explain the continuation of positive relations with Germany (and even Italy) given that maintaining the balance of power in Europe required them to remain together, especially with England and France allying. Because Germany and Austria-Hungary both saw Russia as a threat, balance of threat theory also explains the continuation of the Alliance. However, Austria-Hungary also viewed Italy as a major threat, which fits with binding theory.

More important, that the Alliance changed, particularly compared to German-Italian relations, is difficult to explain without reputation. Austria-Hungary and Germany increased their military coordination, which slightly added to Austria's obligation and delegation to Germany. However, I classify these results as supportive of hypothesis 5, since both measures of alliance variation are significantly less binding than the changes applied to Italy as a result of its lack of support at Algeciras. This is relevant because it again confirms my basic contention that a state's reliability is linked to its relative alliance autonomy.

Neither state had many options other than to keep each other as allies. The German ambassador to Austria wrote to von Bülow, "Personally I have the impression that Austria-Hungary is with us; but we must not overlook the fact that the Dual Monarchy is not inclined or able to act in a military way. This is due to her sorry domestic situation and her reduced circumstances."[69] This is an interesting comment because it simultaneously suggests that Austria-Hungary's reliability was low because of its domestic problems, but that this was a temporary condition, and that for some reason, perhaps because of its previous actions in support of Germany, the Germans still counted on its support. It may have also meant that Germany understood the reality that Austria-Hungary had few other alliance options, and so, despite its low level of capability, Austria-Hungary would still do everything it could to support its lone ally.

Italy

Italy not only failed to support Germany at the Algeciras conference but voted with France. Although Italy's behavior should not have come as a shock, the Italians clearly suffered a loss of reliability, especially in relation to Austria-Hungary. As just one example of the German public's perception

69. Oswald Wedel, *Austro-German Diplomatic Relations, 1908–1914* (Stanford: Stanford University Press, 1932), 37.

of Italy's role at the conference, according to the *Times* (London), "when the eruption of Mount Vesuvius occurred [in Italy in April 1906] the Berlin Press had the bad taste to insinuate that it was so much the worse for a faithless ally."[70]

After the Algeciras conference both Germany and Austria-Hungary took a series of steps to draw their ally closer. The Conference on Commerce and Navigation was held on 11 February 1906 (shortly before the end of the Algeciras conference), at which Italy and Austria-Hungary settled some of their commercial problems. The allies held another conference in Vienna in June 1906, where emphasis was placed on drawing Italy as close as possible to the Central Powers. Then, in October 1906, a visit by the German foreign secretary, Heinrich von Tschirschky, brought with it a demand that Italy spend more on its army and navy.[71] Finally, Anton Monts, Germany's ambassador to Italy, who had earlier advocated dissolution of the Alliance, proposed that Italy be forced to lend diplomatic support to Germany's economic policy in Asia Minor.[72]

Explaining Italian Behavior

Most of the evidence suggests that Italy sided with France during the Algeciras conference for two reasons. Just as the British were concerned that if French control over Morocco were weakened, British control over Egypt would follow suit, the Italians had also recognized French control of Morocco in exchange for Italian control over Tripoli. So commercial interests played a major role in the Italian decision. The other factor is that Italy appeared to be more fearful of war with France and England than with Germany and Austria-Hungary (at least in terms of the ability of England and France to harm Italy). Ironically, although the Italians believed Austria-Hungary posed the greatest threat, geography meant that France and England could do the most damage to Italy in war. In addition, on 4 June 1902, the Italians also made a secret promise to the French that the Triple Alliance contained nothing hostile to them, and on 30 June 1902 the two states pledged neutrality in a war involving one of them.[73]

Of the three alliance theories I examine, only one really explains the Italian decision to side with France at Algeciras. Balance of power theory would expect Italy to side with its Triple Alliance members. And binding

70. "Herr von Tschirschky's Journey," *Times* (London), 9 October 1906.

71. "Italy and Austria-Hungary," *Times* (London), 10 October 1906.

72. Alfred Pribram, *The Secret Treaties of Austria-Hungary, 1879–1914*, vol. 2, *Negotiations Leading to the Treaties of the Triple Alliance* (Cambridge: Harvard University Press, 1921), 139–140.

73. Lee, *Europe's Crucial Years*, 23–43; Taylor, *Struggle for Master of Europe*. 406–407; White, *Transition to Global Rivalry*, 191–192.

theory has some difficulty explaining Italy's lack of support for Germany, especially if Italy perceived Austria-Hungary to be the greatest threat. Only balance of threat theory may be able to explain the Italian decision, since it was going against Germany, but more importantly against the one state that posed a real threat to Italian interests, Austria-Hungary.

Mercer's argument should expect Italy's reputation to decline given that its behavior was unfavorable to Germany. Yet, curiously, in this case, which would be consistent with his argument, Mercer deviates from his own theory to suggest that Italian abandonment was also explained through situation.[74] For him, this would mean that Germany would not expect Italy's support in the future. His argument still does not explain what Germany would do to respond to Italy's declining reliability. Therefore, if the alliance did not change based on these different levels of support, then that strengthens Mercer's claims. If Germany treated its allies according to how much support they gave, then that strengthens the reputation argument.

Regardless of the reason for Italy's lack of support, Italy's reliability clearly declined. In the words of Anton Monts, "If Italy fails us in the relatively unimportant Morocco question, that is a foretaste of what we may expect in really serious times."[75] In addition, the Germans feared that France would call for a second conference on Morocco in the future. On this point, Friedrich von Holstein, a political counselor in the foreign office (and the man responsible for the kaiser's trip to Tangier), claimed, "Such a Conference would be a certain second defeat for Germany. For, with the way the fleet question stands at present, England would adhere to France more than ever. Russia needs a French loan of a billion. *We know how Italy and Spain behave.* And Austria is still angry with us about the 'Seconding' telegram."[76] These points not only illustrate German perceptions of Italy's reliability but also suggest a concern about future crises in which Italy could not be counted on to assist its allies.

But concern about Italy was not exclusive to Germany. Italy's behavior at Algeciras also got the attention of its other ally in the Triple Alliance. General Moritz von Auffenberg, an Austrian army general and later minister of war, stated that "in case of war Italy would explode against us like a keg of powder."[77]

74. Mercer, *Reputation and International Politics*, 89.

75. G. P. Gooch, *Before the War: Studies in Diplomacy*, vol. 1, *The Grouping of the Powers* (London: Longmans, Green, 1936), 258.

76. Cited in Norman Rich and M. H. Fisher, *The Holstein Papers* (Cambridge: Cambridge University Press, 1955–1963), Holstein to Bülow (25 August 1908), no. 1121, 556, emphasis added.

77. J. Lepsius, A. Mendelssohn-Bartholdy, and F. Thimme, eds. *Die Grosse Politik der Europaischen Kabinette, 1871–1914*, vol. 30 (Berlin: Deutsche Verlagsgesellschaft für Politik und Geschichte, 1922–1927), 514, trans. in Sidney Fay, *The Origins of the World War*, vol. 1 (New York: Macmillan, 1928), 346; Manhart, *Alliance and Entente*, 64.

Consequences of Italy's Behavior

Italy is a difficult case for my argument because it is situated in a strategically important geographic position, and it therefore makes sense that it would be a desirable ally, regardless of its prior behavior. Moreover, Italy's allies have few options for other alliances, so they would be less likely to punish Italy for its reputation. But, based on my hypotheses, Italy should suffer a decline in its reputation and therefore also in its alliance autonomy. Specifically, I expect Italy to have trouble finding new allies (especially reliable ones) and to lose its current allies (both Germany, which it failed to support, as well as Austria-Hungary). If it does keep its allies I expect it to have to give up more obligation, precision, and delegation, especially compared to Austria-Hungary.

Both balance of power and balance of threat theories explain why the Triple Alliance persisted, despite Italy's behavior. Both theories recognize that the more powerful Dual Alliance posed a threat to the Triple Alliance, even without the British, and that it would become an even greater threat if Italy were allowed to remain neutral, much less realign with England and France. Both theories also explain why Germany and Austria-Hungary were willing to remain in an alliance with such an unreliable state. Italy's membership in the Triple Alliance is also a classic case of attempting to bind a state's behavior through an alliance, both for Italy and for Austria-Hungary. Germany was also willing to renew the Alliance despite its lack of faith in Italy in order to avoid being completely dependent on Austria-Hungary as an ally. In other words, because Germany did not have a lot of options, its security depended on having more than one ally, even if one of those allies was unreliable. This suggests again that reputation may be less important for actors that have few alliance options to begin with. In contrast, those with several options may be able to care more about the reliability of current and potential allies, meaning they will also more readily punish unreliable behavior.

Austria-Hungary saw Italy as a threat, and even had military plans in which the government assumed a simultaneous war against Italy and Serbia-Montenegro.[78] Austria-Hungary preferred to maintain the Alliance, despite Italy's lack of reliability, because it feared invasion of its southern frontiers in a war with Russia. As long as Italy at least remained neutral in a war that frontier would remain more secure than if Italy were pushed into the opposing camp. Alfred Pribram supports this view, contending, "If the

78. Referred to as "War Plan I." Graydon Tunstall, *Planning for War against Russia and Serbia: Austro-Hungarian and German Military Strategies, 1871–1914* (New York: Columbia University Press, 1993), 56; Leo Valiani, "Italian-Austro-Hungarian Negotiations 1914–1915," *Journal of Contemporary History* 1, no. 3 (July 1966), 114.

government leaders in Berlin and Vienna advocated the continuance of the Triple Alliance, and persisted in their willingness to make fresh sacrifices for the sake of holding their unreliable ally, they did so because they saw in this alliance the only safeguard against Italy's open defection to the camp of the enemy."[79] This suggests a classic case of tethering, and in such situations reputation probably does matter less because the state never expects the ally to fight but instead forms an alliance simply to prevent the state from joining with an adversary. Because the Alliance was renewed for many reasons, it is not surprising that this case fails to support my hypotheses on alliance termination. But these conventional theories have difficulty explaining the changes that occurred in Italy's relationships with both Germany and Austria-Hungary.

As with the Austria-Hungary case, I cannot test my hypotheses on alliance formation because Italy made no attempt to find new allies. Although Italy did not lose its allies, both the German and Austrian leadership did talk of dissolving the Alliance. According to Pribram, "When Italy supported Germany's adversaries in the Moroccan affair and during the course of the Algeciras conference, many were shaken in this belief [that Italy would support its allies in a war]. . . . Statesmen there were of no mean influence who urged a dissolution of the alliance with Italy and a new orientation of German policy in the direction of a revival of the League of Three Emperors."[80] In May 1906, Anton Monts "confronted the Imperial Chancellor and the Secretary of State [in Berlin] with the question of whether, in view of Italy's attitude, it would not be better to make use of the right of denunciation and dissolve an alliance which afforded disproportionately greater advantages to Italy than to the Central Powers."[81] He argued that the current treaty required heavy obligation from Germany without expecting similar commitments from Italy.

Nevertheless, the Alliance did not end and was actually renewed in July 1907. Part of the reason may be that the Italian case is more complicated than it seems on the surface. First of all, the evidence is contradictory regarding how the Germans perceived Italy's reliability after the crisis.[82] On one hand, Wilhelm is claimed to have disapproved of Italy's double-faced attitude. In a 10 April 1906 letter, Ladislas de Szögyény-Marich, the Austrian ambassador in Berlin, wrote to Agenor Goluchowski, the Austro-Hungarian

79. Pribram, *Negotiations Leading to the Treaties of the Triple Alliance*, 143; Taylor, *Struggle for Mastery in Europe*, 441.

80. Pribram, *Negotiations Leading to the Treaties of the Triple Alliance*, 135–136. The Three Emperors' League was an 1873 alliance between Germany, Austria-Hungary, and Russia, aimed at protecting the monarchs from the increasingly liberal governments in western Europe.

81. Ibid., 139.

82. Mercer, *Reputation and International Politics*, 89.

minister of foreign affairs, of a meeting with the German kaiser. According to Szögyény-Marich, Kaiser Wilhelm "did not wish to waste many words over Italy, and would only give the assurance that if the opportunity should arise—and this was not impossible in view of the unreliable policy of that kingdom—it would give him great satisfaction to join us in administering a salutary lesson to Italy, perhaps even with arms in hand."[83]

On the other hand, von Bülow suggested that "the Italian representatives [at Algeciras] took their stand in certain secondary matters with the Western Powers, and against us. . . . In other more important questions, Italy supported and furthered our point of view."[84] It is unclear why von Bülow felt this way, given that the Italians voted with the French. However, von Bülow seemed to understand that even if Italy was unreliable, it was better to have the Italians as allies than have them facing off against Austria-Hungary or formally aligned with either England or France.[85]

It is also possible that Germany did not perceive the Italians to be less reliable, considering that they did not strictly violate the terms of the Triple Alliance. For one thing, Italy frequently informed its allies that it would not become involved in a war against France or England. And, notably, the language of the Triple Alliance did not require Italy to become involved in a conflict with France.[86] It is precisely this argument that the Italian government made after the First World War to explain why it should not be viewed as having betrayed its allies.[87] The same argument could be made for the Algeciras conference. Yet, even if some Germans were willing to forgive Italian behavior at Algeciras because of its conflicting commitments, perceptions of Italy's reliability should be lower than those of Austria-Hungary. Therefore, even though the Triple Alliance did not end and was even renewed contrary to my expectations, this case still supports hypothesis 5 with the changes made by the Triple Alliance states, aimed especially at Italy.

The attempt to coerce Italian support for Germany in Asia Minor is particularly relevant, because it would have placed Italy in conflict with French and British interests in the region. Therefore, consistent with the argument about obligation, this is an example of a state having to pay higher costs to form—or in this case preserve—an alliance. An additional cost of this change was a potential increase in tension between Italy and the Entente states.

83. Pribram, *Negotiations Leading to the Treaties of the Triple Alliance,* 138.

84. Bernhard von Bülow, *Deutsche Politik* (Berlin: R. Hobbing, 1916), 69, cited in ibid., 136fn317. See also Bülow, *Imperial Germany,* 70.

85. Bülow, *Imperial Germany,* 72–73.

86. "The Triple Alliance: The Kaiser's Visit to Vienna," *Times* (London), 9 June 1906.

87. Italian Library of Information, *Italian Foreign Policy since 1870* (New York: Italian Library of Information, 1940), 14–17.

The Austro-Hungarian government also increased talk of invading Italy. Likewise, von Moltke claimed that the agreements made with Italy "were made so clear and so binding that a doubt as to Italy's faithfulness to the Alliance could scarcely arise."[88] Not only does this suggest that there was a high level of precision with respect to Italy's commitments but the binding nature of the commitments meant that Italy would have less autonomy in deciding whether to support its allies in the future. Therefore, although Germany tried to bind *both* of its allies more closely to it after Algeciras, Austria-Hungary clearly retained more autonomy within the Alliance than did Italy.

French Perceptions of Italian Reliability

Because Italy had an agreement with France concerning Morocco, it is also worthwhile to explore any changes that occurred in the Franco-Italian relationship as a result of Italy's support at the conference. From the French perspective, Italy's reliability should have risen, because even though Italy abandoned an ally, it lived up to its agreement with France. On the other hand, Mercer would argue that because the French saw Italian behavior as favorable, France would explain away Italian support at the conference as a function of strategic interests. More relevant for my hypotheses is whether relations between France and Italy improved after the conference.

Evidence appears to be mixed. Stephen Pichon, France's foreign minister, advocated a policy to detach Italy from the Triple Alliance, believing that France and Italy had common interests.[89] Although Pichon's argument was based more on interests than reputation, it is likely that his desire for such a policy would have diminished had Italy not voted with France at the conference. In contrast, Paul Cambon believed that Italy was unreliable and liked Italy being a part of the Triple Alliance because it weakened Germany and Austria-Hungary, whereas if Italy were to abandon the Alliance, Germany might attempt to reconcile with Russia. According to M. B. Hayne, "Cambon correctly assessed that Italy would remain neutral in the event of a general war until it was possible to distinguish the victorious side."[90] In other words, despite Italy's favorable behavior at the conference, at least some in the French government still perceived Italy to be generally unreliable.

This does bring up an important point regarding the degree to which states share a common perception of another state's reputation. I test

88. Cited in Bernadotte Schmitt, *Triple Alliance and Triple Entente* (New York: H. Holt and Company, 1934), 101; Manhart, *Alliance and Entente*, 64.

89. M. B. Hayne, *The French Foreign Office and the Origins of the First World War, 1898–1914* (Oxford: Clarendon Press, 1993), 184.

90. Hayne, *French Foreign Office*, 109.

whether allies have similar perceptions by my two separate hypotheses on alliance duration—one for the abandoned ally and one for other allies. However, this case is an example of a state having two different commitments and having to choose sides in a crisis.[91] The challenge is that although some perceptions of Italian reputation are a product of one's view of the conference outcome as success or failure, others held a more constant view of Italy's reputation, focused on the abandonment of one ally even though it honored its commitments to France. Despite the mixed beliefs about the desirability of France having Italy as an ally, I found no evidence that relations between France and Italy changed in any way after the Algeciras conference. Although the agreements between Italy and France remained intact, neither England nor France was willing to offer Italy a greater commitment, since it was still generally perceived to be unreliable despite supporting France in this one instance. This case, then, offers the strongest support for Mercer's argument, because, in spite of Italy's support, none of the Entente states saw Italy as reliable or acting for any reasons other than its own interests.

An examination of the First Moroccan Crisis does not neatly conform to all of my hypotheses, though it does lend support to my general propositions regarding the connection between reputation and alliance autonomy. (Table 4.2 provides a summary of results from this chapter.) Five separate observations can be made from the First Moroccan Crisis (one each for England, Russia, and Austria-Hungary, and two for Italy, given that it had agreements with both France and Germany).

Some of the hypotheses receive only mixed support because, as I expect, strategic factors such as power, interests, and geography frequently outweigh reputation as explanations of a state's behavior. However, failing to incorporate reputation misses a significant part of the story. And, although supporting an ally does not always increase a state's autonomy, at least during the First Moroccan Crisis reliable states came away with greater autonomy than the states that failed to fully support their ally. Therefore, this case strengthens my overall contention that leaders who want to preserve their state's alliance autonomy should pay attention to their state's reputation as a reliable ally.

91. A more contemporary example of this dilemma is the United States having to choose sides between Great Britain and Argentina during the 1982 Falklands/Malvinas War. After initially trying to maintain neutrality, the United States ended up supporting Britain. Given that the United States had stronger interests in supporting its NATO ally, its reputation was unlikely to suffer a general decline within the international community. Nevertheless, Argentina's perception of the United States as an ally dropped as a result of these actions during the war. David Feldman, "The United States Role in the Malvinas Crisis, 1982: Misguidance and Misperception in Argentina's Decision to Go to War," *Journal of Interamerican Studies and World Affairs* 27, no. 2 (Summer 1985), 19.

Table 4.2. Review of chapter findings

Observation	French allies: England[a] (up)	French allies: Russia[a] (mixed)	French allies: Italy[a] (up)	German allies: Austria-Hungary[a] (up)	German allies: Italy[a] (up)
H1: alliance formation	+	0	N/A	N/A	N/A
H2: similar reliability	0	0	0	N/A	+
H3: lose abandoned ally	+	0	+	+	–
H4: lose other allies	+	N/A	N/A	+	–
H5: alliance variation	+	+	N/A	+	+

Note: N/A = not applicable to case; – = no support; 0 = mixed findings; + = strong support
[a] State (reliability level)

If we look first at alliance formation, neither Italy nor Austria-Hungary attempted to find new allies, so the test for this hypothesis is limited to the Anglo-Russian entente. British reliability during the crisis did lead to renewed talks on the subject of an entente with Russia. This entente is a small problem for my argument, given the tsar's willingness to abandon its ally for an agreement with Germany. However, this is another example of strategic interests outweighing reputation concerns, since the British thought that they would benefit from an agreement with Russia, and because both sides recognized the growing German threat. That in the end Russia did not abandon France at the Algeciras conference may have reduced some initial concerns about Russia's reputation; for this reason, I consider the Russian side of the Anglo-Russian entente to provide mixed support for my argument.

There is also mixed support for my hypotheses on alliance termination. Although both of Italy's allies discussed leaving the Alliance (not to mention developing plans for attacking Italy), the Triple Alliance was renewed. One can easily imagine that if Germany and Austria-Hungary had other alliance options they would have followed through on the threat to dissolve the alliance with Italy. However, because they had no other alternatives, they were unwilling to let Italy go, despite its poor reputation. At the same time, neither of the states that honored their obligations—England and Austria-Hungary—were even threatened with the loss of an ally.

Next, as we found in the cases in chapter 3, the strongest support is for my hypothesis on alliance variation. Mercer suggests that the French credited neither of its allies with being resolved: "Because they explained allied support in terms of the situation, both France and Germany questioned the support they would be given in the future."[92] However, what Mercer identifies is that the French were uncertain about their allies' capabilities and competence—for example, the speed with which England could put troops on the Continent and Russia's ability to recover from its defeat to Japan. Despite Mercer's claims, the French did not question England's willingness to support France. Nor did the French question whether they would receive at least naval support from the British, considering France's willingness to leave its Atlantic coastal defense in British hands. The real question here is whether the relationships between these states and their allies changed as a result of their behavior during the crisis.

One thing I have tried to show in this case is that France's relationships with England and Russia reflected the degree to which each state supported France at Algeciras. The British were able to preserve a great deal of autonomy, even to the point of believing that the French had become reliant on England. In his annual report on France, Francis Bertie wrote: "I believe that France is now so dependent in matters of foreign policy on England that pressure might be used to bring the French Government to show a more accommodating spirit in some of the questions in which the two countries are at present not entirely agreed."[93] As a result, not only did England's reputation ensure that it had more autonomy within its alliances but it also gave England greater levels of influence over its allies. My basic argument is strengthened when we compare England's relative level of autonomy after the crisis to that of Russia, since the increase in Russian delegation and integration was greater than that required of the British.

Similarly, Germany's attitude toward Austria-Hungary and Italy illustrates the degree to which it perceived its allies to be reliable based on their behavior at Algeciras. Germany received a great deal of support from Austria-Hungary, but Italy voted with France. Italy was not forced to withdraw from the Triple Alliance as hypotheses 3 and 4 might expect. And even though German and Austro-Hungarian leaders did discuss denunciation of the Alliance, or even an invasion of Italy, I consider the hypotheses unsupported in this case. But Germany and Austria-Hungary did try to bind Italy more closely to the Alliance, specifically by demanding that Italy increase its obligation through diplomatic support for German and Austro-Hungarian interests. In addition, Austrian rhetoric about invading Italy increased after the crisis,[94] and when the Austro-Hungarian government annexed Bosnia in

92. Mercer, *Reputation and International Politics,* 109.

93. Cited in Keith Wilson, "The Agadir Crisis, the Mansion House Speech, and the Double-Edgedness of Agreements," *Historical Journal* 15, no. 3 (September 1972), 528.

94. Conrad, Austria's Chief of the General Staff, even referred to Italy as Austria's principal opponent, and suggested that preventive war was an option. Manhart, *Alliance and Entente,* 64; Fay, *Origins of the World War,* vol. 1, 344–345.

1908, it did so without consulting the Italians, despite Italy having clearly expressed an interest in Balkan stability.

In looking at other explanations for the alliance behavior of states, only balance of threat theory explains the British decision to ally with Russia and continue the entente with France, since it was clear that all three states saw Germany and Austria-Hungary as primary threats to their interests. Both balancing theories explain the willingness of Germany and Austria-Hungary to renew the Triple Alliance because they viewed Russia as a common threat. Binding theory also explains Austro-Hungarian and Italian motives for renewing the Alliance.

The arguments by Paul Schroeder and Patricia Weitsman that states sometimes ally to manage a threat receives solid support from the Triple Alliance, but only mixed support from the Triple Entente. Britain and Russia did have disputes that forming the Entente helped resolve, but by the time of the agreement, they no longer perceived each other to be the greatest threat. Although these theories each explain part of the story, we have no explanation for why states sometimes balance and other times ally to manage those threats.

Curiously, alliance behavior in the Triple Entente seems to fit more closely with my expectations than it does for the Triple Alliance. One possible explanation is that Germany and Austria-Hungary had few other alliance options. One can see evidence of this in a statement by Aloys von Aehrenthal, the Austrian foreign minister: "They [the Austrians] could be absolutely sure of Germany . . . for she could now depend on Austria alone."[95] In situations like this, where alliance options are already limited, I expect reputation to play a less significant role in alliance choices. However, it is useful to remember that Germany was limited to an alliance with other unreliable states precisely because of its reputation for being unreliable. Had an Anglo-German alliance formed in 1901, either despite Germany's reputation or if Germany had been more reliable, then I contend that Germany and Austria-Hungary could have dealt with Italy more harshly since they would have had more options.

Germany and Austria-Hungary accepted a tenuous relationship with Italy because they had little choice, and doing so at least prevented Italy from allying against them and leaving Austria-Hungary's southern border vulnerable. What this also suggests is an additional benefit from a reliable reputation—if it improves the chances of forming alliances with reliable states (thus providing other alliance options), it also enables a state to punish its allies for unreliable behavior. In contrast, unreliability decreases a state's options and therefore lessens its ability to punish unreliable behavior

95. Gooch, *Grouping of the Powers*, 394.

by a partner. With an unreliable reputation of its own, Italy too was stuck trying to manage the threat from Austria-Hungary, since none of the Entente states were willing to ally with Italy.

This chapter has clearly gone beyond simply showing that reputation has some influence on alliance choices. Of course, in some instances strategic interests trump reputation, and I have tried to point these out as much as possible. However, that does not detract from the basic argument that a state's reliability influences the behavior of other states. Even if a state does not receive observable benefits from a reliable reputation, states that honor their commitments appear to gain or preserve more of their autonomy than do unreliable states.

The next chapter addresses this puzzle more by examining the Bosnia-Herzegovina Crisis (1908–9) between Russia and Austria-Hungary. This is a more difficult test of reputation because of the growing perception of a coming war and because the European alliances were already much less flexible by 1908 than they had been just three years earlier. Both of these factors suggest that strategic interests should increasingly outweigh reputation as a primary motivation for alliance decisions. Nevertheless, reputation plays an important role in helping us understand the alliance choices of the great powers.

5

The Bosnia-Herzegovina Crisis

Expanding the Entente, 1907–1911

A reputation once broken may possibly be repaired, but the world will always keep their eyes on the spot where the crack was.

Joseph Hall

Important Dates

8 July 1907	Triple Alliance renewed (tacitly)
31 August 1907	Anglo-Russian entente/Triple Entente signed
15–16 September 1908	Russo-Austrian meeting at Buchlau
6 October 1908–22 March 1909	Bosnia-Herzegovina Crisis
9 February 1909	Casablanca agreement signed (France and Germany)
August 1909–June 1911	Anglo-German naval conventions
24 October 1909	Racconigi agreement signed (Russia and Italy)
4 November 1910–19 August 1911	Potsdam convention (Russia and Germany)

Key Actors

Austria-Hungary

Aloys von Aehrenthal	Minister of Foreign Affairs (1906–1912)

Franz Conrad	Chief of the General Staff (1906–1916)
England	
Edward VII	King (1901–1910)
Edward Grey	Foreign Secretary (1905–1916)
Charles Hardinge	Ambassador to Russia (1904–1906); Permanent Under-Secretary for Foreign Affairs (1906–1910)
Arthur Nicolson	Ambassador to Spain (1904–1905); Ambassador to Russia (1906–1910)
France	
Georges Clemenceau	Prime Minister (1906–1909)
Stephen Pichon	Foreign Minister (1906–1909)
Camille Barrère	Ambassador to Italy (1897–1924)
André Tardieu	Foreign Affairs Editor, *Le Temps* (1905–1914)
Germany	
Wilhelm II	Emperor (1888–1918)
Bernard von Bülow	Chancellor (1900–1909)
Helmuth von Moltke	Chief of the General Staff (1906–1914)
Anton Monts	Ambassador to Italy (1902–1905)
Italy	
Tommaso Tittoni	Foreign Minister (1906–1909); Ambassador to France (1910–1916)

Russia

Alexander Izvolsky	Minister of Foreign Affairs (1906–1910)
Alexander Nelidov	Ambassador to France (1903–1910)

Considerable diplomatic activity took place between the 1905 First Moroccan Crisis and the 1908–9 Bosnia-Herzegovina Crisis: the Triple Alliance was tacitly renewed; England and Russia signed an agreement that effectively created the Triple Entente with France; and England and France engaged in military discussions to develop contingencies for war. Russia and Austria-Hungary also began negotiating an agreement in which Russia would grant Austria-Hungary privileged rights in Bosnia in exchange for Austria's support in reopening the Dardanelles and Bosporus, which had been closed to shipping since the Crimean War (British defense of the Straits Treaty helped Japan during the Russo-Japanese War). An unintended consequence of this negotiation between Russia and Austria-Hungary was another crisis involving Europe's great powers.[1]

On 15 September 1908, the Russian and Austrian foreign ministers met secretly at Buchlau in Moravia to discuss Austria's interest in Bosnia-Herzegovina. Russia's foreign minister, Alexander Izvolsky, agreed to support Austria's plan to annex Bosnia in exchange for a promise by Aloys von Aehrenthal that Austria-Hungary would support an international proposal to reopen the Dardanelles to Russian warships. However, on 5 October 1908, Bulgaria declared its independence from the Ottoman Empire, and, on the following day, before Izvolsky could gain support from the other great powers for an opening of the straits, Austria proceeded with the annexation of Bosnia.[2] In response, the Serbian army mobilized and requested Russian intervention.[3]

The Russian government initially challenged the annexation for a number of reasons. First of all, Izvolsky felt betrayed by von Aehrenthal, so it was a matter of personal honor for him. The government also felt pressure to support its Slavic brothers in Serbia.[4] While Russia was in no position to challenge Austria-Hungary and Germany on its own, Russian leaders believed that they could count on British and French support, at least if

1. An excellent, more complete, account of the crisis can be found in Bernadotte Schmitt, *The Annexation of Bosnia, 1908–1909* (Cambridge: Cambridge University Press).

2. A. J. Taylor, *The Struggle for Mastery in Europe, 1848–1918* (Oxford: Clarendon Press, 1954), 451; "Austria Takes Two Provinces," *New York Times*, 7 October 1908.

3. "Servian Assembly Meets," *New York Times*, 11 October 1908.

4. "Austria and Servia Are near a Clash," *New York Times*, 24 February 1909, 1.

Germany became involved in the conflict. And because the agreement at Buchlau was conducted in secret, Russia's allies were unaware that Izvolsky had been negotiating to give Bosnia away.

The crisis lasted for six months, during which time Italy and France led the call for a conference of the great powers, similar to the one that solved the First Moroccan Crisis. Germany and Austria-Hungary opposed a conference in the belief that they would once again be outnumbered as they were at Algeciras.[5] Britain also initially opposed a conference, at least until the issues to be addressed were clearly spelled out.[6] The British government did tell Izvolsky that while it could not support Russia's desire to open the strait at that time, it would consider discussing the matter at a later date. More important was the British promise that Izvolsky could count on their support against Austria-Hungary and Germany. In contrast, the French failed to back their ally, even signing another agreement with Germany, in which German concessions over Morocco were granted in exchange for French neutrality with respect to Bosnia.

As for the Triple Alliance, Italy felt betrayed by the annexation and gave little support to Austria-Hungary. At the same time, Germany stood by its ally, going so far as to give Austria assurances of German support regardless of how the crisis played out. This "blank check" emboldened Austria to stand firm against Russia.[7] On 21 March, Izvolsky also received an ultimatum from Germany demanding that Russia accept Austria's proposal for annexation.[8] Germany also threatened to release documents from Buchlau that would have embarrassed Izvolsky because they pointed to his backroom dealings over Bosnia and the Dardanelles. The next day, Izvolsky reversed his previously tough stance and gave in to Austrian demands.[9]

The conventional wisdom is that because Russia received little support from France and only diplomatic backing from England, Izvolsky felt the need to back down and accept a humiliating defeat. However, in this chapter we will see that while Russia did perceive France to be unreliable—not only because of its lack of support in 1908 but going back to its failure to

5. "Article 4," *New York Times*, 25 February 1909.

6. G. Gooch and Harold Temperley, eds., *British Documents on the Origins of the War, 1898–1914*, vol. 5, *The Near East: The Macedonian Problem and the Annexation of Bosnia, 1903–9* (London: His Majesty's Stationery Office, 1928), no. 314 (6 October 1908), 396; no. 317 (6 October 1908), 397; no. 321 (6 October 1908), 399–400; and no. 333 (7 October 1908), 408–410.

7. Although the term "blank check" is more typically used in association with the 1914 crisis that led to war, it also accurately describes Germany's support for Austria-Hungary in 1908. Kenneth Dailey, "Alexander Isvolsky and the Buchlau Conference," *Russian Review* 10, no. 1 (January 1951), 63; Manus Midlarsky, "A Hierarchical Equilibrium Theory of Systemic War," *International Studies Quarterly* 30, no. 1 (March 1986), 80; John Vasquez and Marie Henehan, *The Scientific Study of Peace and War* (New York: Lexington Books, 1992), 217.

8. "The Balkan Situation," *Times* (London), 29 March 1909.

9. "Peace in Balkans Assured by Powers," *New York Times*, 29 March 1909.

support Russia against Japan in 1904—the Russian government viewed England's behavior to be loyal. These different levels of support parallel changes in Russia's relationship with its two allies.

If my hypotheses are correct, then I expect a number of things to happen as a result of allied behavior during the crisis. If Russia did perceive the British to be more reliable, then it should have been willing to give up more autonomy to the British without demanding more in exchange. Similarly, Austria-Hungary should have given up more autonomy to Germany than to Italy because of the different levels of support it received. In contrast, both Britain and Russia should have demanded that France give up more of its autonomy for the Entente to remain intact, and Italy should have been required to give up still more autonomy to preserve its place in the Triple Alliance.

If reputation does not influence alliance autonomy, then there should be little correlation between state behavior during this crisis and changes to the alliances. Instead, changes in the relationships should be easily attributable to strategic factors, such as changing threats or shifts in the balance of power. The conventional view of this time period has been that with each crisis initiated by the Central Powers the Entente states drew closer together out of mutual recognition of the growing threat. My position, however, is that the closeness we observe in the Entente was a result of efforts to bind one another more closely together because of a lack of full reliability during these pre–First World War crises.

France

Initial French reaction to the annexation of Bosnia-Herzegovina was ambiguous. Like Russia during the First Moroccan Crisis, France was unwilling to completely abandon its ally, but at the same time it feared antagonizing the Central Powers. The French government was wary of being dragged into a war between Austria and Russia, or between England and Germany, and sought to play the role of mediator in the crisis. So France went along with Russia's call for a conference of the great powers, but it also informed its ally that it would not go to war over the Balkans. In the end, France worked with Germany to propose an end to the crisis, preferring to avoid war rather than fully support its ally.[10]

The Germans believed that France would support its ally, *unless* the French were given an incentive to stay out of the crisis. So Germany took advantage of this by offering France an agreement on Morocco in exchange

10. Gooch and Temperley, *Near East*, no. 311 (6 October 1908), 395; Graydon Tunstall, *Planning for War against Russia and Serbia: Austro-Hungarian and German Military Strategies, 1871–1914* (New York: Columbia University Press), 62–63.

for its neutrality on the Balkans issue. The deal was signed on 9 February 1909, giving France greater influence over Morocco and temporarily decreasing the chance of war with Germany but further damaging its reputation as a reliable ally.[11] France's decision to abandon its ally was a product of both strategic interests and a response to Russia's limited support in 1905. David Watson suggests that Georges Clemenceau authorized France to sign the agreement with Germany because of "the exposed position in which France found herself, as a result of the weakness and unreliability of Russia and the British refusal to create a serious army that could be used at the outbreak of a Continental war."[12]

There are three questions to address here. The first is how do we explain France's failure to support Russia and acceptance of an agreement with Germany? The second is how does French behavior affect its reputation? Finally, how do we explain the changes to the Triple Entente after the crisis as well as Russia's willingness to sign agreements with both Germany and Italy?

Explaining French Behavior

The Triple Entente formed in August 1907, and because England and Russia were more powerful than the Triple Alliance by themselves, balance of power theory would not be surprised to see France take a neutral position in the crisis, even focusing on its own interests and signing an agreement with Germany over Morocco. (Table 5.1 represents power relations, existing agreements, and behavior during the crisis.)

Balance of threat, on the other hand, has difficulty explaining why France would accept an agreement with Germany while abandoning an ally. Germany and Austria-Hungary both represented growing threats to France, so contrary to balance of power theory, balance of threat theory would expect France to clearly support its allies. Theories that focus on alliances as tools to manage state behavior do the best job of explaining France's decision to side with Germany during the crisis. Clearly balance of power and binding can explain France's behavior during the crisis, but Germany's willingness to sign an agreement with France was also a compelling incentive for France to abandon its ally.

Regardless of the reasons for France failing to support Russia, many of which were strategic calculations, Watson contends that "the French attitude in the Bosnian crisis, together with the agreement [with Germany], revealed them to be *unreliable partners*."[13] Despite initial Russian expectations of

11. "The Franco-German Agreement," *New York Times*, 13 February 1909.
12. David Watson, *Georges Clemenceau: A Political Biography* (Plymouth, UK: Eyre Methuen, 1974), 232.
13. Ibid., 230–231, emphasis added.

Table 5.1. The great powers during the Bosnia-Herzegovina Crisis (1908)

State	Capabilities score	Alliance (combined score)	Behavior
Germany	0.15	Triple Alliance (0.22)	Negotiated Casablanca agreement with France
England	0.12	Triple Entente (0.31)	Strongly supported Russia
Russia	0.12	Triple Entente (0.31)	Primary belligerent
France	0.07	Triple Entente (0.31)	Negotiated Casablanca agreement with Germany
Austria-Hungary	0.05	Triple Alliance (0.22)	Primary belligerent
Italy	0.03	Triple Alliance (0.22)	Mild support for Austria-Hungary

receiving French support, France played a publicly neutral role in the crisis. According to Bernhard von Bülow, Germany's chancellor at the time, "France awaited events and assumed an attitude not unfriendly to Germany."[14] A. J. P. Taylor agrees, suggesting that the French "were a good deal more alarmed than the British [about the crisis] and less high principled."[15] Frank Anderson and Amos Hershey also confirm that Russia received support from Britain and Italy, but only mixed support from France.[16]

Mercer suggests that since French behavior at Algeciras was favorable, the Russians would have explained it away through situation and therefore would not expect France to be resolute during the Bosnian crisis.[17] As a result, France's behavior during the crisis should not have surprised Russia. Nor would Mercer expect France's reputation to decline, since he contends that it was already low. Therefore, Mercer would not expect any changes in Franco-Russian relations after the crisis, or he would at least be able to explain them with strategic interests.

Consequences of French Behavior

Mercer's focus on resolve is different from my emphasis on reliability, and France's resolve toward Germany over Morocco is less important during the Bosnian crisis than its willingness to support an ally—whereas it is

14. Bernhard von Bülow, *Imperial Germany*, trans. Marie Lewenz (Westport, CT: Greenwood Press, 1979 [1914]), 57.

15. Taylor, *Struggle for Mastery*, 454.

16. Frank Anderson and Amos Hershey, *Handbook for the Diplomatic History of Europe, Asia, and Africa, 1870–1914* (Washington, DC: Government Printing Office, 1918), 384.

17. Jonathan Mercer, *Reputation and International Politics* (Ithaca: Cornell University Press, 1996), 137–138.

Russia's resolve that is relevant in this case. In addition, Russian expectations of France are more complicated than Mercer suggests.[18] The changes to the Dual Alliance after Algeciras that bound Russia and France closer together should have increased Russian expectations of French reliability.

If so, then contrary to Mercer's claim that previous French behavior was explained through situation, I propose that Russia did expect to receive French support, given the more binding relationship that evolved after the Russo-Japanese War and the First Moroccan Crisis. Likewise, because the Russians believed their support for France helped resolve Algeciras favorably, they would expect France to return the favor.

Regardless of Russia's expectations of France, the biggest weakness of Mercer's argument is that it does not tell us why Franco-Russian relations changed the way they did after the crisis, particularly in comparison to Anglo-Russian relations (discussed in the next section). Russia held the French largely responsible for its defeat over Bosnia. The question is whether or not this view affected the alliance between Russia and France. As a result of French behavior during the crisis, my general argument expects France's allies would demand France to give up more of its autonomy while being unwilling to give up much of their own. Specifically, because of its behavior during the crisis, my hypotheses would expect France to lose its alliance with Russia (hypothesis 3) and the entente with England (hypothesis 4). Or, to preserve the alliance, I would expect France's allies to demand greater levels of obligation, precision, or delegation (hypothesis 5).

In comparison to my hypotheses, the existing alliance theories have some expectations about Franco-Russian relations after the crisis. Because the Triple Entente was more powerful than the Triple Alliance, balance of power theory would not be surprised to see Russia and France part ways after the crisis. Where the theory differs from my own expectations is that even if the alliance were not to end, balance of power theory would expect France and Russia to become less dependent on each other. Balance of threat theory would not only expect the Triple Entente to continue but would predict that it grow closer after the crisis, possibly even transforming into a defense pact. Finally, while binding theory explains Russia's agreements with Germany and Italy, the timing of the agreement suggests that Russia only opted to manage threats after France again showed itself to be an unreliable ally. The theory also provides no real expectations for changes to the Triple Entente as a result of the crisis.

According to Winston Churchill, after the Bosnian crisis, France and Russia "closed their ranks, cemented their alliance, and set to work to construct with Russian labour and French money the new strategic

18. Ibid.

railway systems of which Russia's western frontier stood in need."[19] At the same time, Russia also hedged its bets by signing agreements with two members of the Triple Alliance. Russia concluded the Racconigi agreement with Italy on 24 October 1909 to secure cooperation in the Near East. In addition, Russia began negotiating with Germany in November 1910 over their interests in Persia and the Baghdad Railway.[20] These talks led to the Potsdam convention of 19 August 1911.[21] Although Russia made an effort to assure its allies that the negotiations with Germany would not weaken the Triple Entente, Russia signed the agreement without consulting its allies.[22]

Although Russia did not withdraw from its alliance with France, the Racconigi and Potsdam agreements that Russia signed with Italy and Germany, respectively, were a consequence of France's failure to support Russia during the Bosnian crisis. And, as expected, the Russians also demanded that France give up some of its autonomy. Dwight Lee refers to this tightening of the French alliance as a fundamental guideline of Russian policy, which stands in sharp contrast to Russia's desire to simply "foster the entente with Great Britain."[23]

The railways that the Russians wanted were in need of French loans, which were requested with greater urgency after the crisis. In addition, Russia began a reorganization of its army in 1909.[24] This move was clearly a result of its own weakness, but it also reflected Russia's recognition that it might not be able to count on France or England in a war against the Central Powers—England because its naval might would not be of direct help to Russia, and France because it was growing less reliable. Reorganizing the military was an attempt to regain some of its autonomy while simultaneously showing its allies that they could count on its military capabilities if war did break out in Europe.

All of the existing theories on alliance behavior explain some part of the case, but incorporating reputation helps balance of threat theory explain why Russia signed agreements with Italy and Germany, even though Russia did not abandon the Triple Entente, and it helps binding theory explain the timing of Russia's agreements. Without reputation, all of the existing theories miss a significant part of the story.

19. Winston Churchill, *The World Crisis* (New York: Charles Scribner's Sons, 1923), 31.

20. "Czar Guest of Kaiser," *New York Times,* 5 November 1910; "Fear Russo-German Deal," *New York Times,* 7 January 1911.

21. For thorough discussions of the Potsdam convention, see Dwight Lee, *Europe's Crucial Years: The Diplomatic Background of World War I, 1902–1914* (Hanover, NH: University Press of New England, 1974), 217–220; G. Gooch, *Before the War: Studies in Diplomacy,* vol. 2, *The Coming of the Storm* (London: Longmans, Green, 1938), 291–301.

22. "Britain Scared by Russo-German Deal," *New York Times,* 15 January 1911.

23. Dwight Lee, *Europe's Crucial Years,* 207.

24. Anderson and Hershey, *Handbook for the Diplomatic History,* 471.

It is noteworthy that French perceptions of Russian loyalty were also in decline. Not only did Russia negotiate with Germany during the 1905 Morocco crisis but now Russia nearly dragged its allies into a conflict over Bosnia. By the time of the Potsdam talks, France's foreign minister, Stephen Pichon, had become extremely concerned about Russia's loyalty to the Dual Alliance. According to M. B. Hayne, "had there not been a signed agreement between the two countries . . . one would hardly have known that Russia was France's ally."[25] This point will be important again in chapter 6, when we look at the situation in which France once again had to count on its allies to defend its control over Morocco. And, according to Watson, France's indifference during the Bosnian crisis caused Russia to provide only lukewarm support to France in later crises.[26]

England

The Anglo-Russian entente did not even require British neutrality in the Bosnia-Herzegovina Crisis, since it dealt solely with Central Asia.[27] However, Russia might have expected British support considering England's record of providing assistance to Japan during the Russo-Japanese War and to France during the First Moroccan Crisis.

Despite the limitations of British naval power to affect the outcome of a war in Central Europe that involved Russia and Austria-Hungary, Britain was the deciding factor in Russia's willingness to challenge Austria-Hungary. Had the Triple Entente not existed at the beginning of the crisis, and if Russia had to rely on France alone, it may not have been so quick to challenge Austria. But the entente with England, together with Britain's historical willingness to honor its obligations, likely led Russia to expect British support. The question is whether the British lived up to those expectations.

Analysis of Russia's view of British behavior is mixed. Some claim that Russian opinion of Britain suffered as a result of the crisis. For example, Graydon Tunstall attributes Russia's being forced to back down as a function of French *and* British inaction.[28] And certainly the British government's unwillingness to support Russian proposals for opening the Dardanelles—

25. M. B. Hayne, *The French Foreign Office and the Origins of the First World War, 1898–1914* (Oxford: Clarendon Press, 1993), 183.

26. Watson, *George Clemenceau*, 233.

27. Beryl Williams, "The Strategic Background to the Anglo-Russian Entente of August 1907," *Historical Journal* 9, no. 3 (1966), 361.

28. Tunstall, *Planning for War against Russia and Serbia*, 77, emphasis added. See also Ira Klein, "The Anglo-Russian Convention and the Problem of Central Asia, 1870–1914," *Journal of British Studies* 11, no. 1 (November 1971), 139; M. B. Cooper, "British Policy in the Balkans," *Historical Journal* 7, no. 2 (1964), 258–279.

even though the British exhibited some encouraging signs on this point during the entente negotiations—affected Russia's overall perception of British friendship.

However, in contrast to France's lack of support for its ally in any conflict that did not immediately threaten vital Russian interests, the British did support Russia's opposition to the annexation. And, as with British support for Japan in its war against Russia and for France at Morocco, it went beyond what was required by the terms of the entente. According to von Bülow in his assessment of the Bosnian crisis, "England sided with Russia, and the language of the English Press was almost more impassioned than the utterances of the Russians."[29] In addition, correspondence between the two new allies toward the end of the crisis suggests that the Russians viewed the British as loyal.[30]

The only evidence I found of even a proposed change in Anglo-Russian relations is that the Russians did press the British to convert the Triple Entente into a military alliance. Alexander Nelidov, the Russian ambassador to France, wrote to Izvolsky on 1 April 1909, saying, "The cabinets of Paris and London have therefore drawn the conclusion that Russia, France and England must pay more attention than ever to action in common and at the same time must take the military measures necessary to convince their opponents that they have to deal with a political combination which knows how to insure respect for itself and will carry through its demands."[31] Yet the British were unwilling to agree to a more formal commitment to either France or Russia. The questions here are how do we explain British support for Russia, and how do we explain the nature of Anglo-Russian relations after the crisis?

Explaining British Behavior

Balancing theories are able to explain England's support for Russia, given that by 1908 the combined power of Germany and Austria-Hungary was greater than that of France and Russia (table 5.1) and the German threat to England continued to grow. Theories about managing or tethering have trouble explaining why England supported Russia rather than allying with Germany.

Mercer claims that since British support for France at Algeciras was perceived to be favorable behavior, it was explained away using situation or British interests rather than British reputation.[32] Thus he asserts that the

29. von Bülow, *Imperial Germany*, 62.

30. Gooch and Temperley, *Near East*, no. 571 (15 February 1909), 600–601; no. 701 (17 March 1909), 695.

31. Cited in Schmitt, *Annexation of Bosnia*, 253.

32. Mercer, *Reputation and International Politics*, 108–109.

Russians did not count on British support. He does agree that England supported Russia, but because the Russians saw that support as favorable, he claims that Russia explained it as a function of British interests. As a result, British reliability should not have improved after the crisis.[33]

The British did have a number of strategic reasons for opposing the annexation of Bosnia. Bulgaria's declaration of independence from Turkey—made simultaneously with the annexation—was a blow to the pro-British "Young Turks" movement.[34] The annexation also violated the terms of the 1878 Berlin Treaty, which all the great powers had signed and which the British felt obligated to defend.[35] The most important reason was that the British feared German aggression and believed that Germany was behind Austria's actions. Even Mercer admits that British decision makers learned from Algeciras to "beware the Germans for they are aggressive,"[36] although he fails to acknowledge that a reputation for aggression is itself the result of state actions and can influence the behavior of allies and adversaries alike.

Consequences of British Behavior

Mercer and I both would expect Russia to blame its failure in the Bosnian crisis on its allies, although we disagree about whether that includes England or not. I would predict that British reliability would be recognized by both Russia and France and positively reflected in the postcrisis relations between the three Entente states.

Regardless of the British government's reasons for providing support—and there is no reason to suggest that the British acted for reasons other than their national interest since there was no real obligation to support Russia—England clearly acted more reliably than France. Because the Russians recognized this and responded accordingly, changes to Anglo-Russian relations provide an interesting comparison with those in the Franco-Russian relationship. My argument expects that the British should have been able to preserve higher levels of autonomy than the French. Specifically, England should not lose any of its allies (hypotheses 3 and 4), and it should be able

33. Ibid., 153.

34. Ibid., 120–121.

35. The Treaty of Berlin was signed by the United Kingdom, Austria-Hungary, France, Germany, Italy, Russia, and the Ottoman Empire and recognized the independence of Romania, Serbia, and Montenegro, and the autonomy of Bulgaria (though it was divided into three parts under formal Ottoman control). In addition, Bosnia-Herzegovina was placed under Austro-Hungarian occupation, though it remained a part of the Ottoman Empire. Gooch and Temperley, *Near East*, no. 296 (5 October 1908), 388; no. 302 (5 October 1908), 390; no. 342 (9 October 1908), 415; no. 351 (9 October 1908), 420–421; Taylor, *Struggle for Mastery*, 454; Gooch, *Coming of the Storm*, 46–47.

36. Mercer, *Reputation in International Politics*, 135.

to preserve its autonomy within the Triple Entente while France and Russia willingly give up more autonomy to keep England as an ally (hypothesis 5).

Balancing theories are unable to explain, at least without incorporating reputation, the fact that the Entente never became a more formal defense pact, considering the power of the Triple Alliance and the growing German threat. As I mentioned in the section on France, tethering theories do explain Russia's actions after the crisis, with the signing of separate agreements with Triple Alliance members. However, Russia also sought to strengthen its entente with England, which suggests that Russia would have preferred a binding commitment to the more reliable British than to ally with either Germany or Austria-Hungary.

Consistent with my argument, the Russians and French both supported the creation of a more formal type of alliance that would bind them more closely to the British. A more formal alliance with England would help make up for French unreliability, so Russia's interest in expanding the Entente into an alliance is less about binding England but rather about binding France more tightly, giving up more Russian autonomy to preserve the alliance with the reliable British, while avoiding an alliance with the still unreliable Germans.

This behavior of strengthening an alliance is also consistent with what balancing theories would expect of states facing a rising challenger. But contrary to what traditional alliance theories would predict, the British were unwilling to form a more binding alliance to balance against the Central Powers. Although an alliance would have tied France and Russia's hands more, it also would have bound England more closely to what were quickly becoming unreliable partners with respect to both abandonment and entrapment. When the British believed they could count on French and Russian hostility toward Germany, they were content with a vague agreement having little or no military obligation. However, as Anglo-German antagonism rose, and as the French and Russians both appeared unwilling to fully support their allies yet were perfectly willing to negotiate with Germany for reasons of self-interest, the British favored France and Russia making more binding commitments as long as it did not reduce British autonomy. As a result, England wished to avoid such agreements and instead advocated for less formal agreements that reduced French and Russian autonomy without reducing British autonomy.

British Perceptions of French Behavior

Because England's other ally, France, failed to support Russia during the Bosnian crisis, British perceptions of French reliability are also relevant. Although Mercer claims that British decision makers saw French actions as partly favorable and partly unfavorable, many within the British government, including Grey, Hardinge, and Nicolson, blamed the outcome of the crisis on France's unwillingness to support an ally.[37] In discussing the effect of the Casablanca agreement between France and Germany on the Anglo-French Entente, Thomas Otte states that "Clemenceau's agreement . . . with Germany in Morocco of February 1909, coming at a time of strained Anglo-German relations, was hardly conducive to harmonious relations between the two entente powers."[38] This suggests that not only would Russia have demanded more restraints on French autonomy but that the British should have done the same.

When the Anglo-French military talks resumed in 1910, the British were able to maintain a greater degree of autonomy than did the French. These talks covered such topics as "the size of the British force to be made available, where it was to be sent, and the details concerning its movement—ports, shipping, railway trains and timetables," but P. M. H. Bell contends that they had little effect on British autonomy. According to Bell, these were technical arrangements that did not commit the British to action and "the government's freedom of choice as to whether to intervene in a war, or to put the plans into effect, was to remain unimpaired."[39]

Similarly, Taylor argues that the British did not believe the French and Russians had repaid Britain's loyalty, with respect to their negotiations with Germany.[40] Ensuring that France was dependent on the British navy to protect its Atlantic coast, therefore, helped bind the French more closely to England through delegation, without decreasing British autonomy. In other words, the French government's lack of reliability led to a loss of its autonomy within the Entente, but the British commitment remained comparatively vague and flexible.

Germany

Although Germany eventually supported Austria-Hungary over Bosnia, the annexation initially displeased the Germans, since there was no prior consultation and they disliked the prospect of being dragged into a Balkan conflict.[41] Moreover, much as in the British case, Bulgaria's independence

37. Ibid., 145–146. See also Cooper, "British Policy in the Balkans," 278; Edward Grey, *Twenty-Five Years, 1892–1916,* vol. 1 (New York: Frederick A. Stokes Company, 1925), 167.

38. Thomas Otte, "The Elusive Balance: British Foreign Policy and the French Entente before the First World War," in *Anglo-French Relations in the Twentieth Century: Rivalry and Cooperation,* ed. Alan Sharp and Glyn Stone (London: Routledge, 2000), 22.

39. M. H. Bell, *France and Britain, 1900–1940: Entente and Estrangement* (London: Longman, 1996), 47.

40. Taylor, *Struggle for Mastery,* 462; Gooch and Temperley, *Near East,* no. 764 (24 March 1909), 736–737.

41. Gooch and Temperley, *Near East,* no. 346 (9 October 1908), 417.

posed a threat to German interests in Turkey. However, on 30 October 1908, von Bülow informed the British government that Germany would stand by its ally,[42] and he also gave a blank check to Austria-Hungary saying, "I shall regard any decision taken by you as imposed by circumstances."[43] The crisis eventually ended after Germany issued its ultimatum to Russia. Russia backed down since it did not have the capabilities to challenge Germany and Austria-Hungary on its own and believed that it did not have the full support of France and that British support might be limited to defending the terms of the entente.[44]

The most significant change in the relationship between Germany and Austria was that after the crisis the military staffs of the two allies held talks. But, according to Samuel Williamson, "the two army staffs never really exchanged precise information about each other's war plans. Nor did they trade extensive data about their forces."[45] Von Moltke specifically refrained from outlining specific details regarding German military plans, even though Conrad pressured him to do so.[46]

Explaining German Behavior

Based on the initial German reaction to the crisis, it is difficult to believe that Germany's support for Austria-Hungary was based on German interests. Nor do I find any evidence to suggest Germany specifically cared about its reputation. However, German support was indirectly about reputation because Germany feared that not supporting Austria-Hungary would break up the Triple Alliance, leaving the Germans isolated. At the same time, both balancing theories adequately explain German support.

Balance of power theory is especially valid, considering the widespread belief among the two states that they could not count on Italy providing much support. Balance of threat theory also explains German behavior, given that both Germany and Austria-Hungary considered Russia to be a threat. In contrast, binding theory does not explain Germany's support for Austria-Hungary, since if Germany considered Russia to be a greater threat to its interests, it would have voted with Russia over Austria-Hungary. No-

42. "Balkan Conference Resented in Berlin," *New York Times*, 7 March 1909.

43. Luigi Albertini, *The Origins of the War of 1914*, vol. 1, trans. Isabella Massey (New York: Oxford University Press, 1957), 231; Tunstall, *Planning for War against Russia and Serbia*, 63; Gooch and Temperley, *Near East*, no. 380 (14 October 1908), 444.

44. Gooch and Temperley, *Near East*, no. 748 (23 March 1909), 723–724; no. 753 (23 March 1909), 727–729; no. 761 (24 March 1909), 732–733.

45. Samuel Williamson, *Austria-Hungary and the Origins of the First World War* (London: Macmillan, 1991), 88.

46. Norman Stone, "Moltke-Conrad: Relations between the Austro-Hungarian and German General Staffs, 1909–1914," *Historical Journal* 9, no. 2 (1966), 201–228.

tably, for both balancing theories to work, Germany had to recognize that it did not have many options, so it had to show Austria-Hungary that they could count on their ally and not begin siding with Russia.

According to Mercer's argument, Austria-Hungary would not have expected German support over Bosnia. Even though Germany was initially resolute in challenging France over Morocco, ultimately the Germans backed down. Likewise, Mercer would not expect Germany to get credit for its support of Austria-Hungary during the Bosnian crisis. Despite the favorable outcome created by German support, Mercer would expect the Austrians to explain German support through situation. According to Mercer, the Austrians did not view their success as a result of German reliability but as a result of Izvolsky's weakness.[47] Thus, Mercer would not expect to see any change to the alliance. Or, if anything, because Austria-Hungary felt even more dependent on Germany, he might expect the two states to grow farther apart.[48]

In contrast, I contend that since Germany's support directly contributed to Austria's victory in the crisis, Germany would be able to preserve its autonomy, while Austria-Hungary would be willing to give up autonomy to preserve the alliance. Specifically, the increase to Germany's reliability should have allowed it to preserve its current levels of obligation, precision, and delegation to the Triple Alliance.

Consequences of German Behavior

The reputations that matter in the Bosnian case are the reliability of Austria-Hungary's allies, Germany and Italy, for supporting Austria during the crisis, as well as Austria's reliability, since it potentially could have dragged its allies into a conflict with the Triple Entente. The most relevant question here is whether the nature of the Triple Alliance after the crisis reflects the degree to which each ally supported Austria-Hungary during the crisis.

First I turn to the existing theories of alliance behavior. For balance of power theory, the fact that the two allies remained close after the crisis shows that they could only stand up to the Triple Entente if they remained together. The theory has more difficulty explaining the lack of military integration between the two states, as well as Germany's willingness to sign the Potsdam convention with Russia, unless it was purely an attempt to split up the Entente. Balance of threat theory provides mixed results. Russia clearly posed a threat to both Germany and Austria-Hungary, but most indications are that Italy was perceived to be a greater threat for Austria-Hungary (at least in terms of the risk of war, though clearly Russia was

47. Mercer, *Reputation and International Politics,* 150.
48. Ibid.

more powerful). Balance of threat theory also cannot explain the Potsdam convention. Binding theory can explain the Potsdam convention as an attempt to manage threat, similar to the Casablanca agreement signed with France. Yet binding theory has trouble explaining the nature of the Triple Alliance after the crisis, since it would expect the alliance to grow significantly closer, especially if Austria-Hungary and Italy viewed each other as the greatest threat.

As usual, Mercer would not expect Germany to get credit for its support of Austria-Hungary. When Mercer cites Emperor Franz Joseph as stating that "one must not presume too much of her,"[49] referring to Germany, I suggest that he is not dismissing German support in this crisis. Instead, he is recalling the same history of German behavior that kept the British from allying with Germany in 1901. Moreover, Austria's explanation for success does not mean that German support was unimportant, especially since even Mercer would admit that a lack of German support would have further hurt its reputation and very likely caused Austria-Hungary to back down before Russia. Mercer also points out Germany's fear that Austria-Hungary might defect to the Triple Entente if not given sufficient support. He then suggests this provides evidence that Germany's reputation did not improve, despite its support for Austria-Hungary during the crisis.[50]

Nevertheless, the evidence still suggests that Austria-Hungary counted on German support, not because of reputation but because the Germans had to support its sole real ally. At a 19 August 1908 meeting of Austro-Hungarian ministers, the Chief of the Austrian General Staff, Franz Conrad, claimed that Germany was secure as an ally.[51] This view of Germany does not necessarily suggest that the Austrians considered the Germans to be reliable allies, merely that both states understood the reality that neither had many other alliance options.

Although Austria-Hungary and Germany did create closer military ties after the Bosnian crisis, Austro-German relations for the most part reflected what my hypotheses would expect of an alliance between states that believed they had each other's support. For example, the two states' militaries held staff talks, but these resulted in only vague statements of support. Norman Stone even faults the two states for having done such a poor job of integrating their military plans and thus failing to prepare for war.[52] The amount of autonomy Germany was able to preserve is especially noticeable

49. Ibid.

50. Ibid., 124.

51. Franz Conrad von Hötzendorf, *Aus meiner Dienstzeit, 1906–1918,* vol. 1 (Vienna: Rikola Verlag, 1921), 103, 106, 109, cited in Tunstall, *Planning for War against Russia and Serbia,* 62; Schmitt, *Annexation of Bosnia,* 12–13.

52. Stone, "Moltke-Conrad," 201–228. See also Tunstall, *Planning for War against Russia and Serbia,* 67.

when compared to how Italy's relations changed with its two allies after the crisis.

German Perceptions of Austrian Reliability

There are two aspects of German perceptions of Austria-Hungary. First, they should be somewhat concerned about Austria-Hungary's willingness to drag its allies into war. As a result, I expect that even though Austria-Hungary would view Germany as more reliable because of its support, Germany would try to constrain Austria-Hungary more after the crisis. Second, because of its own reputation, I expect Germany to be concerned about losing Austria-Hungary as an ally, not because allies always view each other to be unreliable, but because of Germany's own history of unreliability and its willingness to sign an agreement with France during the crisis.

Despite Austria-Hungary's support during the previous Algeciras conference, Mercer claims that the Germans would doubt their ally's resolve in later crises,[53] and there is some support for this claim. Mercer even points out that von Bülow and von Holstein "feared that Austria might defect to the entente if not given sufficient support or if Vienna believed that Germany and Russia were becoming too close."[54] Mercer takes this as evidence that Germany's support was explained away during the crisis as imposed by situation and that Germany would not be credited with greater reliability. In contrast, I contend that Germany's history of unreliability was not erased with one instance of support, and therefore it was not Germany's distrust of Austria-Hungary that influenced its behavior during the crisis, as Mercer suggests, but recognition of its own reputation for unreliability.

The Germans believed that even with the inflexible alliance system in place they would lose their ally if they did not provide enough support. It is important here to recognize that Germany's attempt to sign the Björko Treaty with Russia during the First Moroccan Crisis threatened Germany's alliance with Austria-Hungary as much as it did Russia's alliance with France, and likely increased Austrian fears of abandonment. Von Bülow, in assessing the potential for an agreement with Russia, wrote to the kaiser that "[Germany] must be exceedingly careful with all démarches and sounding in Petersburg. If the Russians allow the least bit to reach Vienna, the Austrians will promptly desert us and will join the Anglo-French camp with banners flying."[55]

53. Mercer, *Reputation and International Politics,* 130.

54. Ibid., 124.

55. Bülow to the Kaiser (15 July 1908), quoted in Ralph Menning, "The Collapse of 'Global Diplomacy': Germany's Descent into Isolation, 1906–1909" (PhD. diss., Brown University, 1986), 146.

Italy

Like Germany, Italy felt betrayed by Austria's grab for territory without consultation and censured the annexation.[56] Italy previously approved of Austria-Hungary's administration of Bosnia, but it objected to any action that might drag Italy into a war, especially by 1907 when England was allied with Russia as well as France. Moreover, under the terms of the Triple Alliance, Italy believed it was entitled to some compensation for Austria's actions. But, unlike Germany, Italy never came around to support its ally. In fact, Italy's reaction was to approach the British in an attempt to determine their position on both the annexation and Bulgaria's declaration of independence.[57] Italy also went against its allies when it supported the call for a conference of the great powers.[58] In the end, Italy only accepted the annexation once France asserted its neutrality and Russia backed down.

Two significant decisions were made after the crisis. As a consequence of their behavior during the crisis, the Italians were asked to give up additional autonomy by supporting German economic interests in Asia Minor, which amounted to an increase in Italian obligation. The other important decision is that on 24 October 1909 Italy signed the Racconigi agreement with Russia.[59] This agreement promoted the status quo in the Balkans and also secured Russia's blessing for Italy to take Tripoli. This second point became especially important in 1911, when Italy declared war on Turkey and received greater support from Russia than from its Triple Alliance partners.[60]

Explaining Italian Behavior

The simplest explanation for Italian behavior—as the Germans and Austro-Hungarians believed—is that Italy was just an unreliable ally, in the sense that it was unwilling to risk war over non-Italian interests. Balance of power theory cannot explain the lack of Italian support, since the Triple Entente was more powerful than the Triple Alliance, even with Italy (table 5.1). Balance of threat is a more compelling explanation for Italy's behavior, because if Austria-Hungary viewed Italy as the primary threat, then Italy likely had similar feelings about the Austrians. Therefore, Italy's willingness to side

56. Gooch and Temperley, *Near East*, no. 331 (7 October 1908), 407; Alfred Pribram, *The Secret Treaties of Austria-Hungary, 1879–1914*, vol. 2, *Negotiations Leading to the Treaties of the Triple Alliance* (Cambridge: Harvard University Press, 1921), 146.

57. Gooch and Temperley, *Near East*, no. 307 (5 October 1908), 393–394.

58. "Italy May Support Servia," *New York Times*, 13 December 1908.

59. "The Racconigi Meeting," *Times* (London), 26 October 1909.

60. Gooch and Temperley, *Near East*, no. 336 (8 October 1908), 413; no. 354 (10 October 1908), 422; no. 401 (22 October 1908), 462; Tunstall, *Planning for War against Russia and Serbia*, 79; Taylor, *Struggle for Mastery*, 463.

with France over Morocco, and Russia over Bosnia, probably reflects Italian concerns about its Triple Alliance partners gaining too much power. Tethering theory does perhaps explain Italy's continued alliance with Germany and Austria-Hungary, but it does not account for its repeated behavior that could have resulted in the end of the alliance.

Mercer barely mentions Italy in his analysis of the Bosnian crisis, but its lack of support for Austria-Hungary provides an important comparison to Germany's high level of involvement. Because Italy's behavior would be viewed as unfavorable by both Germany and Austria-Hungary, Mercer might expect a decline in Austrian and German attitudes toward Italy, which would also be consistent with my argument. Yet, if states always see their allies as having a poor reputation, Austria-Hungary should not have expected Italy's support and should not have been surprised by its behavior nor sought to punish Italy after failing to get support during the crisis.

Even before the crisis, von Aehrenthal viewed Italy with suspicion and believed that it would be an unreliable ally in war.[61] Similarly, William Askew suggests that the Italian and Austro-Hungarian militaries mistrusted each other.[62] And France's ambassador to Italy, Camille Barrère, even described Italy and Austria-Hungary as "enemy-allies."[63] Unlike the previous crisis, when Italy had commitments to both Germany and France, Italy did not have a separate agreement with Russia through which it could legitimately ignore its commitment to the Triple Alliance. Therefore, I suggest that even though Italy already had a reputation for being unreliable because of its previous failures to support its allies, its reliability would once again suffer after the Bosnia-Herzegovina Crisis. And my hypotheses once again expect that Austria-Hungary and Germany would dissolve their alliance or at least impose greater constraints on Italy.

Consequences of Italian Behavior

Although Italy's failure to support an ally did not lead to the dissolution of the Triple Alliance, combining reputation and interests helps identify why the Triple Alliance persisted, with some changes to offset continued Italian unreliability. More important, this case once again provides some compelling results for my specific hypotheses, as well as for my general argument about alliance autonomy and its link to reputation.

61. William Askew, "The Austro-Italian Antagonism, 1896–1914," in *Power, Public Opinion, and Diplomacy: Essays in Honor of Eber Malcolm Carroll by his Former Students*, ed. Lillian Wallace and William Askew (Durham: Duke University Press, 1968), 190–191.

62. Askew, "Austro-Italian Antagonism," 175.

63. Ministère des Affaires Étrangères, *Documents Diplomatiques Français, 1871–1914*, 2nd ser., vol. 11 (Paris: Imprimerie Nationale, 1931), (19 March 1908), 526–527.

To explain the persistence of the Triple Alliance, balance of power identifies how Germany and Austria-Hungary needed Italy to preserve the balance. Balance of threat also explains the alliance, at least for Germany. But if Austria-Hungary and Italy saw each other as threats, then the theory has trouble explaining the continued alliance without considering that Austria-Hungary had few other options and that none of the Entente states appeared to desire an alliance with Italy. That Italy and Russia later signed an agreement at Racconigi was also likely a consequence of their mutual distrust of Austria-Hungary.[64] Binding theory by itself can explain the continuation of the alliance, but then, like all of the existing alliance theories, it cannot explain the particular nature of the alliance or how relations between the allies changed after the crisis.

Conrad still advocated preventive war against Italy,[65] and Askew suggests that Britain was "impressed with the fact in October, 1909, that the relations of Italy and Austria could not be worse."[66] In June 1909, there was even some discussion of bringing Romania into the Triple Alliance, primarily as a substitute for Italy should it fail to agree to renew the alliance.[67] This lends support to the argument about unreliable states losing their existing allies. However, Germany and Austria-Hungary continued to see some strategic benefit in an alliance rather than pushing Italy toward the Entente.

Contrary to my expectations, relations between Italy and Austria ultimately improved once Italy accepted the annexation without pressing for compensation. According to Askew, von Aehrenthal even "expressed pleasure that Italo-Austrian relations had emerged undamaged."[68] This represents probably the biggest challenge for my hypotheses, since reputation cannot account for the improved relations between Italy and Austria-Hungary unless changes to the Alliance after the Bosnian crisis were so dramatic that they offset Italy's unreliability.

Given Germany and Austria-Hungary's lack of alliance options, it is also plausible that the effects of reputation were less than if other allies had been available. Therefore, while this observation fails to support most of the hypotheses, it does conform to the assumption about reputation being less relevant when states have limited alliance options. The only other way to explain this is through the costs Germany and Austria-Hungary would have incurred if they allowed Italy to ally with the Entente powers, such as throwing off the balance of power even more.

64. "The Racconigi Meeting," *Times* (London), 28 October 1909.

65. Leo Valiani, "Italian-Austro-Hungarian Negotiations, 1914–1915," *Contemporary History* 1, no. 3 (July 1966), 114.

66. Askew, "Austro-Italian Antagonism," 194, 217.

67. "Roumania May Join Triple Alliance," *New York Times,* 13 June 1909.

68. Askew, "Austro-Italian Antagonism," 194; Williamson, *Austria-Hungary and the Origins of the First World War,* 93.

One component of this observation that strongly supports the hypotheses on alliance variation is that Italy was asked to increase its obligation to the alliance. Specifically, this included demands for Italy to support German interests in Asia Minor (as Anton Monts, Germany's ambassador to Italy, recommended after the First Moroccan Crisis).

Italian action after the crisis also lends some support to my argument about alliance termination. The Italians blamed Austria-Hungary for not consulting with the allies prior to the annexation. Therefore, not only did Italian reputation suffer but so did Italy's perception of Austria-Hungary's reliability as an ally, as they believed, even more strongly, that Italy could be dragged into war with France and England as a result of the Triple Alliance. As a result, we should expect to see Italy trying to preserve its autonomy, or seeking more reliable partners elsewhere. Italy's foreign minister, Tommaso Tittoni, denied in June 1909 that the Triple Alliance would be renewed before its expiration.[69] Italy's signing of the Racconigi agreement with Russia on 24 October 1909 (only six months after the resolution of the crisis) is also consistent with what I expect of a state that was losing trust in its allies. Curiously, it is the less reliable Russians that Italy turned to, rather than the British, even though either state could have given Italy its blessing to take Tripoli. But because of Italy's reputation, it is unclear that England would have accepted an alliance, or else, according to my argument, Italy would have needed to give up a great deal of autonomy to secure an alliance with the British.

By examining European alliance behavior from 1907 to 1911, this chapter has provided additional support for the argument that a state's reputation is an important factor affecting the alliance choices of other states. (Table 5.2 summarizes the findings from this chapter, which includes four separate observations of Russia's two allies and Austria-Hungary's two allies.) The success rates are notably lower here than those found in chapters 3 and 4, which I attribute to the increased division of Europe and to strategic interests beginning to outweigh reputation even more.[70]

While my hypotheses are less successful in this chapter, there are still substantively significant findings that support my general argument

69. "Tittoni Defends Armament," *New York Times*, 24 June 1909.

70. This may also be consistent with the argument that historical cycles influence international norms regarding the degree to which agreements will be honored; specifically, as war becomes more likely, norms for honoring commitments are less influential. Charles Kegley and Gregory Raymond, "The Long Cycle of Global War and the Transformation of Alliance Norms," *Journal of Peace Research* 26, no. 3 (August 1989), 265–284; Charles Kegley and Gregory Raymond, *When Trust Breaks Down: Alliance Norms and World Politics* (Columbia: University of South Carolina Press, 1990).

Table 5.2. Review of chapter findings

Observation	Russian allies		Austro-Hungarian allies	
	England[a] (up)	France[a] (down)	Germany[a] (up)	Italy[a] (down)
H1: alliance formation	N/A	+	N/A	–
H2: similar reliability	0	0	0	+
H3: lose abandoned ally	N/A	0	N/A	–
H4: lose other allies	N/A	–	N/A	–
H5: alliance variation	+	+	+	+

Note: N/A = not applicable to case; – = no support; 0 = mixed findings; + = strong support
[a] State (reliability level)

about reputation, especially in the area of alliance variation. Also, since none of the conventional theories can explain all of the alliance choices in this case, incorporating reputation provides additional insight into alliance behavior.

The dominant view on pre–First World War Europe is that the great powers formed two tight alliances that divided Europe and increased the probability of war because realignment became unlikely. If true, then by 1908 any crisis should be a fairly difficult test of reputation, because when alliances are inflexible a state's reputation for reliability should have less influence on its alliances than when states can freely switch allies. However, evidence from the Bosnian crisis shows not only that reliability was still influential but also that fears of abandonment were significant for the states with unreliable allies, even if the alliances were perceived to be inflexible. In other words, while *realignment* may have been unlikely, *dealignment* or buck-passing was enough of a concern for states in both the Triple Alliance and Triple Entente to suggest that reputation still mattered.

The least successful hypotheses, once again, are those concerning the role of reputation on alliance termination. Only one instance shows even mixed success—when Russia signed an agreement with Germany and Italy after France's lack of support, yet Russia did not leave the Triple Entente. The other three observations all fail to support my argument that unreliable states will lose the ally they abandon as well as their other allies.

French behavior during the Bosnian crisis, and the subsequent response by Russia, provide several findings consistent with those of previous chapters. There was discussion of making the Entente more of a defense pact, though there was never much support in England for giving up any more of its own autonomy. In other words, strategic interests explain British willingness to form an entente with first France and then Russia, but their mixed reliability prevented England from accepting a more formal commitment to these allies.

France's near failure to support Russia, even signing an agreement with Germany, caused Russia to approach both Germany and Italy as possible alternative allies. While no realignment occurred, this does give limited support to the argument that unreliable states can lose allies, even when Europe was supposedly divided into two inflexible camps. There is less evidence that the British considered withdrawing from the Triple Entente, either because of France's lack of support or because of Russia potentially dragging England into war. Yet both England and Russia did demand more of France after the crisis. More important, the French were expected to provide the funds to help build Russian railways, a form of increased obligation. In addition, joint military talks between England and France made the French even more dependent.

The British did not attempt to form any new alliances, so this does not test hypothesis 1. And, although the British found themselves in an entente with unreliable states, challenging hypothesis 2, I consider the hypothesis to have mixed results for two reasons. First, this was not an attempt at formation or renewal, so the unreliability of existing allies is less of a comment on the argument than that the British would not sign a more formal alliance now that it understood its partners were less reliable than originally believed. Second, strategic interests and the lack of reliable alternative allies are clearly important. Abandoning the Entente was unattractive since it would have meant either allying with the less reliable—and now more threatening—Germans or, alternatively, returning to isolation. Because the British still believed France and Russia would be reliable allies in a war against Germany (which posed the most serious threat to England), preserving the Entente was still the most attractive option. Therefore, I consider hypothesis 2 to have mixed results.

Similarly, because England supported Russia during the Bosnia-Herzegovina Crisis, this does not test the hypotheses on alliance termination, even though one might argue that since the Entente persisted after British support was given, then that is evidence that a positive reputation helps preserve an alliance. However, especially in this case, there is no evidence that either France or Russia had ideas of withdrawing from the Entente only to change their mind because of British support during the crisis. While lukewarm French support prompted the Russians to negotiate with Germany, I consider the British case to not even be a test of alliance termination.

What is successful is the argument about alliance variation, since the British were not only able to preserve their autonomy within the Triple Entente but to emerge especially well in comparison to the less reliable French. Not only did the British impose more military dependence on France to offset its reputation but Russia increased French dependence by ensuring that the western railway (necessary if Russia's military were able to challenge Germany) required French financing. Those loans also made Russia more dependent on France, which correlates with both of the Dual Alliance states having lower levels of trust in each other than they had in their British ally.

As for the Triple Alliance, Germany did not attempt to form any new alliances, so the first hypothesis cannot be tested. I consider hypothesis 2 to have mixed results since Germany was able to retain its alliance with Austria-Hungary, yet it would still have been unable to form an alliance with a more reliable state such as England. In addition, the hypotheses on alliance termination are not tested since Germany supported its ally.

Because of its support during the crisis, Germany was able to preserve its existing levels of obligation and precision in the Triple Alliance. Because the military staff talks held between Germany and Austria-Hungary amounted to even less of an exchange of information than that which occurred between England and France, I also consider Germany to have retained its low level of delegation to the alliance.

Within the Triple Alliance, the Italians once again showed themselves to be an unreliable partner, even signing an agreement with Russia shortly after the crisis. The results of the Italian case are the weakest, since only two hypotheses receive any support—that of demands for greater Italian obligation and Italy's alliance with other unreliable states. However, none of the other hypotheses have even mixed success at explaining alliance behavior after the crisis. In fact, some of the changes that occurred after the crisis move in the opposite direction from what I predict. Tension between Austria and Italy appeared to decline somewhat after the crisis, and the increase in military commitment that did take place occurred between Austria-Hungary and the more reliable Germany (although these military talks amounted to an insignificant loss of autonomy for both states).

I mentioned in chapter 3 that it is plausible that England cared more about reputation than did other countries. Certainly the British willingness to stand by allies—as well as the reluctance to ally with unreliable states—supports that claim. It may also be true that Italy cared least about reputation among Europe's great powers. That does not explain why the results of the Italian case provide such little support for my argument. Though it is noteworthy that even the minimally successful hypotheses in this case are substantively useful because Italian autonomy did continue to suffer after each failure to support its ally and its loss of autonomy was relatively greater than that of any of the states that backed their allies.

In the end, the most plausible explanation for the Italian case is simply the lack of alternatives, because given the reputation of the Central Powers—not only for unreliability but also for initiating crises—none of the Entente states was willing to completely abandon the Entente and realign, at least not to the point where Germany and Austria-Hungary could afford to punish Italy for its lack of reliability. Italy could perhaps afford to be unreliable because it might have had the option of allying with France or Russia (though this is debatable given the universal view of Italy as an unreliable ally).

One curious observation from this chapter is that my hypotheses are less successful at explaining the consequences of unreliable behavior (France and Italy) than in honoring states that have kept their commitments (England and Germany). On the face of it, if unreliable states suffer few consequences for their behavior, then this might strengthen Mercer's claim that states should not be concerned about their reputation. However, since it appears that reputation becomes less relevant when states have limited options for realignment, then it makes sense that the hypotheses will have more difficulty explaining instances in which states failed to honor their commitments. Russia, for example, was unwilling to drop its alliance with France, because doing so would have increased its vulnerability to Germany and Austria-Hungary, since its only potential ally with a reputation for being reliable was the British, who were themselves unwilling to commit to a more formal agreement (at least partly because of Russia's reputation). The same holds true for Italy in the Triple Alliance.

Certain hypotheses may also be less successful because of the multilateral nature of the alliances. In the two previous chapters, most of the observations were related to bilateral agreements. In contrast, by 1907 the great powers were consistently allied with two allies who often provided very different levels of support. Given that such relationships are inherently more complicated, it is not unexpected that some hypotheses are less successful. Thus, some refinements of the argument may be necessary in future studies to deal with multilateral agreements, such as NATO, specifying, for example, whether a decline in one member's reliability affects the autonomy of all the members or the alliances as a whole.

6

The Agadir Crisis

Rolling toward War, 1910–1914

Character is like a tree and reputation like its shadow. The shadow is what we think of it; the tree is the real thing.

ABRAHAM LINCOLN

Important Dates

4 November 1910	Potsdam convention signed (Russia and Germany)
21 May 1911–4 November 1911	Agadir (Second Moroccan) Crisis
20 July 1911	Dubail-Wilson agreement signed
8 January 1912	British Naval War Staff established
8–12 February 1912	Haldane Mission to Berlin
13 July 1912	Franco-Russian military protocol signed
16 July 1912	Franco-Russian naval convention
23 July 1912	Anglo-French naval agreement signed
November 1912	Repositioning of Anglo-French navies
22 November 1912	Austro-German military conversations
5 December 1912	Triple Alliance formally renewed

Summer 1913	Franco-Russian military agreement
2 August 1913	Naval agreement signed (Austria, Italy, and Germany)
15 February 1914	Secret Franco-Russian convention signed
May 1914	Anglo-Russian naval talks
15 June 1914	Secret Anglo-German convention signed
28 June 1914	Assassination of Archduke Franz Ferdinand

Key Actors

Austria-Hungary

Karl von Stürgkh	Prime Minister (1911–1916)
Aloys von Aehrenthal	Minister of Foreign Affairs (1906–1912)

England

Edward VII	King (1901–1910)
Herbert Asquith	Prime Minister (1908–1916)
Edward Grey	Foreign Secretary (1905–1916)
Richard Haldane	Secretary of State for War (1905–1912); Lord Chancellor (1912–1915)
David Lloyd George	Chancellor of the Exchequer (1908–1915)
Winston Churchill	Home Secretary (1910–1911); First Lord of the Admiralty (1911–1915)
Charles Hardinge	Permanent Under-Secretary for Foreign Affairs (1906–1910); Viceroy of India (1910–1916)

Arthur Nicolson	Ambassador to Russia (1906–1910); Permanent Under-Secretary for Foreign Affairs (1910–1916)
Edward Goschen	Ambassador to Austria-Hungary (1905–1908); Ambassador to Germany (1908–1914)

France

Georges Clemenceau	Prime Minister (1906–1909)
Joseph Caillaux	Minister of Finance (1906–1909); Prime Minister (1911–1912)
Raymond Poincaré	Minister of Finance (1906); Prime Minister and Foreign Minister (1912–1913)
Joseph Joffre	Chief of the General Staff (1911–1916)
Georges Louis	Ambassador to Russia (1909–1912)
Jules Cambon	Ambassador to Germany (1907–1914)
Camille Barrère	Ambassador to Italy (1897–1924)

Germany

Wilhelm II	Kaiser (1888–1918)
Theobald von Bethmann-Hollweg	State Secretary for the Interior (1907–1909); Chancellor (1909–1917)
Anton Monts	Ambassador to Italy (1902–1905)

Russia

Alexander Izvolsky	Minister of Foreign Affairs (1906–1910)

Sergei Sazonov	Assistant Minister of Foreign Affairs (1909–1910); Minister of Foreign Affairs (1910–1916)
Alexander Benckendorff	Ambassador to England (1903–1917)

The 1911 Agadir Crisis, or Second Moroccan Crisis, was a renewal of tensions between Germany and France that began with the First Moroccan Crisis in 1905 over which state controlled Morocco, and was only temporarily suspended by the Algeciras conference (1906) and the Casablanca agreement (1909). Yet Morocco remained an unresolved issue because of France's desire to create a protectorate there combined with Germany's unwillingness to allow that to happen, at least without compensation. A. J. P. Taylor claims that this case was the dividing line between the diplomatic crises that occurred before 1911 and the prewar crises that began with Agadir.[1] If my assertion is accurate that the availability of other alliance options affects the degree to which reputation matters, then this fourth and final case study should be the most difficult test of reputation. However, even as late as 1911 a case can be made for a state's reputation for reliability affecting its alliance autonomy.

In January 1911, a rebellion began in Morocco that threatened French political and commercial interests there.[2] On 28 April, Jules Cambon, the French ambassador in Berlin, informed the German government that France might have to send troops to the Moroccan capital of Fez to maintain order, even though such an action technically violated the agreements that France and Germany signed at Algeciras and Casablanca.[3] French troops then occupied Fez on 15 May, which France justified on the grounds that it was a temporary move but necessary to preserve stability in Morocco,[4] though they never provided any kind of timeline for withdrawal of the troops.

The German government stated that it would consider the Algeciras and Casablanca agreements void if French troops remained in Fez for an extended period of time, although it also failed to specify what it viewed to be an "extended period." On 7 June 1911, the German government sent France a note emphasizing that Morocco's sovereignty had to be respected.[5] Then on 1 July the German government informed the other European powers

1. A. J. Taylor, *The Struggle for Mastery in Europe, 1848–1918* (Oxford: Clarendon Press, 1954), 473.
2. "Capture of Fez Reported in Spain," *New York Times*, 22 April 1911.
3. "Action in Morocco Urgent, Says France," *New York Times*, 28 April 1911.
4. Ibid.; "The French in Morocco," *New York Times*, 1 May 1911.
5. "Another Warning to France," *New York Times*, 8 June 1911.

that it had sent the gunboat *Panther* to the south Moroccan harbor of Agadir,[6] claiming that the ship was deployed to protect citizens at the request of German firms.[7]

According to A. J. P. Taylor, the Germans believed that Agadir was far enough south of Gibraltar not to alarm the British.[8] This is interesting in itself, since it suggests that Germany did not expect England to support France unless its own interests were at stake. Not only does this challenge Mercer's claim that adversaries will always be thought of as resolute but it also challenges my reputation argument since the British had already backed allies several times and should have been expected to do so again.

In any event, on 4 July 1911, the British cabinet authorized the foreign secretary, Edward Grey, "to tell Germany that Britain must be involved in any discussions about Morocco, and to tell France that Britain would honour her obligations under the 1904 agreement, but expected the French to make some proposals for a settlement."[9] By this the British were once again attempting to strike a balance between supporting France while remaining distant enough that France would not act too aggressively. When the German government neglected to respond to British concerns over the incident, the path was cleared for David Lloyd George, chancellor of the exchequer, to deliver a warning against further German activities. On 21 July, the cabinet authorized Grey to remind Germany that Britain had not received a reply concerning British interests in Morocco and that the British government must participate in any settlement they were expected to accept.[10] Grey relayed that message to the German ambassador that afternoon.

In addition, Lloyd George gave a public speech that evening at Mansion House, the official residence of the Lord Mayor of the City of London, England, and the location of the chancellor of the exchequer's annual speech regarding the state of the British economy.[11] He claimed that British prestige was on the line:

> I conceive that nothing would justify a disturbance of international good will except questions of the gravest national moment. But if a situation were

6. "German Gunboat Sent to Morocco," *New York Times*, 2 July 1911.

7. "Two War Clouds Menace Europe," *New York Times*, 6 July 1911. Ironically, no Germans were in Agadir until the government ordered the nearest German to head to the port, where he was "rescued" by the *Panther*.

8. G. Gooch and Harold Temperley, eds., *British Documents on the Origins of the War, 1898–1914*, vol. 7, *The Agadir Crisis* (London: His Majesty's Stationery Office, 1932), no. 339 (1 July 1911), 322–323; Joanne Mortimer, "Commercial Interests and German Diplomacy in the Agadir Crisis," *Historical Journal* 10, no. 4 (1967), 441–442; Taylor, *Struggle for Mastery*, 467.

9. M. H. Bell, *France and Britain, 1900–1940: Entente and Estrangement* (London: Longman, 1996), 44.

10. Ibid.

11. "Say Germany Went Too Far," *New York Times*, 23 July 1911.

> to be forced upon us in which peace could only be preserved by the surrender of the great and beneficent position Britain has won by centuries of heroism and achievement, *by allowing Britain to be treated where her interests were vitally affected, as if she were of no account in the Cabinet of nations, then I say emphatically that peace at that price would be a humiliation intolerable for a great country like ours to endure.*[12]

Not only was this statement a signal of British reliability directed at Germany in an attempt to deter war but it was also an assurance of Britain's loyalty to its ally, not because France doubted British reliability, as Mercer might argue, but because the British doubted France's reputation and felt the need to bolster French resolve and reliability.

Germany accepted French proposals for a negotiation in early August.[13] Then, on 4 November 1911, a compromise was reached resulting in yet another agreement over Morocco. France gave Germany part of its possessions in the Congo in exchange for Germany's willingness to accept a French protectorate in Morocco and a claim that Germany had only economic interests there.[14] While both France and Germany claimed victory, public opinion in both states viewed their government as giving up too much.[15] This attitude, combined with the further tightening of Europe's alliances, helped push the great powers even closer to war.

As in previous cases, the main issues are how the allies behaved during the crisis and whether their actions influenced the nature of the alliances afterward. Similar to the First Moroccan Crisis, the principle disputants over Agadir were Germany and France, so I am interested in the behavior of England and Russia toward France, as well as Austria and Italy toward Germany.

Jonathan Mercer divides the Agadir Crisis into four stages, including: (1) the French march toward Fez, which violated the terms of France's earlier treaties with Germany; (2) the dispatch of the German gunboat *Panther* to the region; (3) David Lloyd George's Mansion House speech linking the outcome of the crisis to British prestige; and (4) the agreement between France and Germany that brought an end to the crisis.[16] To simplify the

12. David Lloyd George, *War Memoirs of David Lloyd George,* vol. 1 (Boston: Little, Brown, and Company, 1933), 41fn–42fn, emphasis added.

13. "Germany and Morocco," *Times* (London), 2 August 1911; "The French Cabinet and Morocco," *Times* (London), 26 August 1911.

14. "Moroccan Treaty Terms Disclosed," *New York Times,* 4 November 1911; Taylor, *Struggle for Mastery,* 472; Jonathan Mercer, *Reputation and International Politics* (Ithaca: Cornell University Press, 1996), 160.

15. "France Gratified by Morocco Coup," *New York Times,* 6 November 1911; "Kaiser's Son Shows Anger at Treaty," *New York Times,* 10 November 1911.

16. Mercer, *Reputation and International Politics,* 155–156.

analysis, and to be consistent with previous chapters, I treat the crisis as a single case rather than dealing with each stage separately. Also following the structures of chapters 4 and 5, I deal with each ally as a separate observation.

The British response during the crisis was to offer complete support to France, consisting primarily of Lloyd George's Mansion House speech. Despite claims after the Bosnia-Herzegovina Crisis that Russia would not back down to the Central Powers again (illustrating Jervis's deterrence paradox discussed in chapter 2), the Russian government only supported France in private, offering to provide full public support only in the event of war. As a result, I expect England would emerge from the crisis able to preserve its alliance autonomy while Russia and France both would lose more autonomy to preserve the Triple Entente.

Germany, on the other hand, was essentially abandoned by both of its allies. Germany probably expected more support from Austria-Hungary before the crisis. But what is interesting is that Austria suffered more loss of autonomy for its lack of support than did Italy. This may illustrate Glenn Snyder's contention that unexpected behavior is likely to cause the greatest change in perception,[17] suggesting that a state perceived to be reliable that fails to support an ally will lose more autonomy than the state that is expected to abandon its commitments and merely lives up to those expectations. This also seems to fit the idea, common in the business literature, that it is easier to suffer a loss of reputation than it is to develop a positive one.[18]

England

Three reputations related to the Anglo-French relationship are relevant during the Agadir Crisis. Mercer argues that the British were primarily concerned about French resolve in standing up to Germany during the crisis. While true, more pertinent for this book is that the British were also concerned about French reliability, fearing that France would not just back down to Germany but that it also might abandon its allies and defect from the Entente. The third reputation is British reliability in supporting France against Germany.

According to Stephen Lee, with the Mansion House speech and a declaration to Parliament by Grey, the Entente was tightening into something

17. Glenn Snyder, *Deterrence and Defense: Toward a Theory of National Security* (Princeton: Princeton University Press, 1961).

18. Paul Herbig, John Milewicz, and Jim Golden, "A Model of Reputation Building and Destruction," *Journal of Business Research* 31, no. 1 (September 1994), 23–31.

more closely resembling an alliance.[19] Even before the crisis ended, attention was directed toward renewing military conversations, which had been only on the periphery since the end of 1905. Specifically, changes were made to Anglo-French military plans in 1911 to broaden the scope of cooperation. This involved increasing the level of precision within the relationship while still preserving the high level of British autonomy.[20] In addition, naval conversations between France and England resumed in August and September 1911.

The British also began naval reforms toward the end of the crisis. Winston Churchill, who became First Lord of the Admiralty in October 1911, introduced the concept of a naval war staff in January 1912.[21] Then, "in November 1911 the Cabinet . . . accepted a ruling by [British prime minister Herbert] Asquith that no communications between the British and French staffs would commit Britain, directly or indirectly, to military or naval intervention. . . . But Grey told the Prime Minister that while staff talks implied no commitment, to stop them would indicate a change in policy and so alienate the French."[22] From these talks came the understanding that in the event of war with Germany the French fleet would control operations in the Mediterranean. This understanding was formalized on 23 July 1912, when an agreement was reached that France would concentrate its fleet in the Mediterranean, while Britain concentrated on her home waters, including France's Atlantic coastline.[23] This naval understanding then expanded in early 1913 to include provisions for naval cooperation in the Strait of Dover and the English Channel. These measures helped increase precision, thus lowering British autonomy, but only in that one aspect of the Anglo-French relationship. Even this, though, was more an exchange of notes than a formal agreement and, according to Thomas Otte, represented France's near total dependence on British naval defense of the French channel coast.[24]

Also after the crisis, Lord Chancellor Richard Haldane went to Germany from 8–12 February 1912, where he offered colonial concessions and a political agreement if the German naval program was not increased. However,

19. Stephen Lee, *Aspects of British Political History, 1815–1914* (London: Routledge, 1994), 264. See also Keith Wilson, "British Power in the European Balance, 1906–14," in *Retreat from Power: Studies in Britain's Foreign Policy of the Twentieth Century*, ed. David Dilks (London: Macmillan, 1981), 21–41.

20. George Manhart, *Alliance and Entente, 1871–1914* (New York: F. S. Crofts & Co., 1932), 50–51; Ministère des Affaires Étrangères, *Documents Diplomatiques Français*, 3rd ser. (Paris: Imprimerie Nationale, 1931) vol. 2 (29 March 1912), 267–271.

21. Richard Haldane, *Before the War* (London: Cassell and Company, 1920), 160.

22. Bell, *France and Britain*, 46.

23. Ibid., 48; Taylor, *Struggle for Mastery*, 480–481.

24. Thomas Otte, "The Elusive Balance: British Foreign Policy and the French Entente before the First World War," in *Anglo-French Relations in the Twentieth Century: Rivalry and Cooperation*, ed. Alan Sharp and Glyn Stone (London: Routledge, 2000), 26–27.

the Germans wanted a promise of neutrality during a continental war, rather than a simple declaration of friendship.[25] The French were alarmed by these talks, which may have been one British objective. But, despite England's willingness to negotiate with Germany, the British were unwilling to sign any agreement that was perceived to weaken the Entente. As a result, the negotiations with Germany ended in March with the British and French growing closer to one another. The French did reach an agreement with Germany over the Baghdad Railway in February 1914. Only after that did the British finally reach an agreement with Germany in June 1914. From the German point of view, both France and England seemed to be siding with Germany against Russia on the issue of Turkey.[26] The result was that it appeared to weaken the Entente, and, as I argue in the concluding chapter, it made a challenge by the Central Powers more likely.

Explaining British Behavior

Because I have suggested that reputation may become less important as alliances tighten and as war becomes more likely, it follows that other explanations of state behavior should be even more important in this case. (Table 6.1 illustrates the power, relations, and behavior of the major powers during the crisis.) British support for France can be explained with balance of power theory since France and Russia were less powerful than the Triple Alliance without British support. Likewise, balance of threat adequately explains British support for France, since Germany was perceived to be the common threat to all three members of the Triple Entente.

Because Mercer would see British support for France as favorable, he would not expect England to be rewarded with an improved reputation after the crisis. Mercer also claims that the French did not count on British military support, despite England having supported France at Algeciras, as well as Russia during the Bosnian crisis. Instead, he suggests that the French explained British behavior according to British interests. Taylor seems to agree, arguing that "the French never acted on the confident assumption that Great Britain would support them in a continental war, whatever its cause."[27]

What Mercer and Taylor observe in believing that France did not count on British support is more about the inability of British ground forces to

25. Haldane, *Before the War,* 103–112, 145–148; G. Gooch, *Before the War: Studies in Diplomacy,* vol. 2, *The Coming of the Storm* (New York: Russell & Russell, 1967), 82–86, 227–238; Taylor, *Struggle for Mastery,* 477.

26. Taylor, *Struggle for Mastery,* 518.

27. Mercer, *Reputation and International Politics,* 169, 183–186; Taylor, *Struggle for Mastery,* 481.

Table 6.1. The great powers during the Agadir Crisis (1911)

State	Capabilities score	Alliance (combined score)	Behavior
Germany	0.14	Triple Alliance (0.21)	Primary belligerent; negotiates Potsdam convention with Russia
England	0.12	Triple Entente (0.31)	Strongly supports France
Russia	0.12	Triple Entente (0.31)	Weakly supports France; negotiates Potsdam convention with Germany
France	0.07	Triple Entente (0.31)	Primary belligerent
Austria-Hungary	0.04	Triple Alliance (0.21)	Little support to Germany
Italy	0.03	Triple Alliance (0.21)	Little support to Germany

alter the situation on the European Continent, not an unwillingness by the British government to support its allies. Therefore, even if France did not count on British support, this was a result of British capabilities not British reputation. For instance, in a 1913 military plan presented to the French Defense Council, Gen. Joseph Joffre, the Chief of the French General Staff, made the assumption that France could not count on British land forces given the British government's unwillingness to make a formal commitment in writing. This seems to confirm Mercer's claim. However, Joffre *did* assume that the French would receive British naval assistance.[28] Therefore, France's concern was about England's ability to give assistance in areas where it was weak, namely, its army. In contrast, where the British had the ability to influence events in Europe (or Africa)—through the use of its naval power—the French fully expected to receive British support consistent with England's reputation as a reliable ally.

Mercer is right to claim that the French assumed British support was a function of its interests.[29] The British government feared that if it did not support France, the Germans would gain a foothold in Morocco. However, as I have emphasized throughout this book, one cannot dismiss reputation simply because strategic interests are involved. According to Sergei Sazonov, the Russian foreign minister in 1910, the preservation of the Entente had become more important to the British than some of their economic interests. The relevant point here is that if reputation matters, then part of a state's strategic interest will become the preservation of that very reputation. In this case, Sazonov even believed that he could exploit this "weakness" of the British concern for their reputation to play England and

28. Bell, *France and Britain,* 49.
29. Mercer, *Reputation and International Politics,* 170, 183–184.

Germany off against each other, thus gaining more influence in Persia while preserving the Entente.[30] This is a noteworthy point that is addressed in more detail in the concluding chapter. But essentially, it suggests that while a state's reliability can preserve autonomy within its alliances, reliability can also be detrimental if it is so high that it emboldens an ally to challenge an adversary.

In contrast, the British publicly supported France with the Mansion House speech. France also proved its loyalty to the Entente by not giving away any part of Morocco, particularly since Grey intimated early in the crisis that granting Germany certain concessions in the French Congo would not be contrary to British interests.[31] At the same time, British fears of abandonment once again rose because of a crisis initiated by an ally. Therefore, I would expect the Anglo-French agreement to remain vague, particularly when compared to Franco-Russian relations, and, while I would expect France to continue pushing for a more formal agreement, I also would expect the British to continue to demand high levels of autonomy.

But British actions that strengthened reliability were perceived to be a means of both enhancing the deterrent power of the Entente and strengthening France's willingness to remain within the Entente. Evidence of this appears in a 2 August 1911 letter to Nicolson in which Charles Hardinge, his predecessor as permanent under-secretary for foreign affairs and at this time viceroy of India, stated, "I suppose we can trust the French, but it will be a very difficult position for us if France and Germany come to some agreement together unbeknown to us which, in our opinion, is disadvantageous to our interests."[32] To enhance French awareness of British support, Grey considered sending a ship to Agadir or to the nearby port of Mogador. However, the cabinet overruled this action on the grounds that it was too provocative.[33] Instead, Lloyd George was granted approval by the cabinet to deliver the Mansion House speech.

There is some debate regarding the purpose of that speech. While the conventional view sees Germany as the target,[34] Taylor claims that it was directed at France. According to him, rather than a pledge to support France

30. Serge Sazonov, *Fateful Years, 1909–1916* (New York: Frederick Stokes Company, 1928), 33–34; Sazonov to Poklevsky (Teheran), 8 October 1910. *Benckendorffs Schriftwechsel*, 1, cited in Taylor, *Struggle for Mastery*, 463.

31. Grey to Bertie telegram, 13 July 1909, referenced in Gooch, *Coming of the Storm*, 72.

32. Hardinge-Nicolson, 2 August 1911: Hardinge MSS, vol. 92, cited in Keith Wilson, "The Agadir Crisis, the Mansion House Speech, and the Double-Edgedness of Agreements," *Historical Journal* 15, no. 3 (September 1972), 531. The trust referred to here was that the French would keep the British government informed of its intentions with regard to Morocco.

33. Gooch and Temperley, *Agadir Crisis*, no. 343 (2 July 1911), 325–326; no. 351 (3 July 1911), 330–331; no. 359 (5 July 1911), 336–338; Taylor, *Struggle for Mastery*, 469.

34. Frank Anderson and Amos Hershey, *Handbook for the Diplomatic History of Europe, Asia, and Africa, 1870–1914* (New York: Negro Universities Press, 1969), 404.

against Germany, the speech was a warning to Great Britain's ally that it could not be left out of any new partition of Morocco.[35] Richard Cosgrove refutes this interpretation, citing primary documents that suggest British leaders were completely engaged with the Triple Entente and that Taylor's claim would require a "complete reversal for Grey and the Foreign Office to have allowed Lloyd George's language to be directed against French interests."[36] Lloyd George himself gives no clear indication as to the target of the speech, though the tone of his memoirs suggests that he was focusing on limiting German ambitions.[37]

Concerns about France's perception of British reputation clearly influenced British behavior during the crisis. In a note to Grey, Arthur Nicolson, who had been ambassador to Russia and was now permanent under-secretary for foreign affairs, provided a specific argument in favor of giving full British support to France: "Were [France] to *come to distrust us*, she would probably try to make terms with Germany irrespective of us, while Germany who would soon detect our hesitation would be inclined to impose harder terms than may be the case at present. In any case, France would never forgive us for having failed her, and *the whole Triple Entente would be broken up.*"[38] Nicolson clearly believed that a failure to support France would not only destroy that relationship, as well as the entente with Russia, but would push France into the German camp.

Consequences of British Behavior

Because England supported France in the First Moroccan Crisis and gave support to Russia over the Balkans, France should have expected British support. I also do not expect the British government to have put much faith in either of its allies, considering they both failed to fully support each other in crises and both negotiated with Germany without consulting each other or England. In the end, the British were rewarded with a greater French obligation while being able to preserve its autonomy: "Poincaré proposed to declare that England and France would 'co-operate, if necessary, to maintain the European balance.' Grey would only express a wish 'to co-operate in maintaining European peace.'"[39]

35. Taylor, *Struggle for Mastery,* 471.

36. Richard Cosgrove, "A Note on Lloyd George's Speech at the Mansion House, 21 July 1911," *Historical Journal* 12, no. 4 (December 1969), 699.

37. Lloyd George, *War Memoirs of David Lloyd George,* vol. 1, 39–43.

38. Gooch and Temperley, *Agadir Crisis,* no. 409 (21 July 1911), 386, emphasis added; Fritz Fischer, *War of Illusions: German Policies from 1911 to 1914* (New York: Norton, 1975), 79. Also cited in Mercer, *Reputation and International Politics,* 177.

39. Taylor, *Struggle for Mastery,* 478.

Mercer highlights that despite the Mansion House speech, the British repeatedly told the French that England would not go to war over Morocco. He interprets this to mean that the French never counted on full British support. The French should have been confident in British support, given that England went beyond its required commitments with France in 1905–6 and Russia in 1909. In addition, Grey made it clear to the French that while the British would not unconditionally go to war with Germany over Morocco, they would support France at a conference, in accordance with the terms of the 1904 entente.[40] I have also shown that keeping its commitments intact by supporting an ally frequently became a major British interest in itself, and when reputation and interests become intertwined as they frequently did for the British, we cannot easily separate behavior according to either reputation or interests.

What it also means, though, is that the British understood the balancing act they had to play between giving an ally enough support to deter a challenger like Germany and giving an ally so much support that the British would get dragged into a war. Mercer suggests that the French were annoyed that they did not receive more support from the British.[41] Yet they clearly received enough to emerge from the crisis on top while avoiding war. Therefore, more important for reputation than repeated words of caution from the British are British actions during the crisis and the French response to British behavior, especially compared to France's response to Russian behavior.

That England, once again, was able to preserve more autonomy than Russia, and that this correlates with the level of support that each state provided to France, is difficult to explain using Mercer's argument. As for the existing alliance theories, balance of power has trouble explaining the persistence of the Triple Entente, given that it clearly threw off the balance in Europe; the changes to the Entente; and the willingness of all three states to negotiate agreements with Germany while remaining in the Entente. Balance of threat theory is supported by the Triple Entente remaining intact as well as the changes to the Entente, considering the growing German threat. However, the theory has trouble explaining the willingness of each member of the Entente to negotiate with Germany. Binding theory does a better job of explaining these negotiations, but not their timing, since they could have engaged in them much earlier. Nor can the binding argument explain why the Triple Entente persisted, much less the specific changes in state relations after the crisis.

40. Wilson, "Agadir Crisis," 517–518, 523. See also Joanne Mortimer, "Commercial Interests and German Diplomacy in the Agadir Crisis," *Historical Journal* 10, no. 4 (1967), 443; Cosgrove, "Note on Lloyd George's Speech," 701.

41. Mercer, *Reputation and International Politics*, 185.

If we incorporate reputation into our explanations of alliance choices, we improve not only our ability to explain why changes occurred to the alliance but also some of the specific alliance choices, such as the changes that were made in Anglo-French relations and the willingness and timing of the Entente members to each negotiate agreements with Germany, even while preserving the Entente. For example, Russia and France were willing to negotiate with Germany after being abandoned by each other. Even the British ultimately signed an agreement with Germany, but only after its two allies had already done so without consultation.

Assessing British expectations of France, Mercer again conflates resolve and reliability. According to Mercer, "Bertie feared that if the French doubted British support, they would come to terms with Germany."[42] Although Mercer and I do not disagree about British perceptions of French reliability, the problem is that Mercer uses France's own lack of reliability as a basis to question French expectations of British reliability. In other words, Mercer finds that the French do not expect the British to intervene, but his evidence is based on British concerns about French unreliability, not on England's own reputation.

British Perceptions of its Allies

Mercer points out that throughout the three crises he covers, the British never stopped worrying about the possibility of France defecting to the Triple Alliance.[43] He interprets this to mean that the British gave the French no credit for standing up to Germany during the First Moroccan Crisis. He also suggests that the British made no mention of France's failure to support Russia in 1909.[44] However, this simply illustrates the difference between resolve and reliability. It is the lack of French support over Bosnia, as well as France's willingness to sign an agreement with Germany during the Bosnian crisis, that increased British concerns about a French defection from the Entente.

Indirectly, even Mercer agrees. He suggests that the British did not see the Germans as irresolute but, instead, recognized that Germany sought to break up the Entente.[45] Not only does this suggest that the British once again attributed a reputation for aggression to the Germans but it also indicates German recognition that the Entente could be broken up, probably as a result of French unreliability toward Russia during the Russo-Japanese War and the Bosnia-Herzegovina Crisis, as well as Russian unreliability toward France over Morocco.

42. Ibid., 166.
43. Ibid., 207.
44. Ibid., 167.
45. Ibid., 164.

Because France stood up to Germany at Algeciras, it should have a reputation for *resolve*—its allies would expect France to stand up to Germany again, especially over Agadir. At the same time, because France failed to support Russia during the Bosnian crisis—even making an agreement with Germany—its allies should not have expected France to be a *reliable* ally in its confrontation with Germany. In other words, they did not expect France to back down to German threats, but they did fear that France would be willing to weaken the Entente to reach an accord with Germany if it served French interests. This compelled the British to issue the Mansion House speech, and then to negotiate with Germany after the crisis.

Even Mercer acknowledges that "because they neither trusted France, nor thought it capable of resisting Germany alone, Crowe, Nicolson, and Bertie all felt it imperative to give France unqualified support."[46] Therefore, British perceptions of French reliability are consistent with France's past behavior, which not only suggests that reliability was a separate issue from resolve but also provides contradictory evidence to the conventional wisdom that the pre–First World War alliances were inflexible, since fears of realignment (or at least dealignment) were present throughout the prewar years.

What matters is that the Mansion House speech was interpreted by Germany as an assurance of British resolve and by France as a signal of Britain's reliability. The British were particularly concerned that the French would come to terms with Germany if there was any doubt about British support.[47] This does not mean that France had any thoughts that England was unreliable, particularly given past British behavior. But that did not prevent the British from being concerned about French realignment, given France's past behavior. According to P. M. H. Bell: "Early in 1911 Grey had tried to dissuade the French from military action in Morocco, and then he urged them to withdraw their troops from Fez. But he felt bound to offer France diplomatic support, partly because it was specified in the 1904 agreement, and even more because he dare not risk weakening the entente."[48]

According to Taylor, "the Triple Entente was far from being a perfect arrangement from the British point of view. They had to be loyal to France; yet Russia was not loyal to them. Improved relations with Germany would, it was hoped, lessen the tension between Germany and France; at the same time, they would make it easier to oppose Russia in Persia."[49] Therefore, because of French and Russian action in failing to fully support each other and in negotiating with Germany, even the British sought to hedge their bets by pursuing an agreement with Germany after the crisis.

46. Ibid., 166.

47. Gooch and Temperley, *Agadir Crisis*, no. 376 (12 July 1911), 359; Bertie to Crowe (21 July 1911), quoted in Cosgrove, "Note on Lloyd George's Speech", 699.

48. Bell, *France and Britain*, 43–44.

49. Taylor, *Struggle for Mastery*, 477.

Another problem in Mercer's analysis is that he claims that the British did not see the Germans as irresolute, even though Germany had backed down during the First Moroccan Crisis. His argument is that because German behavior was favorable, the British explained it through situation, rather than German irresolution. However, many in the French and British governments believed that Germany *would* back down again, but only if it believed that France's allies were reliable. In a 29 April 1911 letter to Nicolson, Edward Goschen, the British ambassador in Berlin, offered the following opinion:

> Germany is watching (the attitude of England) very narrowly and . . . if she sees that France will at the present juncture receive the same support from the Powers as she did at Algeciras then she will hold her hand and not make trouble. If on the contrary she sees any likelihood of that support being withdrawn or given grudgingly she will at once proceed to make trouble and turn the situation to her own advantage.[50]

In correspondences with one another, Bertie, Nicolson, and Grey expressed similar views.[51]

Another factor that Mercer misses is the relevance of the new French government that took office on 1 July 1911. Joseph Caillaux, the new prime minister, was convinced that neither Russia nor Great Britain would support France, and rather than risk war, preferred to offer French cooperation on the Baghdad Railway in exchange for Germany dropping its interests in Morocco.[52] However, it is relevant to point out that Caillaux was jailed near the end of the First World War because his radical pacifist stance led him to commit treason. This is pertinent because it suggests that his views about England were more likely to be personal opinion than the result of any real British behavior or reputation. As a result, not only were French perceptions of Britain's reliability influenced by those in power but British perceptions of French reliability would have also been influenced by Caillaux's personal unwillingness to risk war. This, then, helps explain why the French government might *appear* to not trust British loyalty. If Britain had not supported France at Algeciras or Russia during the Bosnian crisis, Caillaux might have had even lower expectations of British loyalty, and more members of the French government would have agreed with him.

In addition, while I cannot explain how Caillaux developed his view of British reliability (it may simply be a product of his pro-German leanings),

50. Goschen-Nicolson, 29 April 1911: Carnock MSS, F.O. 800/348, cited in Wilson, "Agadir Crisis," 514–515. See also Gooch and Temperley, *Agadir Crisis*, no. 265 (13 May 1911), 237.

51. Gooch and Temperley, *Agadir Crisis*, no. 376 (12 July 1911), 359; no. 407 (21 July 1911), 383–384; no. 409 (21 July 1911), 386.

52. Taylor, *Struggle for Mastery*, 467.

the consequences of that perception are still consistent with my argument about the importance of a reputation for being reliable, because his belief that the British were unreliable led him to seek an agreement with Germany. In addition to pointing out one of the difficulties of studying reputation, this case also suggests that if another French government had been in power at the time, it might have had a more favorable view of British reliability. The point is that new governments do not necessarily subscribe to the same perceptions as previous governments, so that one state's reputation can change with a new government, but also perceptions of that state can change when its ally forms a new government.

Russia

The Russians gave France some support over Agadir but avoided providing the kind of full public support given by England. One possible result of weak Russian support is that it may have led many of the great powers to believe that Russia was about to withdraw from the Entente, and the Russians used that to their advantage. According to Taylor: "In view of [Russia's] equivocal policy during the Agadir crisis, no Power would oppose her [securing control of the straits]—Great Britain and France from fear, Germany and Austria-Hungary from hope, that she was about to desert her present partners."[53] This provides still further evidence that the alliances were not as inflexible as is commonly believed, or at least they were not perceived that way at the time by those states that feared any possible shift in the balance of power.

Several agreements were made in the wake of the crisis. Some were designed to bind the allies more closely together. For example, a naval convention between France and Russia was concluded on 16 July 1912.[54] Other agreements were signed between adversaries. The Potsdam convention between Germany and Russia, which began on 4 November 1910, lasted until an agreement was reached on 19 August 1911.[55] The result was an Open Door for German trade in Persia and recognition of Russia's sphere of influence in northern Persia.[56] Sazonov stated that these discussions with

53. Ibid., 474.

54. For the draft text of the convention, see Alfred Pribram, *The Secret Treaties of Austria-Hungary, 1879–1914,* vol. 2, Negotiations Leading to the Treaties of the Triple Alliance (Cambridge: Harvard University Press, 1921), 222–225.

55. "The Tsar and the German Emperor: Meeting at Potsdam," *Times* (London), 5 November 1910.

56. Even this meeting illustrates the effects of German reputation, because built into the agreement was a Russian safeguard to protect against Germany going back on the commitment. Anderson and Hershey, *Handbook for the Diplomatic History,* 407–408.

Germany did not threaten the stability of the Triple Entente, but the entente between England and Russia was weakened at least with regards to Persia.

On 2 December 1911, Grey threatened to resign from office and allow the entente with Russia to dissolve, believing that the next government would assign significantly less value to England's partnership with Russia.[57] This threat was based largely on declining Anglo-Russian relations as a result of Russian activities in Persia and the Russo-German agreement at Potsdam. Russia's approach to Germany was especially offensive, given that Britain had previously avoided completion of an agreement with Germany out of concern for its allies.[58] In response, England agreed to hold negotiations with the Germans in February 1912.[59] Nothing emerged from the talks because the Germans pressed England for a promise of neutrality in any war involving Germany. The British realized that such an agreement would be tantamount to completely abandoning France and Russia, and they were unwilling to take such drastic steps.[60]

Explaining Russian Behavior

As with previous cases, conventional alliance theories can explain part of the case but not all of it, and they do not account for changes in Franco-Russian relations. Neither balance of power nor balance of threat theory can explain Russia's willingness to negotiate with Germany during the crisis, based on the growth of German power and perceptions of the continuing German threat. Binding theory might explain Russia's willingness to negotiate with Germany, but not why greater attention was given to strengthening the Triple Entente after the crisis.

Donald Mathieu suggests that Russian support may have been intentionally low to prevent Austria-Hungary from siding with Germany.[61] Mercer also suggests that Russia may have avoided lending full support to France over concern that Austria-Hungary would support Germany in the crisis rather than remain neutral.[62] Although he makes this point in relation to Russia's lack of support for France, if true, then it has even greater relevance for perceptions of Austria-Hungary's reliability as a German ally.

57. Grey believed that his successor would sign an agreement with Germany on Persia, effectively ending England's relationship with Russia. Taylor, *Struggle for Mastery,* 475.

58. Edward Grey, *Twenty-Five Years, 1892–1916,* vol. 1 (New York: Frederick A. Stokes Company, 1925), 245–246.

59. "Lord Haldane in Berlin: An Unofficial Visit, Meeting with the Imperial Chancellor," *Times* (London), 9 February 1912; "Mr. Churchill's Speech: German Comment, Departure of Lord Haldane from Berlin," *Times* (London), 12 February, 1912.

60. Anderson and Hershey, *Handbook for the Diplomatic History,* 415.

61. Donald Mathieu, "The Role of Russia in French Foreign Policy, 1908–1914" (PhD. diss., Stanford University, 1968), 56.

62. Mercer, *Reputation and International Politics,* 171.

If the Russians truly believed this, then they probably arrived at this belief as a result of Austrian support for Germany during the First Moroccan Crisis. Even if valid that reason should not have prevented Russia from suffering certain consequences for its behavior, unless there is evidence that France and England were aware of this tactic. However, I have been unable to find any such information.

Based on Mercer's test of reputation, France would not expect Russia's support against Germany because of Russia's unwillingness to stand up to Austria-Hungary and Germany over Bosnia.[63] Because Mercer does not believe states expect loyalty from their allies, after the crisis the Russians should not have been punished for their failure to support France, both compared to England, which did provide strong support, and compared to the effects of mixed Russian support during the First Moroccan Crisis.

One question is whether France expected Russian support. Unlike the high level of support Britain historically provided to its allies in Asia and Morocco, and then Bosnia, Russia provided only mixed support for France during the First Moroccan Crisis, particularly with its negotiations for the Björko Treaty with Germany. Because Russian support was mixed during the 1905 Moroccan crisis, I would not expect France to rely heavily on Russia. But I suggest that France perceived Russia to be more reliable than Mercer asserts. This argument is based on Russia's mixed reliability during the First Moroccan Crisis, rather than its lack of resolve during the Bosnia-Herzegovina Crisis. In addition, changes in the Franco-Russian relationship after the previous crises should have reduced Russian autonomy, thus leading France to have more faith that Russia would be compelled to honor its commitment.

Consequences of Russian Behavior

The primary question for my hypothesis is whether Russia's low level of support during the crisis resulted in any type of change to Franco-Russian relations. The hypotheses on alliance termination and variation would expect France to withdraw from the Dual Alliance, or at least to demand greater constraints on Russia. If Russia was perceived to be seriously considering withdrawal from the Triple Entente, then I would expect French and British concerns about that to limit how much they would punish Russia for its lack of support over Agadir (just as Italy's allies consistently worried about its realignment). Instead, we might even see France offering Russia more to remain in the alliance. On one level, this challenges my hypotheses. On another, I suggest Russia's willingness to consider realignment was largely a consequence of concern over French reliability.

63. Ibid., 188–190.

As for the existing alliance theories, balance of power has trouble explaining the continuation of the Triple Entente, and especially the strengthening of the Entente. Balance of threat can explain both of these choices, but not the decision of each member to negotiate agreements with Germany. Finally, binding theory has trouble explaining everything except the agreements with Germany, but without reputation it cannot even explain the timing of the agreements.

The Franco-Russian naval convention increased the level of delegation on both sides, but for the first time the French government indicated that France would support Russia against Germany, even if the conflict was begun by a Russian attack on Austria-Hungary.[64] Raymond Poincaré, who became France's premier and foreign minister on 14 January 1912, told Alexander Izvolsky, the Russian foreign minister, that "if Russia fights France will also because we know that in this question Germany is behind Austria."[65]

This lowered the French government's autonomy by increasing its commitment. Although this appears to contradict my hypotheses, this expanded commitment is also a consequence of previous French actions as much as a result of Russian behavior. According to Georges Louis, the French ambassador to Russia, the Russians were getting back at France for its lack of support during the Bosnian crisis.[66] The French realized the damage caused by their prior behavior (on both Russian and British perceptions of French reliability) and sought to impose constraints on themselves. Strictly speaking, this still fails to support my hypothesis for this observation, but over the course of the fourteen years examined in chapters 3–6, it is not surprising that France kept losing autonomy as a result of its frequently unreliable behavior, as it had twice failed to support Russia and twice dragged its allies into unwanted crises.

At the same time, there is still support for my hypothesis on alliance variation, because after the crisis France placed two new conditions on its loans to Russia that effectively punished Russian behavior by increasing its obligations, thus decreasing its autonomy more than what France gave up. One demand was that Russia immediately begin construction of new rail lines. From 1912 onward, the French put tremendous pressure on the Russian government to construct strategic railroads directed toward Germany. Ironically, according to D. N. Collins, this attempt at improving Russian railways not only *increased* the possibility of war but also diverted funds

64. Manhart, *Alliance and Entente, 1871–1914,* 53–54; Taylor, *Struggle for Mastery,* 488; Pribram, *Negotiations Leading to the Treaties of the Triple Alliance,* 222–225.

65. Again we see reference to Germany's aggressive reputation, this time from France. Fischer, *War of Illusions,* 425.

66. Mercer, *Reputation and International Politics,* 189.

from other parts of the economy, thus preventing Russia from growing more economically powerful.[67] The second French condition was for Russia to increase the strength of its peacetime army,[68] which likely had similarly costly effects on the Russian economy. The point is that France's making these demands is typical of how state behavior is influenced by reputation, in that Russia's low level of support resulted in increased demands for a greater Russian obligation.

Russia's failure to fully support France also contributed to British concerns about Russian loyalty. Contrary to the conventional wisdom regarding the inflexibility of the prewar alliances, but consistent with my argument about unreliable states losing their allies (hypothesis 4), Russian behavior almost led Britain to withdraw from the Entente. Mercer claims that "Russia's irresolution in 1909 did not govern Nicolson's expectations of Russian behavior in 1911."[69] Instead, he suggests that the British believed Russia would support France and strengthen the Entente. But this misses the point of separating out different types of reputation. If England believed that Russia would support France, it was a result of Russia's ultimate willingness to support France during the First Moroccan Crisis despite its initial attempt to sign a separate agreement with Germany. It has less to do with Russia's behavior during the 1909 Bosnian crisis, since that was more about Russian resolve. But because Russia did not fully support France during the Agadir Crisis, I would expect France and England to demand that Russia give up more autonomy after the crisis in order to keep the Entente from breaking apart.

The fact that the Russians asked England for an alliance in 1914, while the British were still unwilling to make a formal commitment to Russia, supports my hypotheses on alliance formation, especially given England's history of reliability and Russia's reputation for unreliability. According to Otte: "Even Nicolson, the most ardent advocate of closest ties with Russia, began to doubt [Russian] reliability."[70] Moreover, British relations with Germany seemed to improve in 1913–14, while tension grew between England and its allies. The German government sought to take advantage of this, believing that as long as France was left alone, Great Britain could be turned away from Russia.[71]

Grey did agree to hold Anglo-Russian naval talks in return for better Russian behavior in Persia. Sazonov even offered to surrender Persia's

67. D. N. Collins, "The Franco-Russian Alliance and Russian Railways, 1891–1914," *Historical Journal* 16, no. 4 (December 1973), 786–788.

68. Fischer, *War of Illusions*, 426–437.

69. Mercer, *Reputation and International Politics*, 189.

70. Otte, "Elusive Balance," 28.

71. Taylor, *Struggle for Mastery*, 519.

neutral zone to the British and to give a guarantee to India.[72] This lends support to my hypothesis on alliance obligations, since Britain's reliability contributed to its continued autonomy with both of its partners, while Russia was forced to give up greater concessions to preserve not only the alliance with France but also its entente with Britain.

Austria-Hungary

During the Second Moroccan Crisis, Germany received less support from its allies than it had in 1905. Even Austria-Hungary remained relatively aloof during the crisis. According to Fritz Fischer, "Count Aehrenthal made no secret of his view that a Franco-German war over Morocco did not constitute a casus foederis. He thought that the Monarchy could render better service as a neutral power than as a military ally. Therefore, he told the French government right from the start that he sympathized with their stand."[73]

Unlike the willingness of both France and Russia to sign agreements with Germany after the crisis, to the detriment of the Triple Entente, we do not see Austria-Hungary engaged in activities that would weaken the Triple Alliance. Instead, they simply failed to support Germany during the crisis, and this probably had a great deal to do with Germany's decision to back down during the crisis.

Despite the lack of support from the allies, the Triple Alliance was formally renewed for a third time (for another six years) on 5 December 1912.[74] One major change that occurred after the crisis was the development of Austro-German military conversations on 22 November 1912. Austria-Hungary also increased the size of its military in 1912–13,[75] which I contend was a result of strategic interests but also a signal to Germany that it was willing to pay greater costs to ensure the continuation of the Triple Alliance.

Explaining Austrian Behavior

Balancing theories have difficulty explaining the lack of Austrian support, because the Triple Alliance was less powerful than the Triple Entente, so all of the members should have supported each other. Balance of threat theory provides mixed results, since Austria-Hungary saw both Russia and Italy as threats. As a result, not only are the conventional theories nonspecific about how Austria should have been expected to behave but without reputation

72. Ibid., 511–513.
73. Fischer, *War of Illusions*, 85.
74. Manhart, *Alliance and Entente*, 68.
75. Anderson and Hershey, *Handbook for the Diplomatic History*, 471.

they have difficulty explaining several aspects of Germany's response to its ally's lack of support.

Taylor suggests that Austria-Hungary's behavior was at least partly a response to German concessions to Russia in the Potsdam convention, which was already underway when the crisis began.[76] Similarly, Austria may have been annoyed at Germany's lack of consultation prior to the crisis,[77] and this would negate any goodwill obtained by Germany's support during the Bosnian crisis. In other words, it becomes clear during this crisis that while Germany might not abandon Austria-Hungary, it would not hesitate to drag its ally into war. Frank Anderson also suggests that the Russo-German discussion was partly a German reaction to Austria's willingness to drag Germany into conflict with Russia, suggesting that the Potsdam convention "furnished a lever against Austrian unruliness."[78]

Mercer claims that Germany did not give Austria a reputation for resolve after Bosnia and thus did not expect Austrian support during the Agadir Crisis.[79] Likewise, if Germany did not expect its allies to provide support because allies are always believed to be unreliable, then it should not punish them for unreliability during the crisis. Contrary to Mercer's argument, I suggest that Germany should have expected support from its ally, based on Austria-Hungary's support of Germany during the First Moroccan Crisis, not to mention Germany's whole-hearted support of Austria-Hungary over the Bosnian crisis. However, if Germany did not expect Austrian support, I posit that it would have been for some reason other than Austria's reputation, such as domestic turmoil or Austrian fears about dragging Russia into a war over Morocco.

We do see a clear shift in the German government's perception of Austria-Hungary's reliability after the crisis. In addition, Theobald von Bethmann-Hollweg, von Bülow's successor as German chancellor, said, "Let us hope that if there is a war the attack will be aimed against Austria which will then need our assistance and not against us so that it is not left to Austria to decide whether to be loyal to the alliance or not."[80] Bethmann-Hollweg eventually got his wish in 1914, because Austria-Hungary's resolve, rather than its reliability, was tested over the assassination of Archduke Franz Ferdinand in

76. Taylor, *Struggle for Mastery*, 468.

77. Mercer, *Reputation and International Politics*, 199.

78. Anderson and Hershey, *Handbook for the Diplomatic History*, 408.

79. Mercer, *Reputation and International Politics*, 148–149, 196–197.

80. Cited in Fischer, *War of Illusions*, 86. A slightly different version of this quote, but with the same sentiment regarding Austrian reliability is: "Should extreme things come to pass, it would be better if the first attack were directed against Austria, which will then need *our* help, and not against us, so that [the outcome] does not depend upon Austria's [decision] if it wants to be loyal." Konrad Jarausch, *The Enigmatic Chancellor: Bethmann Hollweg and the Hubris of Imperial Germany* (New Haven: Yale University Press, 1973), 131, cited in Mercer, *Reputation and International Politics*, 196–197.

1914, and it was Germany's reliability that was tested, just as it was during the Bosnia-Herzegovina Crisis. That this lack of support over Agadir lowered German perceptions of Austria-Hungary's reliability is further support of the premise that a state's behavior influences its reputation. The question is whether this translated into German behavior toward its allies.

Consequences of Austrian Behavior

Regardless of why Austria-Hungary failed to support Germany, the fact that Germany did not receive the level of support that it expected from its ally should have had a negative effect on the relationship between the two states. Balance of power theory can explain Austria's willingness to remain in the Triple Alliance. Balance of threat theory could conceivably explain realignment with the Triple Entente, to balance against Italy, or remaining in the Triple Alliance to balance against Russia. Binding theories also depend on who is perceived to be the greater threat. (If Italy, then staying in the Triple Alliance makes sense; if Russia, then we should have seen realignment, or at least a willingness to negotiate with Russia.)

I would expect Germany to withdraw from the Triple Alliance or demand more binding conditions. Contrary to my hypotheses on alliance termination, not only was the alliance not terminated but the Triple Alliance was renewed. Yet Germany's dealings—discussed earlier in this chapter—with all three of the Entente powers were a result of Austria's failure to support Germany during the Agadir Crisis. Consistent with the hypothesis on alliance variation, Austro-German military conversations increased the levels of delegation and obligation required of Austria-Hungary. Curiously, we see this with Austria-Hungary but less so with Italy. Likewise, I would also expect Italy to question Austria-Hungary's reliability as a result of its lack of support.

E. C. Helmreich also suggests that the military conversations that took place between the allies in November 1912 were not perceived as any type of extension to the treaty.[81] This effectively preserved German autonomy while drawing Austria-Hungary closer. There is also evidence that Austria-Hungary's leaders believed that Germany was loyal to the alliance. Just prior to the outbreak of the First World War, Count Ladislaus von Szögyény-Marich, the Austrian ambassador to Germany, suggested that "even if it [Austrian action against Serbia] should come to war between Austria and Russia, we could be convinced that Germany would stand by our side with her accustomed faithfulness as an ally."[82] This view was based primarily

81. E. C. Helmreich, "An Unpublished Report on Austro-German Military Conversations of November, 1912," *Journal of Modern History* 52 (June 1933), 205.

82. Cited in Taylor, *Struggle for Mastery,* 521.

on past German behavior in support of its ally and completely contradicts Mercer's general argument that allies always perceive each other as likely to back down in a crisis.

Italy

As a member of the Triple Alliance, Italy was obligated to support its ally in the crisis. However, Italy's agreement with France was also still valid. Therefore, nobody should have anticipated that Germany would receive Italian support, based on both its record in previous crises and on its other existing commitments. And, as expected, Italy once again failed to support Germany during the crisis. Again, the question is whether or not this affected Italy's relationship with either Germany or Austria-Hungary after the crisis.

As with his analysis of the First Moroccan Crisis, Mercer's discussion of the Agadir Crisis also omits Italy. Even though he ignores Italy's behavior during the crisis, we can again infer what his theory would suggest. As before, because Italy's failure to support its allies would be unfavorable, its behavior would again be explained by its reputation. But because Germany should not have expected support, it should not have been surprised by the lack of Italian support and not treated Italy differently after the crisis.

Explaining Italian Behavior

Balance of power theory would expect Italy to support its allies, given that the Triple Entente was more powerful than the Triple Alliance. Only balance of threat theory can claim to explain Italy's failure to support Germany during the crisis, since Italy was threatened by Austria-Hungary, and one of its main fears was being dragged into war against France and England. As a result, its unwillingness to support Germany against France is perfectly reasonable and predictable. But because of Italy's concerns about Austria-Hungary as a threat and getting dragged into a war by Germany, binding theory would expect Italy to have supported Germany in the hope that it would gain more control over Germany's behavior, possibly to prevent war with France and England.

Mercer's view of Italy does not differ dramatically from mine—all of Italy's allies should not expect it to be particularly reliable, and therefore they should not be surprised when it failed to support Germany during the crisis. Yet, as before, Mercer's argument cannot explain how Germany reacted to Italy's unreliability, since having no expectation of Italian support should not cause Italy's allies to alter the alliance as a result of its behavior.

In contrast, my hypotheses provide some explanation of the changes that occurred between Italy and its allies. Germany was unlikely to expect Italian support in the crisis, given that Italy repeatedly failed to support its allies in previous cases. But the failure to support Germany once again should have further diminished perceptions of Italian reliability, thus causing Germany and Austria-Hungary to demand still further changes to their relations with Italy that would continue to bind Italy even more to the Triple Alliance.

Consequences of Italian Behavior

Balance of power theory would expect Italy to remain a part of the alliance. Since Austria-Hungary posed the greatest threat to Italian interests, balance of threat theory would expect Italy to realign with the Triple Entente, while binding theories would expect Italy to draw closer to its allies after the crisis, especially to Austria-Hungary. What none of these conventional theories explain is the response of Italy's allies to its unreliability.

My hypotheses would expect Italy to lose its allies, or at the very least to be even more constrained by its allies. Challenging my hypotheses on alliance termination, as I discussed in the Austria-Hungary section above, the Triple Alliance was formally renewed for a third time. However, the German leadership did attempt to bind Italy more closely to the alliance. One example is the 2 August 1913 naval agreement between Germany and its two allies.[83] Another is the 11 March 1914 meeting between German and Italian military leaders in which they outlined the Italian military commitment.[84] Specifically, Italy's Third Army was pledged to assist Germany and would involve 200,000 soldiers, including 150,000 combatants. There was even a proposal that Italy might send troops to help Austria.[85] This suggests an increase in the precision of Italy's commitment to the Triple Alliance, but it did not require Germany or Austria-Hungary to give up any of their autonomy, since they were unlikely to have counted on those troops when developing their war plans.

Nevertheless, Italy's military promise amounted to nothing more than cheap talk, for it imposed no costs on Italy that would have prevented it from declaring neutrality at the outbreak of the First World War, or even from allying with the Entente powers. Greater integration of Triple Alliance

83. Alfred Pribram, *The Secret Treaties of Austria-Hungary, 1879–1914,* vol. 1, *Texts of the Treaties and Agreements* (Cambridge: Harvard University Press, 1920), 282–305.

84. George Manhart places this meeting in May 1914. Manhart, *Alliance and Entente,* 68–69.

85. William Askew, "The Austro-Italian Antagonism, 1896–1914," in *Power, Public Opinion, and Diplomacy: Essays in Honor of Eber Malcolm Carroll by his Former Students*, ed. Lillian Wallace and William Askew (Durham: Duke University Press, 1968), 181fn25; Luigi Albertini, *The Origins of the War of 1914,* vol. 1, trans. Isabella Massey (New York: Oxford University Press, 1957), 555–565.

forces might have prevented Italy from abandoning its allies. However, such a demand might also have pushed Italy out of the alliance altogether, and Germany was unwilling to risk that given its lack of strategic alternatives to an alliance with unreliable Italy.

What is interesting is Austria-Hungary's response. Italy's naval staff held formal conventions with Austria-Hungary in 1913, and an agreement was reached that provided for a union of the two fleets.[86] However, by 2 August 1914, tension between Italy and Austria-Hungary once again dominated their relations. Austria's prime minister, Karl von Stürgkh, even suggested that rather than wait for Italy to betray Austria, it would be better "to deceive her with a kind of secret agreement. . . . No diplomatic trick is too low in dealing with such brigands as the Italians now are." And, of course, Italy was already conducting negotiations with the Entente powers to intervene against Austria-Hungary.[87]

French Perceptions of Italian Behavior

It is also useful to briefly examine Franco-Italian relations in response to Italy's support during the crisis. France might have expected Italian support, given its behavior during the Algeciras conference. And, although Italy failed to support its Triple Alliance partner, it did support French control over Morocco. Nevertheless, much of the evidence suggests that France still viewed Italy as unreliable.[88] This seems to fit Mercer's argument that because Italian behavior benefitted the French, its actions were explained by situation, whereas the Germans saw Italian behavior as a function of unreliability since they viewed its actions unfavorably.

A third explanation is given by Paul Halpern, who suggests that while France was aware of the tension between Italy and Austria-Hungary, the French government was also suspicious of Italy's reliability as an ally.[89] The French were aware of Italy's willingness to abandon its allies when it was in its interest to do so. As a result, while France would have been pleased with Italian support, it would not have changed French perceptions, since to support France, Italy also would have to abandon an ally. As a result, I would not have expected anyone to fully trust Italy. This point challenges Mercer's assertion that the favorability of an act matters more than the state's reputation. Italy was perceived to be unreliable by all the

86. Paul Halpern, "The Anglo-French-Italian Naval Convention of 1915," *Historical Journal* 13, no. 1 (March 1970), 107.

87. Leo Valiani, "Italian-Austro-Hungarian Negotiations, 1914–1915," *Contemporary History* 1, no. 3 (July 1966), 119–120.

88. Halpern, "Anglo-French-Italian Naval Convention," 106.

89. Ibid.

Table 6.2. Review of chapter findings

	French allies			German allies	
Observation	**England[a] (up)**	**Russia[a] (mixed)**	**Italy[a] (mixed)**	**Austria-Hungary[a] (down)**	**Italy[a] (down)**
H1: alliance formation	N/A	+	N/A	N/A	N/A
H2: similar reliability	0	0	0	+	+
H3: lose abandoned ally	N/A	0	N/A	–	–
H4: lose other allies	N/A	0	N/A	–	–
H5: alliance variation	+	+	0	+	+

Note: N/A = not applicable to case; – = no support; 0 = mixed findings; + = strong support
[a] State (reliability level)

states, regardless of whether its actions were favorable or not, just as prior to signing the ententes, both France and Russia perceived England to be reliable because of its support for Japan during the Russo-Japanese War, even though that support was unfavorable to the Dual Alliance.

This fourth and final case study should provide the most difficult test of reputation, yet we continue to see a connection between a state's behavior in a crisis and its alliance autonomy after the crisis. (Table 6.2 summarizes the results from this chapter, which included five separate observations: France's three allies and Germany's two allies, counting Italy in both camps.)

The conventional wisdom is that the inflexibility of Europe's great power alliances contributed to the outbreak of the First World War. Although fears of states realigning with an adversary may have been low, there appeared to be a great deal of concern that an ally might remain neutral. As Taylor puts it: "The existing alliances were all precarious. Italy was only the extreme example—renewing the Triple Alliance and making exaggerated promises of military support to Germany on one side; seeking to negotiate a Mediterranean agreement with France and Great Britain on the other."[90] Ironically, this fear of abandonment—fed at least partly by the failure of several states to fully support their allies during the prewar crises—caused the alliances to become increasingly binding, which is ultimately what dragged all of the states into a general war.[91]

90. Taylor, *Struggle for Mastery*, 518.

91. This finding is consistent with Kenneth Waltz's argument about the instability of multipolar systems such as existed before the First World War, since his claim relies on the assertion that states followed inflexible military policies precisely because they knew the alliances were flexible. Kenneth Waltz, *Theory of International Politics* (New York: McGraw-Hill, 1979), 166–167.

England did not try to find any allies, so this case does not test the first hypothesis. The British remained in their ententes with states having mixed reliability. Yet I do not consider that to completely falsify hypothesis 2, since the alternative was an alliance with even less-reliable states (or isolation). The British case does provide interesting results for alliance termination, because both Russia and France had mixed reliability, so one might expect a state to withdraw from the alliance. England's decision not to withdraw but to pursue an agreement with Germany similar to the agreements signed between Germany and the other members of the Triple Entente is decent support for the argument. However, England did this not as a result of the crisis but as a result of its allies already pursuing similar agreements. Therefore, I do not consider this to be a completely valid test.

Although the changes that did occur to the Anglo-French relationship do not strictly fit my hypotheses on alliance variation, since British reliability should not have led to any loss of its autonomy as we found in previous chapters, the relative change of autonomy is critical. And compared to Russia, which provided much less support to France, British autonomy remained relatively high.

Russia lost a great deal of its alliance autonomy because of its repeated lack of full, open support. Despite being able to preserve the entente with England and the alliance with France, the British continued to avoid a full alliance with Russia. In addition, the high costs imposed on Russia after the crisis strongly support my hypothesis on alliance variation. Both of Russia's partners also considered withdrawing from their agreements but they avoided doing so, probably because of the lack of reliable alternatives as well as Russia's willingness to give up more autonomy to preserve its relations with England and France.

The Russians, like the British, were also worried about France's reliability and its willingness to throw over its allies in favor of an agreement with Germany. French negotiations during the two Moroccan crises were less responsible for this reputation than its repeated willingness to negotiate with Germany, even while Russia was involved in a crisis with Austria-Hungary. As a result, even though none of the Entente states were interested in an alliance with Germany, they all expressed an interest in signing some type of agreement with Germany rather than risk being abandoned by other members of the Entente. As a result of these alliance choices, many of which were a consequence of reputation, the Entente grew more binding, although Germany and Austria-Hungary continued to see it as something that could be challenged and torn apart.

As for the Triple Alliance, more changes occurred between Austria-Hungary and Germany than between Italy and Germany, even though Germany received little support from either of its allies. It may be that since Germany did not expect to receive Italian support, the lack of support had little effect on Germany's perception of Italian reliability. In contrast, because Austria-Hungary's loyalty was expected based on its past behavior, its lack of support had a more pronounced effect on German perceptions of its ally's reliability. This at least explains why Austria-Hungary's autonomy suffered more than Italy's. In addition, consistent with my scope conditions, since Italy did have agreements with France, it had to be dealt with carefully or Germany risked losing an ally, whereas Austria-Hungary had few other alliance options and could be treated more harshly for its abandonment of Germany.

As we found in previous chapters, the Italian case is the least supportive of my arguments. But the Italian case still provides strong support for the hypotheses on alliance variation. Most prominent is the added precision resulting from the specific promise of Italian troops to its allies in the event of war. Other measures added more obligation and delegation to both Italy and Austria-Hungary during the three-way naval agreement.

Not all of the hypotheses are supported, and the arguments about alliances ending as a result of a state's unreliability once again are the weakest hypotheses in the chapter. The hypothesis on alliance variation still receives considerable support even as Europe was growing closer to the outbreak of the First World War.

7

Summary and Expansion of Findings

A good name is more valuable than money.

Publius Cyrus, 42 b.c.

The puzzle posed at the beginning of this book was whether a state's reputation influences the behavior of other states, given the differences between the conventional wisdom and more critical scholarship on reputation published in the 1990s and the first decade of the twenty-first century. The general argument of this book is that states with reputations for being reliable allies will have greater autonomy in making their alliance choices than states with unreliable reputations. Although some of the specific hypotheses tested are more successful than others, the cases examined clearly show that a state's reputation does influence its alliance autonomy. As a result, if government leaders care about their freedom of action in making alliance decisions, then they will pay attention to their state's reputation as an ally.

In this concluding chapter I will first summarize my findings from the four case study chapters, as well as addressing one of the findings that was not one of my original hypotheses—regarding the connection between reputation and the outbreak of conflicts—but which provides a new perspective on the outbreak of the First World War. I then apply my findings to two later cases in which reputation should influence state behavior—the North Atlantic Treaty Organization (NATO) during the cold war and the U.S. "war on terror." This is done to illustrate the applicability of my findings for other eras, including both bipolar and unipolar international systems. Finally, I discuss some other ways in which scholars can expand on this work, as well as additional areas of international relations that would benefit from further research on reputation, such as nonmilitary agreements and dealing with various forms of internal violence, including terrorism.

Summary of Findings from Case Studies

To generate hypotheses for testing the role of reliability on state behavior, I have drawn heavily from the business literature, where positive reputations are believed to be crucial to the health of a firm, and where numerous scholarly works support the validity of that belief. If actors in the economic market are influenced by reputation, even though their commitments can be legally enforced, then states in the international political arena should also be influenced by reputation, since international commitments are self-enforcing and since prior behavior is frequently the only way to evaluate a state's intentions under the condition of anarchy in the international system. Alliances in particular can improve a state's security, but they can also leave a state more vulnerable. As a result, there should be observable differences in a state's behavior toward those with reputations for reliability compared to those with reputations for being unreliable.

My general argument is that as a state's reliability is perceived to increase, it will have greater autonomy in its alliance choices. In contrast, as a state's reliability is perceived to decline, it will be forced to give up autonomy while its allies will be less willing to part with their own. To test these general claims, I devised the five hypotheses presented in chapter 2. The first two hypotheses address gaps in our understanding of alliance formation: specifically, how states choose between different alliance strategies, such as balancing and bandwagoning, and also how they choose their alliance partners. Balance of power, balance of threat, and binding theories help us identify some of the strategies behind a state's alliance choices, but they do not always explain situations in which states prefer one strategy over another, nor can they explain why states sometimes opt to not ally at all. In addition, even if we can identify why a state selects a particular strategy, it is often difficult to explain its choice of partners or the timing of its decisions.

My first hypothesis predicts that states with a reputation for being unreliable will have more trouble finding allies than states with a reputation for reliability. *Ceteris paribus*, if states have a choice in alliance partners, they should prefer to ally with the more reliable state, since an agreement with that ally is more likely to enhance the state's security. The market analogy behind this hypothesis is that firms with positive reputations have an easier time attracting employees, customers, and investors. If true, then states may balance against power or threat if a potential partner is reliable. If not, then bandwagoning or buck-passing will be safer moves.

My second hypothesis on alliance formation is based on the observation that even unreliable states do sometimes find allies. As such, I draw on the market observation that reputations are easily transferred from one actor to another. The implication of this in business is that reputable actors tend to interact only with other reputable actors, while those with negative reputations are left to deal with one another. As a result, I hypothesize that reliable states are more likely to ally with other reliable states, leaving unreliable states to ally with each other.

The second category of alliance behavior focuses on the choice to end an alliance. There are a number of explanations for the duration of alliances, but scholars still have trouble explaining specific cases of alliances falling apart (or being preserved when we expect them to end). In business, firms that suffer a decline in their reputation lose customers, employees, and investors. If this translates into international relations, then states that fail to honor their commitments should have trouble keeping their allies. Hypothesis 3 suggests that states will lose the allies that they abandon. This particular argument focuses only on the ally and the state it abandons, but it is also plausible that abandoning one ally will affect a state's other alliances. As a result, hypothesis 4 tests the more general argument that unreliable states lose allies, even beyond those that are abandoned.

The third category focuses on the variation that exists between alliance institutions. The business literature identifies a number of ways in which firms with a positive reputation have greater freedom, not only to act but also to ask more of their employees and consumers. As a result, reliable states should also have greater freedom of action within their alliances. Hypothesis 5 tests whether or not reliable states have more autonomy within their alliances than do unreliable states.

Chapters 3 through 6 test these five hypotheses against four case studies, each of which provides multiple observations of Europe's great powers before the First World War. Because the results of the cases are examined at the end of each chapter, here I only briefly discuss the most relevant points of the cases, as well as how each of the five hypotheses fared.

Chapter 3 applied my hypotheses to England's search for an ally at the beginning of the twentieth century. The British government realized that its long-held policy of splendid isolation was becoming dangerous because its global interests were growing more vulnerable to its European rivals. The British first approached Germany for an alliance, since they had a common interest in checking Russian expansion into Asia. However, the British ultimately abandoned hopes of an alliance, not only because German demands would have required the British to give up too much autonomy but also because the German government proved itself unwilling to support England against Russia. As a result, the British opted for an alliance with Japan instead.

In one of the best examples of reputation influencing state behavior, the Japanese evaluated British reliability and offered an alliance only after Britain's reputation was confirmed. Moreover, Britain's "benevolent neutrality" helped contribute to the Japanese victory over Russia, which rewarded the British with a greater Japanese commitment. Another consequence of Britain's reliability was the development of an entente with France, which feared that its commitment to Russia would bring about a war with England.

Shortly thereafter, British reputation was tested again when Germany and France clashed over Morocco. This Moroccan crisis, the subject of chapter 4, allowed me to examine how the behavior of states during a crisis influences their relations with allies. In this case, France received solid support from England but only mixed support from Russia, since the tsar also negotiated a treaty with the German kaiser. Although the British did appear to lose some autonomy after the crisis, they preserved much more freedom of action than Russia did. While this does not perfectly conform to the hypotheses, it still suggests that a state's autonomy is influenced by its reliability as an ally. Moreover, British support for France helped generate Russian interest in a similar agreement with the British, resulting in the Triple Entente.

The Germans also received full support from Austria-Hungary, but Italy voted against Germany at the Algeciras conference. Although Italy was able to preserve its place in the Triple Alliance, this is partly explained by Italy also having an agreement with France and that it had made it clear to its allies well before the crisis that it would not join in a war against France. As a result, Germany did not expect Italian support and therefore did not perceive Italy's behavior to be a form of abandonment. Nevertheless, Italy still suffered a loss of its autonomy in order to remain in the Triple Alliance.

Chapter 5 begins with Austria-Hungary's annexation of Bosnia and the Russian attempt to reverse the move. The British once again supported their ally, but the French failed to support Russia and even signed an agreement with Germany over Morocco in exchange for French neutrality in the crisis. As expected, the British were able to preserve more autonomy in their relations with Russia than were the French. Austria-Hungary received support from Germany. In fact, it was the German ultimatum that finally forced Russia to back down. In contrast, the Italians once again failed to support an ally. While Germany was able to preserve its autonomy, the Italians were again asked to increase their obligation to the Triple Alliance. Germany and Austria-Hungary also continued to discuss fitting punishments for their unreliable Italian partner, which even included invasion. However, the lack of other possible allies for Germany probably prevented Italy from being punished too harshly for its lack of reliability.

The final case study chapter focused on yet another clash between France and Germany over Morocco. The proximity of this crisis to the First World War, as well as the conventional wisdom that the divisions in Europe were growing increasingly less flexible, suggest that this should be the most difficult test of reputation. While the hypotheses are less successful in chapter 6 than in the previous three chapters, reputation continues to be for certain alliance choices. This time Germany was abandoned by of its allies, resulting in a loss of autonomy for both Austria-Hungary and Italy within the Triple Alliance. The French received strong support from England but very little public support from the Russians. As a result, both France and England questioned Russian reliability and subsequently negotiated commercial treaties with Germany. The French also demanded that Russia pay more to maintain the relationship, specifically insisting that Russia accelerate the construction of its strategic railways and increase its military manpower. In contrast, changes to the Anglo-French Entente made France even more dependent on the British without seriously decreasing British autonomy.

While my hypotheses do not explain every alliance choice made by the great powers, they fit a number of actions that cannot be explained by conventional alliance theories alone. Also, if we take all of the cases together and focus on the overall reliability of each state, it is clear that the British should have had the best reputation since they consistently supported their allies, while Italy should have had the worst since it failed to do so in every case. In between those two, from most reliable to least reliable, are Germany, Austria-Hungary, Russia, and France. If we apply the hypotheses on alliance variation to these states over the eleven years covered in this book, Britain ended up with the highest level of autonomy, while Russia, France, and Italy had the least autonomy. Therefore, taking all the cases together as part of the pre–First World War environment, it is clear that the states that supported their allies preserved the most autonomy, while those that lost the most were the ones that failed to live up to their commitments.

Throughout my four cases, the hypotheses on alliance formation and variation received the strongest support. Whereas the least successful hypotheses are the two related to alliance termination. (Table 7.1 provides the comparative numbers for each hypothesis in each case.) The first set of numbers in each box represents the number of observations in the chapter that show full support, mixed support, or no support for that hypothesis. The two percentages in each box represent, first, the percentage of observations that show full support, and then the percentage that do not show any support.

The most successful hypothesis overall is hypothesis 5 on variation (95.2% of the observations show full support), followed by hypothesis 1 on alliance formation (72.7%). The second hypothesis on alliance formation receives full support on 38.1 percent of the cases. While these numbers are not statistically significant, especially considering the relatively low number of observations that I was able to examine, they do represent substantive significance, particularly given that these cases were selected to be difficult tests of reputation. But if we combine the observations that show full support with those that show mixed support, then several of the hypotheses are

Table 7.1. Summary of results

	Chapter 3	Chapter 4	Chapter 5	Chapter 6	Total
Alliance formation					
H1	5/1/0	1/1/0	1/0/1	1/0/0	8/2/1
	83.3%	50.0%	50.0%	100%	72.7%
	0.0%	0.0%	50.0%	0.0%	9.1%
H2	4/4/0	1/3/0	1/3/0	2/3/0	8/13/0
	66.7%	25.0%	25.0%	40.0%	38.1%
	0.0%	0.0%	0.0%	0.0%	0.0%
Alliance termination					
H3	1/1/0	3/1/1	0/1/1	0/1/2	4/4/4
	50.0%	60.0%	0.0%	0.0%	33.3%
	0.0%	20.0%	50.0%	66.7%	33.3%
H4	0/0/0	2/0/1	0/0/2	0/1/2	2/1/5
	0.0%	66.7%	0.0%	0.0%	25.0%
	0.0%	33.3%	100.0%	66.7%	62.5%
Alliance variation					
H5	8/0/0	4/0/0	4/0/0	4/1/0	20/1/0
	100.0%	50%	100.0%	80.0%	95.2%
	0.0%	0.0%	0.0%	20.0%	0.0%
Total	18/6/0	11/5/2	6/4/4	7/6/4	42/21/10
	75.0%	61.1%	42.9%	41.2%	57.5%
	0.0%	11.1%	28.6%	23.5%	13.7%

Note: H = hypothesis. The first numbers in each cell indicate the number of observations that are successful/with mixed success/failed tests (i.e., chapter 3 sees a total of 18 successful observations, 6 with mixed success, and 0 failed tests).

above, or very near, what would be considered statistical significance in a large-n study (H1 = 90.9%; H2 = 100.0%; H5 = 100.0%).

The limited support for both of the hypotheses on alliance termination is interesting and useful because it is partly consistent with Mercer's findings, to the extent that he actually tests alliance reliability. What these results suggest is that states may not need to be concerned about losing their allies simply because they fail to support them. If we were to stop our analysis there, it would fit with Mercer's overall argument that states should not be concerned about their reputations. Digging deeper into how alliances are designed and transform, though, tells us more about the importance of reputation. Specifically, as my hypothesis on alliance variation illustrates, even if unreliable states do not lose their allies, there is still some utility in preserving a reputation for reliability, at least if leaders value freedom of action in their state's alliance choices.

As expected, there is also a clear decline in the validity of my hypotheses with each successive crisis, from 75.0 percent receiving full support and 0.0 percent receiving no support in chapter 3, to only 41.2 percent receiving full support and 23.5 percent failing to receive support in chapter 6. This is consistent with my contention that as a European war became more likely, reputation became less important than other factors that influence state alliance behavior, such as power, threat, and geography. Another explanation for this decline is that as a state's alliance options shrink, reputation's influence on state behavior also falls. If a state has only one potential ally, that ally's reputation will be a minor factor in the decision to ally, or to remain allied with it. However, as a state's options increase, it can afford to be more selective, which will include a preference for allying with the most reliable state that can help it attain its strategic goals. States with options can also afford to impose harsher punishments on their unreliable allies.

This may explain why the findings for the Triple Entente generally follow my hypotheses better than those for the Triple Alliance; including chapters 4 through 6, the observations involving the Triple Entente states show either full or mixed support in 22 out of 23 observations (or 95.7% of the time), while those involving the Triple Alliance show full or mixed support in only 13 out of 22 observations (or 59.1% of the time). Once France and Russia allied, and once England abandoned its negotiations with Germany, the perception was that Austria-Hungary was Germany's only protection from isolation. As a result, it makes sense that Germany was unable to be overly harsh with its allies and risk alienating them. In contrast, the Entente powers all believed that they had other options, and thus they assigned greater importance to the reliability of their allies.

This finding has implications for other time periods. According to Snyder, fears of abandonment are considerably diminished during bipolar periods because the possibility of realignment is much lower.[1] If true, then reputation should be less important during the cold war than in the multipolar period leading up to the First World War. On the other hand, James Alt, Randall Calvert, and Brian Humes contend that reputations are important for hegemons,[2] but the unanswered question is whether a hegemon needs to care about the reliability of its allies. Therefore, future research should expand on the cases studied here to include periods in which the international system was organized differently, such as the tripolar interwar years, the bipolar cold war, and the unipolar post–cold war era. I explore this in more detail in the brief application of my findings to the case of NATO and to the war on terror.

1. Glenn Snyder, *Alliance Politics* (Ithaca: Cornell University Press, 1997).

2. James Alt, Randall Calvert and Brian Humes, "Reputation and Hegemonic Stability: A Game-Theoretic Analysis," *American Political Science Review* 82, no. 2 (June 1988), 445–466.

Reliability and Moral Hazard

The common thread between all of the hypotheses examined in the previous chapters is the importance that states place on their autonomy. Although I suggest several ways in which having a reputation for reliability improves a state's freedom of action, a potential downside of reliability emerges in several of the cases. A moral hazard problem exists when an actor that is insured is more likely to take risks, which means the insurer will receive more claims than it bargained for. Individuals with no-fault automobile insurance and those with more safety features on their cars are more likely to drive recklessly than those without.[3] The parallel to this in international politics seems to be that when a state has reliable allies, it displays a greater willingness to challenge or stand up to its rivals than it would if it were alone or if it could not count on its allies.

This point is politically important because if a reliable reputation encourages a state's allies to challenge adversaries, then some leaders will assign less value to their state's reliability, particularly if they are more concerned about entrapment than they are about abandonment. In addition, this point may help explain findings by several scholars who suggest that there is a strong correlation between the existence of alliances and the outbreak of wars. Karl Deutsch and David Singer argue that alliances reduce the opportunities for interaction in the international system and therefore enhance the prospects for conflict.[4] Bruce Bueno de Mesquita contends that states often have a positive value from attacking their own allies, and that as a result wars among allies are three times more likely than chance would predict.[5] Making more nuanced arguments, Ido Oren finds that alliance membership contributes to the expansion of wars rather than their outbreak, and Brett Ashley Leeds finds that the connection between alliances and war has to do with the nature of the alliance, focusing on the level of commitment.[6] Jack Levy contends that the relationship between alliance formation and war is

3. David Loughran, *The Effect of No-Fault Auto Insurance on Driver Behavior and Auto Accidents in the United States* (Santa Monica, CA: RAND, 2001); Russell Sobel and Todd Nesbit, "Automobile Safety Regulation and the Incentive to Drive Recklessly: Evidence from NASCAR," *Southern Economic Journal* 74, no. 1 (July 2007), 71–84. Charles Cohen and Eric Werker also show how the presence of international aid decreases the likelihood that a government will prepare well for natural disasters. Charles Cohen and Eric Werker, "The Political Economy of 'Natural Disasters,'" *Journal of Conflict Resolution* 52, no. 6 (December 2008), 795–819.

4. Karl Deutsch and David Singer, "Multipolar Power Systems and International Stability," *World Politics* 16, no. 3 (April 1964), 390–406.

5. Bruce Bueno de Mesquita, *The War Trap* (New Haven: Yale University Press, 1981).

6. Ido Oren, "The War Proneness of Alliances," *Journal of Conflict Resolution* 34, no. 2 (June 1990), 208–233; Brett Ashley Leeds, "Do Alliances Deter Aggression?: The Influence of Military Alliances on the Initiation of Militarized Interstate Disputes," *American Journal of Political Science* 47, no. 3 (June 2003), 427–439.

spurious, because alliances often form in response to rising tensions and anticipation of war.[7] Still another possibility is that the formation of an alliance creates a security dilemma that compels other states to act, either building up their own military capabilities or creating counterbalancing coalitions, either of which can result in a higher incidence of war.[8]

The explanation I offer here is that the scholars who find a connection between alliances and war are capturing a moral hazard problem associated with being a reliable ally. The cases here show several examples where expectations of allied support did lead to tension between adversaries, while expectations of not getting support led states to back down. From chapter 3 it is apparent that Japan was emboldened to challenge Russia, not just by the alliance with England itself, but specifically because of British reliability. The Japanese belief that their ally would honor its obligation and prevent other states from supporting Russia played a major role in Japan's initial decision to offer an alliance, and then it contributed to its decision to attack Russia on 8 February 1904. If the British had been perceived to be less reliable, the Japanese might have been more reluctant to engage the Russians, therefore reducing the likelihood that England would be drawn into war. At the same time, the alliance with Japan might not have been concluded in the first place, and the British would have been forced to either remain neutral or to ally with an unreliable Germany on German terms.

The Entente Cordiale also appears to have emboldened France against Germany, because the French now had a more reliable ally (at least regarding Morocco) than Russia had been. Mercer suggests France and England were not seen as resolved or reliable by the Germans because their behavior was explained through situation. Yet he also provides several examples of how England's support for France was what made France stand up to Germany. For instance, he cites Holstein: "As soon as France is no longer sure of having the English fleet at her side in case of war, she will pursue a peaceful attitude."[9] Not only does this illustrate how the French perceived British reliability but it also illustrates how British reliability greatly influenced

7. Jack Levy, "Alliance Formation and War Behavior: An Analysis of the Great Powers, 1495–1975," *Journal of Conflict Resolution* 25, no. 4 (December 1981), 581–613.

8. Hans Morgenthau accepted that alliances could create uncertainty about the balance of power that could lead to wars of miscalculation. At the same time, he recognized it could also make leaders more cautious. Hans Morgenthau, *Politics among Nations: The Struggle for Power and Peace,* brief ed., rev. Kenneth Thompson. (Boston: McGraw-Hill, 1993[1948]), 205–210. See also Morton A. Kaplan, *System and Process in International Politics* (New York: Wiley, 1957), 24; Ole Holsti, P. T. Hopmann, and J. D. Sullivan, *United and Disintegration in International Alliances: Comparative Studies* (New York: Wiley and Sons, 1973), 33; Quincy Wright, *A Study of War* (Chicago: University of Chicago Press, 1965), 774.

9. Jonathan Mercer, *Reputation and International Politics* (Ithaca: Cornell University Press, 1996), 94.

This finding also indicates that the key for governments that wish to avoid war may be to make allies believe that they are relatively unreliable, while convincing adversaries that they are highly reliable. Unfortunately, the situation leading up to the First World War was the exact opposite—each state believed it had at least one reliable ally and one that was bound tightly to them, while simultaneously believing that their adversaries' allies were unreliable because of past failure to support their ally.

From Agadir to World War

It is worth making some additional comments about the period between the Agadir Crisis and the outbreak of the First World War. The conventional wisdom has been that the inflexibility of the alliances was one of the main causes of the First World War. However, I suggest that while fears of an ally realigning with the other side may have been low, there was certainly a great deal of concern that an ally might remain neutral. As Taylor puts it: "The existing alliances were all precarious. Italy was only the extreme example—renewing the Triple Alliance and making exaggerated promises of military support to Germany on one side; seeking to negotiate a Mediterranean agreement with France and Great Britain on the other."[14] Ironically, this fear caused the alliances to become increasingly binding, which ultimately dragged all of the states into a general war.

Britain, as usual, supported France at Agadir, and was rewarded with a greater French obligation while being able to preserve its autonomy. While "Poincaré proposed to declare that England and France would 'co-operate, if necessary, to maintain the European balance.' Grey would only express a wish 'to co-operate in maintaining European peace.' "[15] At the same time, the British appeared much closer to France than to Russia, particularly once tensions reemerged over Persia.

On the other hand, while England supported Russia during the Bosnian crisis, France did not. This contributed to Russia's willingness to negotiate with Germany, which created a slippery slope, because Russian agreements with Germany lowered English perception of Russia's reliability. As a result, the German government hoped to take advantage of this, believing that as long as France was left alone, Great Britain could be turned away from Russia.[16]

According to Taylor, "the Triple Entente was far from being a perfect arrangement from the British point of view. They had to be loyal to France; yet Russia was not loyal to them. Improved relations with Germany would,

14. A. J. P. Taylor, *The Struggle for Mastery in Europe, 1848–1918* (Oxford: Clarendon Press, 1954), 518.
15. Ibid., 478.
16. Ibid., 519.

it was hoped, lessen the tension between Germany and France; at the same time, they would make it easier to oppose Russia in Persia."[17] Therefore, because of French and Russian action in failing to fully support each other and negotiating with Germany, even the British sought to hedge their bets by pursuing an agreement with Germany.

Lord Chancellor Richard Haldane went to Germany from 8–12 February 1912, where he offered colonial concessions and a political agreement if the German naval program was not increased. However, the Germans wanted a promise of neutrality during a continental war rather than a simple declaration of friendship.[18] The French were alarmed by these talks, which may have been one objective. But, despite Britain's willingness to negotiate with Germany, the British were unwilling to sign any agreement that was perceived to weaken the Entente. As a result, the negotiations with Germany ended in March with the British moving even more toward France. In contrast, the French reached an agreement with Germany over the Baghdad Railway in February 1914. Only then did the British finally reach an agreement with Germany in June. From the German point-of-view, both seemed to be siding with Germany against Russia on the issue of Turkey.[19] I contend that from the outside this appeared to weaken the Entente and made a challenge by the Central Powers more likely.

In addition, perceived cleavages in the Triple Alliance appeared to be an opportunity for the Entente. Italy's lack of reliability is well-established, and the failure of Austria-Hungary to support Germany at Agadir may have signaled to the Entente that the Central Powers were growing farther apart. And while Germany's having dealings with all three of the Entente powers may have been a result of Austria's failure to support Germany during the Agadir Crisis, the effects are debatable. They may have lowered Austria-Hungary's perceptions of German reliability. For instance, E. C. Helmreich suggests that the Austrian foreign office was uncertain that it would receive German support throughout the 1912–13 Balkan Wars. Moreover, he argues that the military conversations that took place between the allies in November 1912 were not perceived as any type of extension to the treaty.[20]

Other sources suggest that Austria-Hungary's leaders believed that Germany was loyal to the alliance, based primarily on German behavior in support of its ally during the Bosnia-Herzegovina Crisis.[21]

17. Ibid., 477.

18. Richard Haldane, *Before the War* (London: Cassell and Company, 1920), 103–112, 145–148; G. P. Gooch, *Before the War: Studies in Diplomacy*, vol. 2, *The Coming of the Storm* (London: Longmans, Green 1938), 82–86, 227–238; Taylor, *Struggle for Mastery*, 477.

19. Taylor, *Struggle for Mastery*, 518.

20. E. C. Helmreich, "An Unpublished Report on Austro-German Military Conversations of November, 1912," *Journal of Modern History* 5, no. 2 (June 1933), 205.

21. Cited in Taylor, *Struggle for Mastery*, 521.

As for Italy, its naval staff held formal conventions with Austria-Hungary in 1913, and an agreement was reached that provided for a union of the two fleets.[22] However, by 2 August 1914, tension between Italy and Austria-Hungary once again dominated their relations.[23] And, of course, Italy was already conducting negotiations with the Entente to intervene against Austria-Hungary.

Most accounts of the causes of the First World War involve some mention of Germany's blank check, its guarantee to support Austria in 1914. Based on Germany's prior behavior during the Bosnian crisis and changes to their relationship, Austria clearly found this promise reliable and was therefore willing to go to the brink of war. In addition, the British have taken some of the blame for not issuing a stern enough warning to Germany. However, I suggest that Britain's prior behavior should have been enough to convince the European powers of its reliability. The real weakness in the Triple Entente was the perceived lack of French and Russian reliability—Russia's Björko Treaty negotiation with Germany during the First Moroccan Crisis, France's lack of support during the Bosnia-Herzegovina Crisis (including the Casablanca agreement with Germany over Morocco), and Russia's agreement with Germany at Potsdam along with its mixed support for France during the Agadir Crisis. This history created the belief in the German and Austrian governments that France and Russia might not support each other in war, especially if they could be enticed to remain neutral.

Although increased commitments to each other may have further improved Russia's perception of French reliability, it also ultimately encouraged Russia to begin the mobilization against Austria-Hungary that eventually plunged Europe into general war. Yet Germany's perception was that France would continue to abandon its allies if it meant achieving French interests. These contradictory images of French reliability may have prompted Germany to push for war, whereas a better French reputation might have deterred the July 1914 crisis from escalating. In addition, Russian negotiations with Germany over Central Asia were conducted without British knowledge, whereas the British were themselves hamstrung by the Anglo-Russian Entente and their unwillingness to violate the agreement. In November 1911, for example, Grey warned the Russian minister in London that the government might be forced to disavow Russian activities that potentially destroyed the entente.[24] At the same time, had the British been

22. Paul Halpern, "The Anglo-French-Italian Naval Convention of 1915," *Historical Journal* 13, no. 1 (March 1970), 107.

23. Leo Valiani, "Italian-Austro-Hungarian Negotiations, 1914–1915," *Contemporary History* 1, no. 3 (July 1966), 119–120.

24. The British government was also limited in its dealings with Russia in terms of what could be negotiated, owing to its commitments to Japan. Ira Klein, "The Anglo-Russian Convention and the Problem of Central Asia, 1870–1914," *Journal of British Studies* 11, no. 1 (November 1971), 126–128.

less reliable, the Russians might have been less willing to challenge Austria in 1914.

Before the war, both sides believed they would receive support from their allies in war, either because of their prior willingness to honor commitments (Britain), their lack of alternatives (Germany and Austria-Hungary), or because of the institutional changes that were made (France, Russia, and Italy). Yet both sides viewed the other alliance as likely to fall apart. Because the causes of the First World War are highly overdetermined, I make no grand claims about this argument other than to suggest that it is interesting enough to warrant future research.

State Reliability during other Time Periods

Before turning to some of the policy implications of my findings, I briefly discuss two later cases and how applying the findings from this book helps evaluate the importance of reliability during other time periods, under different international conditions. Specifically, I discuss the role of state reputation on and within NATO, and on the war on terror initiated by the United States after the 9/11 terrorist attacks.

North Atlantic Treaty Organization

A discussion of the influence of reliability during the cold war could be a book in itself. Here, I simply focus on some of the implications of my findings to better explain the behavior of NATO states during the cold war. Despite the bipolar nature of the system, I expect states during the cold war to respond to concerns about reliability much the same way states did prior to the First World War. While the United States and its allies were not particularly concerned about any states realigning with the Soviet Union, there was concern about states pursuing neutrality. Punishment for unreliability would not have been too severe, and we should find little support for the hypotheses on alliance termination. Yet, I still expect the relationships to transform as a result of shifts in reliability—particularly in terms of obligation, precision, and delegation.

The hypotheses on alliance formation are not only useful for explaining the initial establishment of NATO in 1949, given the vague nature of the North Atlantic Treaty, but also the conditions under which other states were later admitted into the alliance, namely, Greece and Turkey (both in 1952), West Germany (1955), Spain (1982), and several former Soviet republics and Eastern Bloc states after the cold war.[25] While early expansions of NATO

25. These included the Czech Republic, Hungary, and Poland (1999), Bulgaria, Estonia, Latvia, Lithuania, Romania, Slovakia, and Slovenia (2004), and Albania and Croatia (2009).

were primarily based on strategic interests to counter Soviet influence and power in Europe, later expansion, beginning with Spain, appears to heavily focus on the democratic nature of the government. This ties to reputation in that Kurt Gaubatz and Brett Ashley Leeds both find that democracies are generally better allies,[26] which suggests that perceptions of reliability changed with the democratization of Spain and later entrants, making them more acceptable as allies.

One question is whether the other states that were brought into the alliance for strategic reasons—for example, Germany, Turkey, and Greece—were asked to pay more to ensure their reliability in the alliance? One of the main promises made by West Germany was to rearm itself (obligation), as well as its acceptance of continued NATO troops on the ground in West Germany (delegation). Likewise, French calls for a European Defense Community would have put the German military under direct EDC control (delegation). The German constitution also prohibited any offensive military action (precision), suggesting that concerns by some NATO members about German reputation were as much about Germany's history of aggression as the possibility it might not support other NATO states against the Soviet Union.

NATO's cohesion was also tested on several occasions, which provide useful extensions of my hypotheses on alliance variation. Although the initial treaty had fairly vague precision and limited obligation for any of the members, there were doubts throughout the cold war about U.S. reliability—its willingness to honor the agreement, especially if it meant "trading New York for Paris,"[27] as well as concerns about the United States dragging its allies into an unwanted war.[28] There are four cases in particular that should be illustrative tests of reputation. First of all, U.S. support for Germany during the Berlin airlift (June 1948–September 1949) should have enhanced U.S. reputation and therefore allowed the United States to retain existing levels of autonomy. Conversely, lack of support for England and France during the Suez Crisis (July 1956–March 1957) should have hurt U.S. reliability and generated calls for greater U.S. obligation, precision, and delegation. The Bay of Pigs invasion

26. Kurt Gaubatz, "Democratic States and Commitment in International Relations," *International Organization* 50, no. 1 (Winter 1996), 109–139; Brett Ashley Leeds, "Alliance Reliability in Times of War: Explaining State Decisions to Violate Treaties," *International Organization* 57, no. 4 (Fall 2003), 801–827.

27. A phrase generally attributed to Charles de Gaulle, president of France from 1959 to 1969, which illustrates the concern among many Europeans that the U.S. would allow the Soviet Union to take western Europe rather than risk a nuclear exchange that would destroy the United States.

28. Drew Middleton, "Global Reaction; Allies Rally to the U.S. Cause but Neutrals Are Less Sure," *New York Times,* 17 July 1960; Drew Middleton, "British Note Peril," *New York Times,* 23 October 1962; Joseph Biden, Jr., "Calming the Allies' Jitters," *New York Times,* 3 February 1988.

(April 1961) and the Cuban Missile Crisis (October 1962) should have resulted in increased U.S. obligation and precision and lower delegation, since the crises could have dragged NATO into a shooting war. Finally, the Vietnam War (1964–1973) could have had two different effects on U.S. reliability. On the one hand, because there was a risk of escalation, there could have been fears of the United States entrapping its allies. On the other hand, because the United States illustrated its willingness to fight for ten years and lose more than 58,000 lives over a relatively unimportant ally (at least in strategic terms),[29] we should also see other allies of the United States assign it greater reliability and thus grant it more autonomy.

As just one example of how these events influenced the alliance, within one year of the Suez Crisis, France wanted NATO to expand to include French territories outside the North Atlantic area, such as Algeria.[30] Failing to obtain these changes to the alliance, France then proceeded to develop an independent defense, including nuclear weapons.[31] The French eventually announced withdrawal from NATO's integrated military command on 12 March 1966 (to be completed by 1969).[32] Although it did not withdraw from the entire alliance, and did support the United States during the Cuban Missile Crisis, France's decisions were consistent with a perceived drop in U.S. reliability.[33]

Further analysis of NATO and other cold war alliances, such as the Southeast Asia Treaty Organization, are likely to illustrate a similar level of support for my findings.[34] Likewise, building on my findings about the moral hazard of reliability, it would be useful in future work to identify whether cold war shifts from détente to tension corresponded with

29. Figures taken from, "U.S. Military Operations: Casualty Breakdown," http://www.globalsecurity.org/military/ops/casualties.htm, accessed 1 March 2010.

30. Harold Callender, "The Question of Algeria," *New York Times,* 1 April 1956.

31. Kathleen Teltsch, "France to Develop Her Own Atom Bomb in Absence of Arms Pact, U.N. is Told," *New York Times,* 23 October 1957; Hanson Baldwin, "French Nuclear Force," *New York Times,* 8 January 1963.

32. Henry Tanner, "De Gaulle Insists on Rule of Bases of NATO in France," *New York Times,* 22 February 1966; "France Explains Bid for Removal of Foreign Bases," *New York Times,* 13 March 1966.

33. Drew Middleton, "Unity of the Allies Is Improved but Problems Remain," *New York Times,* 14 April 1963.

34. SEATO was established by eight states in 1955, largely in an attempt to duplicate the success of NATO, but also to signal to the Soviet Union that the United States, England, and France were committed to protecting Southeast Asia from Communism. However, when in 1965 the United States attempted to use SEATO to intervene in Vietnam, the action was blocked by France and the Philippines. That Australia, New Zealand, and Thailand did send a few thousand troops provides an opportunity to test the hypotheses on alliance variation, which would expect U.S. relations with the states that assisted in Vietnam to improve relative to U.S. relations with France and the Philippines.

increased perceptions of allied reliability, thus emboldening one or both of the superpowers to challenge the other.

The War on Terror

A great deal has been made of the states that supported the 2003 invasion of Iraq and the U.S. allies that failed to provide support. However, if we focus first on the immediate response to 9/11, it is clear that U.S. allies should have benefitted from improved reliability. NATO, for the first time, invoked Article V of the North Atlantic Treaty, which stipulated that an attack on one member of the alliance would be considered an attack on all members.[35] The alliance also deployed airborne warning and control system (AWACS) surveillance flights on 9 October 2001 as part of Operation Eagle Assist to help protect the U.S. homeland,[36] enacted Operation Active Endeavor on 26 October 2001 to use NATO air and sea assets to patrol the eastern Mediterranean,[37] and created the Partnership Action Plan against Terrorism on 21 November 2002.[38] In addition, on 11 August 2003, NATO took command of the International Security Assistance Force (ISAF) in Afghanistan, for which it oversees roughly eighty thousand troops from all twenty-eight NATO members as well as sixteen other states.[39]

As a result, I would expect the United States to view its allies favorably, which ironically may have given the United States more confidence to invade Iraq (if the argument on moral hazard made earlier in this chapter is correct). That several states did not support the invasion of Iraq is also useful, because even though no state was required to support it, U.S. relations with those who did provide consistent support—for example, England, Italy, Poland, Australia—appeared much stronger afterward than its

Pakistan not only withdrew from the organization in 1973 over the lack of allied support against India, but it grew closer to Communist China. France also withdrew in 1974. The alliance finally fell apart in 1976, just one year after the Vietnam War ended. At least with this cursory examination, we can see evidence of reputation influencing not only the creation of the organization but also the behavior of states withdrawing from the agreement when its members proved to be unreliable. Whether U.S. relations with SEATO members reflected different levels of reliability is a more extensive project than I can address here, but it would be useful to examine the question to further advance our understanding of reputation.

35. Suzanne Daley, "For First Time, NATO Invokes Joint Defense Pact with U.S.," *New York Times*, 13 September 2001.

36. Suzanne Daley, "Europeans Pledge Troops, if Necessary," *New York Times*, 9 October 2001; Eric Schmitt, "NATO Planes to End Patrol of U.S. Skies," *New York Times*, 2 May 2002.

37. "Operation Active Endeavor," http://www.nato.int/cps/en/natolive/topics_7932.htm, accessed 10 March 2010.

38. "The Partnership Action Plan against Terrorism," http://www.nato.int/cps/en/SID-2D8D5965–998324AA/natolive/topics_50084.htm, accessed 10 March 2010.

39. "NATO's Role in Afghanistan," http://www.nato.int/cps/en/natolive/topics_8189.htm, accessed 10 March 2010; see also the ISAF website, http://www.isaf.nato.int/.

hose states that did not support it. For example, an agree- under President George W. Bush for a U.S. missile defense e to be located in Poland.[40] The United States also helped grade its armed forces. In contrast, states that failed to support United States paid a price.[41] Therefore, even though several U.S. allies supported the war on terror, those that failed to support the United States in Iraq saw relations strained, whereas those that supported the United States both in Afghanistan and in Iraq were more likely to see their relations with the United States improve.

Comparing the importance of reputation in earlier periods to its role in a unipolar system is interesting. But because the war on terror deals primarily with a nonstate actor, it is not clear that we should take the assessment too far. Yet there appears to be evidence that states in a unipolar system still pay attention to whether or not their partners live up to their expected obligations. This case is particularly challenging because it is ongoing and therefore requires some predictive ability. However, based on the findings of this book, I can make a couple of important points.

First, because a hegemonic state does not need its allies to ensure its security, it should be less concerned about its own reliability as an ally (whether or not it is punished by its allies for being unreliable). Second, if theories about hegemonic stability are valid, then as a hegemon's power increases we should see it demanding more reliability from its allies and punishing those states that do not live up to their commitments. At the same time, a hegemon in decline should refrain from inflicting too much punishment on its unreliable allies for fear of losing those allies (possibly to a balancing coalition). Whether or not the United States is in decline, and whether or not these expectations hold true, are questions for other research projects. The point is that incorporating reputation into our studies of alliances provides us with a novel view of state behavior, regardless of the nature of the international system.

Additional Applications of Reputation

Although I have shown that reliability is a factor in state alliance choices, sometimes in unanticipated ways, this book leaves a number of unanswered

40. Thom Shanker and Nicholas Kulish, "U.S. and Poland Set Missile Deal," *New York Times*, 15 August 2008. This plan was shelved by President Barack Obama on 17 September 2009, and another plan was implemented to put the missile interceptors in Romania. Peter Baker, "White House Scraps Bush's Approach to Missile Shield," *New York Times*, 18 September 2009; Nicholas Kulish and Ellen Barry, "Romanians Accept Plan for Basing of Missiles," *New York Times*, 5 February 2010.

41. Ron Hutcheson, "Administration Deals Payback to Leaders Who Crossed Bush on Iraq," *Knight Ridder/Tribune Business News*, 7 May 2003; Mark Steyn, "Payback Time for the Axis of Weasels," *Sunday Telegraph* (UK), 13 December 2003.

questions. I address some of those questions here, as well as discuss how my argument is applicable to other areas of international relations scholarship and how it may be useful for policymakers. Specifically, I discuss whether state reputations survive a change of leadership, the role of reputation in nonmilitary agreements, the possibility that reputation helps explain the difficulty of resolving internal conflicts, and the value of reputation for responding to terrorism.

Reputation and Political Change

This book does not directly deal with the question of whether reputations are assigned to states or to individual leaders. I assume for the sake of simplicity that both have reputations, but there is evidence from my cases that perceptions of a state's reputation can change as a result of new leadership. Some initial work has been done on the differences between national and individual reputations,[42] but more is needed. Despite the relatively few changes in leadership in that time, the pre–First World War period does provide some interesting observations about the relative importance of individual versus national reputations. The British fear prior to the First Moroccan Crisis was that Delcassé would lead France to war with Germany, thus entangling Britain in an unwanted war. Mercer suggests that the resignation of Delcassé because of German requests was a sign of France being irresolute. However, British fears of entrapment were decreased, which not only suggests that reputations of individuals are somewhat relevant for the state but also that the British were more willing to bind themselves to France after Morocco because there was a new person in charge of French foreign policy. Similarly, I briefly discussed in chapter 6 the effect that the pacifist Joseph Caillaux had on Anglo-French relations and how it altered not only British perceptions of France but also French perceptions of its allies.

In a couple of cases, I even found evidence to suggest that a political party was perceived to have its own reputation. According to L. W. Fuller, "the French Government had been somewhat concerned at the accession of the Liberals to power in England, knowing their traditionally pacifist views. Paul Cambon, therefore, approached Edward Grey with a view to the continuation of the military conversations and, if possible, the securing of a definite pledge of aid in case France were involved in war with Germany."[43] Although this complicates studies of reputation if different parties

42. Alexandra Guisinger and Alastair Smith, "Honest Threats: The Interaction of Reputation and Political Institutions in International Crises," *Journal of Conflict Resolution* 46, no. 2 (April 2002), 175–200.

43. L. W. Fuller, *The Effect of the First Moroccan Crisis on Anglo-German Relations* (Colorado Springs: Colorado College Publication, 1932), 27.

ific reputations, it is still compatible with my hypotheses. When a y less reliable party came to power in England (or at least a party liability was so far untested), the French sought a more binding commitment from that new party. In much the same way, each domestic group within Germany had a preferred ally and adversary, and this divide influenced each group's perception of the reliability of states.[44]

In another instance, if we expand our focus to include other types of reputation, it is clear that the perceptions of England, France, and Russia concerning a growing German threat did not change when Bethmann-Hollweg took over as chancellor from von Bülow in 1909. This change had little influence on Germany's reputation as an aggressive state, or at least it was not considered significant because of the reputations of the other German leaders who remained in power.

That individual or group reputations may outweigh a state's reputation provides a possible explanation for the continued ability of Italy to find allies during the interwar years. Despite Italy's poor reputation leading up to the First World War, it was approached by numerous states seeking alliances before the Second World War. Alliances during this period are also described as being much more flexible than those prior to the First World War, so my suggestion is that, overall, the reliability of allies should have even more influence on state behavior. This would explain British reluctance to ally with either France or the Soviet Union, as well as French unwillingness to ally with the Soviets. Their main concern with the Soviet Union was not just about allying with a communist state; they should also have been influenced by Russia's actions during the First World War, abandoning England and France to sign a separate peace treaty with Germany on 3 March 1918 (the Treaty of Brest-Litovsk).

The obvious puzzle is why anyone, especially the Germans, would have wanted to ally with Italy. Not only did Italy fail to support its allies in repeated crises before the First World War but it also exploited German preoccupation over Morocco in 1911 to launch its own war against Turkey to gain Tripoli (which resulted in a weakening of the Ottoman Empire, allowing the Balkan states to begin their own wars).[45] According to George Manhart, "in general, it is thought here that neither the Triple Entente nor the Triple Alliance can count on the loyalty of Italy."[46] Nevertheless, the Italians were kept within the Triple Alliance until they abandoned their allies yet again during the First World War. However, despite this obvious

44. Taylor, *Struggle for Mastery*, 519.

45. "Turkey and Italy," *Times* (London), 28 September 1911; "The War," *Times* (London), 2 October 1911.

46. George Manhart, *Alliance and Entente, 1871–1914* (New York: F. S. Crofts & Co., 1932), 64.

Italian unreliability, they were still courted by both sides prior to the Second World War.

At least part of the answer may lie in the fact that reputations are assigned to individual leaders as well as to the states themselves. While Italy may have had an unreliable reputation, Mussolini as a leader was unlikely to have been perceived as unreliable, particularly by Hitler with whom he had similar interests and a common ideology. That still does not explain why other states approached Italy, but Mercer may provide part of the answer by suggesting that the favorability of an action also effects the reputation. Since Italian abandonment repeatedly favored the Entente states, they might have seen Italy as slightly more reliable than either Germany or Austria-Hungary believed them to be.

Reputation and Nonmilitary Agreements

In this book I have focused exclusively on military alliances because these types of agreements provide a difficult test of reputation. States joining an alliance may have to give up a great deal of sovereignty and risk their survival. Since I find that reputation influences the behavior of states within alliances, it is worthwhile to expand on this to include other types of international institutions that may be less threatening to a state's sovereignty. Just as we see future balancing behavior focusing more on economic and diplomatic power rather than military power (e.g., the European Union forming to economically balance against the United States, or the coalition of states on the UN Security Council that joined to oppose the U.S. invasion of Iraq), it is possible that nonsecurity agreements will grow increasingly more important within the international community, especially if the power of the United States declines.

As with works on deterrence, much of the international institutions literature traditionally assumed that a state's reputation mattered, without ever testing that assumption. However, since my hypotheses on alliance variation are drawn from studies on the differences between international institutions, it would be interesting to test these hypotheses on nonsecurity agreements. One possibility would be to examine whether a state's willingness to honor its trade agreements influences its relations with other trade partners. The World Trade Organization, for instance, would provide a useful test of certain types of state reputations. One would expect states with reputations for honoring their trade agreements to be treated differently by current and potential trade partners from states that fail to do so. The WTO publishes reviews of state trade policies, and although violations of free trade are commonly the result of domestic political considerations, it would be interesting and worthwhile to determine if factors such as obligation and precision in trade agreements are influenced by these trade reviews. Moreover, since the WTO provides an arena for dispute settlement between trade partners, this might provide further means for evaluating a state's reliability and for determining whether that affects the behavior of its trade partners.

Other types of international situations that would be appropriate tests of state reputation include environmental agreements such as the Kyoto Protocol on climate change. In addition, a state's willingness to sign an arms control treaty may be influenced by the reputation of the other state to live up to its commitments. Certainly, reputation influences how states deal with potential nuclear proliferators such as North Korea and Iran. Agreements with such states closely parallel alliances in the sense that failing to adequately understand the other actor's intentions can threaten a state's survival.

Reputation and Internal Violence

If a reputation for reliability influences a state's ability to attract allies, or if it affects a state's autonomy, then reputation should also contribute to our understanding of nonstate violence, such as terrorism and civil wars. Several international relations scholars have discussed the effect of security dilemmas on various aspects of internal conflict, including its origins and the difficulties surrounding its resolution.[47] A potential problem with this is that it applies an explanation of state behavior in the international system to domestic situations. As a result, the security dilemma may be an inappropriate analogy for internal conflict for two reasons. First, internal violence may occur in conditions other than a state of complete anarchy. There are numerous instances of effective states suffering from internal violence (e.g., Sri Lanka, Spain, England). Even in cases of state failure, such as Somalia and Yugoslavia, anarchy could be the result of internal conflict, rather than a necessary condition for it.[48] Second, the actors may not be as uncertain

47. Barry Posen, "The Security Dilemma and Ethnic Conflict," *Survival* 35, no. 1 (Spring 1993), 27–47; Stephen Steman, "Negotiation and Mediation in Internal Conflict," in *The International Dimensions of Internal Conflict*, ed. Michael Brown (Cambridge: MIT Press, 1996), 344–345; Joanna Spear, "Arms Limitations, Confidence-Building Measures, and Internal Conflict," in Brown, *International Dimensions of Internal Conflict*, 377–410; Stephen Saideman, "The Dual Dynamics of Disintegration: Ethnic Politics and Security Dilemmas in Eastern Europe," *Nationalism and Ethnic Politics* 2, no. 1 (Spring 1996), 18–43; Stephen Saideman, "Is Pandora's Box Half Empty or Half Full?: The Limited Virulence of Secessionism and the Domestic Sources of Disintegration," in *The International Spread of Ethnic Conflict: Fear, Diffusion, and Escalation*, ed. David Lake and Donald Rothchild (Princeton: Princeton University Press, 1998), 134–139; Jack Snyder and Robert Jervis, "Civil War and the Security Dilemma," in *Civil Wars, Insecurity, and Intervention*, ed. Barbara Walter and Jack Snyder (New York: Columbia University Press, 1999), 15–37.

48. David Lake makes a similar point about the problems of applying IR theories to internal violence. David Lake, "International Relations Theory and Internal Conflict: Insights from the Interstices," *International Studies Review* 5, no. 4 (December 2003), 81–89.

about each other's intentions as they often are in international politics. As a result, there may be other factors that contribute to internal conflict, and reputation could improve our understanding, not only of why these conflicts occur in the first place but also why they are frequently difficult to resolve.

Some scholars have begun to look at the role of reputation to explain why those involved in internal conflicts have difficulty trusting each other enough to reach a negotiated settlement. James Fearon suggests that actors face a commitment problem when trying to resolve internal disputes.[49] Because this is similar to the problem facing states that have alliances, in some cases it will be exacerbated by problems of reliability. And Barbara Walter argues that separatist movements face particularly tough challenges from states that want to build a tough reputation rather than face challenges from separatist groups (similar to the chain store paradox discussed in chapter 1).[50] Although Walter focuses more on credibility than reliability, as I distinguish the two types of reputation in this book, the overall advantage of incorporating reputation is that it is not exclusive to any particular domain, since it appears to explain the behavior of actors in markets and political systems alike.

In addition, one of the reasons internal conflicts are difficult to solve is that the actors frequently come to distrust each other because of their previous interactions. For example, before his death, many perceived Yasser Arafat to be unreliable.[51] As a result, Arafat may have had greater difficulty negotiating a settlement than another Palestinian leader who was perceived by the Israeli government to be more willing and/or more capable of honoring commitments. The Troubles in Northern Ireland offer another example of this, where attempted solutions, such as the Good Friday agreement or the Irish Republican Army's plan to unilaterally disarm, were often unsuccessful because the history of the conflict provided numerous examples of both sides reneging on promises. More work on how one side's reputation influences the behavior of the other could help identify ways to alleviate some of the distrust that makes internal conflicts so difficult to resolve. In addition, future work could examine the many ways in which firms preserve and build their reputations to identify how

49. James Fearon, "Commitment Problems and the Spread of Ethnic Conflict," in Lake and Rothchild, *International Spread of Ethnic Conflict*, 107–126. See also Tony Addison and Mansoob Mershed, "Credibility and Reputation in Peacemaking," *Journal of Peace Research* 39, no. 4 (July 2002), 487–501.

50. Barbara Walter, *Reputation and Civil War: Why Separatist Conflicts Are So Violent* (Cambridge: Cambridge University Press, 2009).

51. Barbara Slavin, "Events in Mideast, Afghanistan Strain U.S.-Iran Ties," *USA Today*, 10 January 2002; Associated Press, "U.S. Looks to Deal with a Younger Palestinian Leader," *Dallas Morning News*, 6 June 2002.

domestic groups and governments involved in internal conflicts can do the same thing.

Reputation and Counterterrorism

Finally, there is debate, both in the literature and among state leaders, regarding the most effective counterterrorism policies. Some contend that states must develop a reputation for being tough on terrorism as a way of deterring future acts because soft policies encourage more violence.[52] Israel's policy of using military force to punish acts of terrorism is a perfect example of a state trying to create a reputation for being tough on terrorism. One illustrative example was the Israeli government's mission to find and kill those members of Black September responsible for the killings of the Israeli athletes at the 1972 Munich Olympics.[53]

Others argue that tough policies only encourage terrorism, compel moderates to support terrorist activities, and help to create cycles of violence, whereas conciliatory policies that ensure moderates are part of society are more likely to prevent people from engaging in terrorist acts.[54] As a result, we clearly have a puzzle regarding the best way for states to deal with terrorism, and reputation can play a useful role in evaluating the best counterterrorist policies. If states cannot change their reputations, as Mercer suggests, then policies designed to deter terrorism through harsh measures may be ineffective.

This puzzle also has real-world implications, considering the change in U.S. counterterrorism policies after 9/11 and with some U.S. allies (such as Spain) pulling out of Iraq as a result of terrorist demands.[55] Preliminary research relating to this puzzle suggests that domestic terrorist groups are

52. William O'Brien, "Counterterrorism: Lessons from Israel," *Strategic Review* 13, no. 4 (Fall 1985), 32–44; Caleb Carr, "Terrorism as Warfare: The Lessons of Military History," *World Policy Journal* 13, no. 4 (Winter 1996–97), 1–12; William Betts, "The Soft Underbelly of American Primacy," *Political Science Quarterly* 117, no. 1 (Spring 2002), 33.

53. Neil Amdur, "Games Suspended; Rites in Arena Set," *New York Times,* 6 September 1972; George Jonas, *Vengeance: The True Story of an Israeli Counter-Terrorist Team* (New York: Simon and Schuster, 1984).

54. Ruud Koopmans, "The Dynamics of Protest Waves: West Germany, 1965 to 1989," *American Sociological Review* 58, no. 5 (October 1993), 637–658; David Charters, ed. *The Deadly Sin of Terrorism: Its Effect on Democracy and Civil Liberty in Six Countries* (Westport, CT: Greenwood Press, 1994); Jeremy Ginges, "Deterring the Terrorist: A Psychological Evaluation of Different Strategies for Deterring Terrorism," *Terrorism and Political Violence* 9, no. 1 (Spring 1997), 170–185; Sidney Tarrow *Power in Movement: Social Movements and Contentious Politics* (New York: Cambridge University Press, 1998); Philip Heymann *Terrorism in America: A Commonsense Strategy for a Democratic Society* (Cambridge: MIT Press, 1998).

55. Edward Luttwak, "Rewarding Terror in Spain," *New York Times,* 16 March 2004; Marlise Simons, "Spanish Premier Orders Soldiers Home from Iraq," *New York Times,* 19 April 2004.

less likely to be deterred by harsh policies and that states that use violence against their own population frequently create cycles of violence.[56] However, conciliatory policies are much less effective against terrorist groups that are transnational, since their members are unlikely to benefit from concessions. Moreover, early findings suggest that a state's reputation for being tough has much greater influence on the behavior of groups with ideological motivations—such as the Red Army factions that operated in West Germany during the 1970s and 1980s, and the Ku Klux Klan—than against nationalist or religious groups, like the IRA, the Palestinian Liberation Organization, or al-Qaida. Clearly, this is another area in which a greater understanding of reputation is valuable, not only for scholars but for leaders as well.

The purpose of this book has been to challenge the growing trend of scholarship that is critical of reputation, not only by examining one type of reputation that is often overlooked but also by evaluating specific ways in which a state's reliability will influence its autonomy in developing new alliances or preserving existing alliances. By studying the alliance behavior of Europe's great powers before the First World War, I have found that while reputation does not influence every alliance decision, it does have some important effects on the ability of states to form alliances with other reliable states, to preserve their freedom of action within their alliances, and possibly also on the willingness of allies to stand up to adversaries. As a result, incorporating reputation into our existing theories of alliance behavior tells us more about how states choose their allies or opt for neutrality, why alliances change over time, and why there appears to be a connection between alliances and war. More work is still needed on all aspects of reputation, but it is my hope that this book provides useful findings in cases that should be difficult tests of reputation, leading to solid evidence that state leaders should be concerned about their state's reliability as an ally if they hope to preserve their state's autonomy.

56. Gregory Miller, "Confronting Terrorisms: Group Motivation and Successful State Policies," *Terrorism and Political Violence* 19, no. 3 (Fall 2007), 331–350.

Appendix A

First Treaty of Alliance between Austria-Hungary, Germany, and Italy, 20 May 1882

Their majesties the Emperor of Austria, King of Bohemia, etc., and Apostolic King of Hungary, the Emperor of Germany, King of Prussia, and the King of Italy, animated by the desire to increase the guaranties of the general peace, to fortify the monarchical principle and thereby to assure the unimpaired maintenance of the social and political order in Their respective States, have agreed to conclude a Treaty which, by its essentially conservative and defensive nature, pursues only the aim of forestalling the dangers which might threaten the security of Their States and the peace of Europe.

To this end Their Majesties have appointed, to wit, His Majesty the Emperor of Austria, King of Bohemia, etc., and Apostolic King of Hungary,

Count Gustavus Kálnoky, General, His Minister of the Imperial Household and of Foreign Affairs:

His Majesty the Emperor of Germany, King of Prussia,

Prince Henry VII of Reuss, Aide-de-Camp General, His Ambassador Extraordinary and Plenipotentiary to His Imperial and Royal Apostolic Majesty,

His Majesty the King of Italy,

Count Charles Felix Nicolis de Robilant, Lieutenant-General, His Ambassador Extraordinary and Plenipotentiary to His Imperial and Royal Apostolic Majesty,

Who, furnished with full powers, which have been found in good and due form, have agreed upon the following articles:

Article I

The High Contracting Parties mutually promise peace and friendship, and will enter into no alliance or engagement directed against any one of their States.

They engage to proceed to an exchange of ideas on political and economic questions of a general nature which may arise, and they further promise one another mutual support within the limits of their own interests.

Article II

In case Italy, without direct provocation on her part, should be attacked by France for any reason whatsoever, the two other Contracting Parties shall be bound to lend help and assistance with all their forces to the Party attacked.

This same obligation shall devolve upon Italy in case of any aggression without direct provocation by France against Germany.

Article III

If one, or two, of the High Contracting Parties, without direct provocation on their part, should chance to be attacked and to be engaged in a war with two or more Great Powers non-signatory to the present Treaty, the *casus foederis* will arise simultaneously for all the High Contracting Parties.

Article IV

In case a Great Power non-signatory to the present Treaty should threaten the security of the states of one of the High Contracting Parties, and the threatened Party should find itself forced on that account to make war against it, the two others bind themselves to observe towards their Ally a benevolent neutrality. Each of them reserves to itself, in this case, the right to take part in the war, if it should see fit, to make common cause with its Ally.

Article V

If the peace of any of the High Contracting Parties should chance to be threatened under the circumstances foreseen by the preceding Articles, the High Contracting Parties shall take counsel together in ample time as to the military measures to be taken with a view to eventual cooperation.

They engage henceforward, in all cases of common participation in a war, to conclude neither armistice, nor peace, nor treaty, except by common agreement among themselves.

Article VI

The High Contracting Parties mutually promise secrecy as to the contents and existence of the present Treaty.

Article VII

The present Treaty shall remain in force during the space of five years, dating from the day of the exchange of ratifications.

Article VIII

The ratifications of the present Treaty shall be exchanged at Vienna within three weeks, or sooner if may be.

In witness whereof the respective Plenipotentiaries have signed the present Treaty and have annexed thereto the seal of their arms.

Done at Vienna, the twentieth day of the month of May of the year one thousand eight hundred and eighty-two.

Kálnoky H. VII Of Reuss C. Robilant

Additional declaration of Italy that the provisions of the Alliance could not be regarded as directed against England. Rome, May 22, 1882.

Ministerial Declaration

The Royal Italian Government declares that the provisions of the secret Treaty concluded May 20, 1882, between Italy, Austria-Hungary, and Germany, cannot, as has been previously agreed, in any case be regarded as being directed against England.

In witness whereof the present ministerial Declaration, which equally must remain secret, has been drawn up to be exchanged against identic Declarations of the Imperial and Royal Government of Austria-Hungary and of the Imperial Government of Germany.

Rome, May 22, 1882.

The Royal Minister of Foreign Affairs.

Mancini

The information in this appendix is drawn from Alfred Pribram, *The Secret Treaties of Austria-Hungary, 1879–1914*, vol. 1, *Texts of the Treaties and Agreements* (Cambridge: Harvard University Press, 1920), 64–71.

Appendix B

The Anglo-Japanese Alliance, 30 January 1902

The Governments of Great Britain and Japan, actuated solely by a desire to maintain the status quo and general peace in the extreme East, being, moreover, specially interested in maintaining the independence and territorial integrity of the Empire of China and the Empire of Corea, and in securing equal opportunities in those countries for the commerce and industry of all nations, hereby agree as follows:

Article I

The High Contracting parties having mutually recognized the independence of China and of Corea, declare themselves to be entirely uninfluenced by aggressive tendencies in either country. Having in view, however, their special interests, of which those of Great Britain relate principally to China, whilst Japan, in addition to the interests which she possesses in China, is interested in a peculiar degree politically as well as commercially and industrially in Corea, the High Contracting parties recognize that it will be admissible for either of them to take such measures as may be indispensable in order to safeguard those interests if threatened either by the aggressive action of any other Power, or by disturbances arising in China or Corea, and necessitating the intervention of either of the High Contracting parties for the protection of the lives and properties of its subjects.

Article II

If either Great Britain or Japan, in the defence of their respective interests as above described, should become involved in war with another Power, the other High Contracting Party will maintain a strict neutrality, and use its efforts to prevent other Powers from joining in hostilities against its ally.

Article III

If, in the above event, any other Power or Powers should join in hostilities against that ally, the other High Contracting Party will come to its assistance, and will conduct the war in common, and make peace in mutual agreement with it.

Article IV

The High Contracting Parties agree that neither of them will, without consulting the other, enter into separate arrangements with another Power to the prejudice of the interests above described.

Article V

Whenever, in the opinion of either Great Britain or Japan, the above-mentioned interests are in jeopardy, the two Governments will communicate with one another fully and frankly.

Article VI

The present Agreement shall come into effect immediately after the date of its signature, and remain in force for five years from that date.

In case neither of the High Contracting Parties should have notified twelve months before the expiration of the said five years the intention of terminating it, it shall remain binding until the expiration of one year from the day on which either of the High Contracting Parties shall have denounced it. But if, when the date fixed for its expiration arrives, either ally is actually engaged in war, the alliance shall, *ipso facto*, continue until peace is concluded.

Notes exchanged between the two Governments, 30 January 1902.

Sir,

M. le Marquis,

In reference to the Agreement concluded by us to-day on behalf of our respective Governments, I have the honour to inform you that the British/Japanese Government recognize that the naval forces of Great Britain/Japan should, so far as possible, act in concert with those of Japan/Great Britain in time of peace, and agrees that mutual facilities shall be given for the docking and coaling of vessels of war of one country in the ports of the other, as well as other advantages conducing to the welfare and efficacy of the respective navies of the two Powers.

At the present moment Japan and Great Britain are each of them maintaining in the Extreme East a naval force superior in strength to that of any third Power. Great Britain/Japan has no intention of relaxing her efforts to maintain, so far as may be possible, available for concentration in the waters of the Extreme East, a naval force superior to that of any third Power.

The information in this appendix is drawn from J. A. S. Grenville and Bernard Wasserstein, *The Major International Treaties of the Twentieth Century: A History and Guide with Texts*, vol. 1 (London: Routledge, 2001), 54–55.

Appendix C

Declaration between the United Kingdom and France Respecting Egypt and Morocco, 8 April 1904

Article I

His Britannic Majesty's Government declare that they have no intention of altering the political status of Egypt.

The Government of the French Republic, for their part, declare that they will not obstruct the action of Great Britain in that country by asking that a limit of time be fixed for the British occupation or in any other manner, and that they give their assent to the draft Khedivial Decree annexed to the present. Arrangement, containing the guarantees considered necessary for the protection of the interests of the Egyptian bondholders, on the condition that, after its promulgation, it cannot be modified in any way without the consent of the Powers Signatory of the Convention of London of 1885.

It is agreed that the post of Director-General of Antiquities in Egypt shall continue, as in the past, to be entrusted to a French *savant*.

The French schools in Egypt shall continue to enjoy the same liberty as in the past.

Article II

The Government of the French Republic declare that they have no intention of altering the political status of Morocco.

His Britannic Majesty's Government, for their part, recognise that it appertains to France, more particularly as a Power whose dominions are conterminous for a great distance with those of Morocco, to preserve order in that country, and to provide assistance for the purpose of all administrative, economic, financial, and military reforms which it may require.

They declare that they will not obstruct the action taken by France for this purpose, provided that such action shall leave intact the rights which Great Britain, in virtue of treaties, conventions, and usage, enjoys in Morocco, including the right of coasting trade between the ports of Morocco, enjoyed by British vessels since 1901.

Article III

His Britannic Majesty's Government for their part, will respect the rights which France, in virtue of treaties, conventions, and usage, enjoys in Egypt, including the right of coasting trade between Egyptian ports accorded to French vessels.

Article IV

The two Governments, being equally attached to the principle of commercial liberty both in Egypt and Morocco, declare that they will not, in those countries, countenance any inequality either in the imposition of customs duties or other taxes, or of railway transport charges.

The trade of both nations with Morocco and with Egypt shall enjoy the same treatment in transit through the French and British possessions in Africa. An agreement between the two Governments shall settle the conditions of such transit and shall determine the points of entry.

This mutual engagement shall be binding for a period of thirty years. Unless this stipulation is expressly denounced at least one year in advance, the period shall be extended for five years at a time.

Nevertheless the Government of the French Republic reserve to themselves in Morocco, and His Britannic Majesty's Government reserve to themselves in Egypt, the right to see that the concessions for roads, railways, ports, etc., are only granted on such conditions as will maintain intact the authority of the State over these great undertakings of public interest.

Article V

His Britannic Majesty's Government declare that they will use their influence in order that the French officials now in the Egyptian service may not be placed under conditions less advantageous than those applying to the British officials in the service.

The Government of the French Republic, for their part, would make no objection to the application of analogous conditions to British officials now in the Moorish service.

Article VI

In order to ensure the free passage of the Suez Canal, His Britannic Majesty's Government declare that they adhere to the treaty of the 29th October, 1888, and that they agree to their being put in force. The free passage of the Canal being thus guaranteed, the execution of the last sentence of paragraph I as well as of paragraph 2 of Article VII of that treaty will remain in abeyance.

Article VII

In order to secure the free passage of the Straits of Gibraltar, the two Governments agree not to permit the erection of any fortifications or strategic works on that portion of the coast of Morocco comprised between, but not including, Melilla and the heights which command the right bank of the River Sebou.

This condition does not, however, apply to the places at present in the occupation of Spain on the Moorish coast of the Mediterranean.

Article VIII

The two Governments, inspired by their feeling of sincere friendship for Spain, take into special consideration the interests which that country derives from her geographical position and from her territorial possessions on the Moorish coast of the Mediterranean. In regard to these interests the French Government will come to an understanding with the Spanish Government.

The agreement which may be come to on the subject between France and Spain shall be communicated to His Britannic Majesty's Government.

Article IX

The two Governments agree to afford to one another their diplomatic support, in order to obtain the execution of the clauses of the present Declaration regarding Egypt and Morocco.

Secret Articles

Secret Article I

In the event of either Government finding themselves constrained, by the force of circumstances, to modify their policy in respect to Egypt or Morocco, the engagements which they have undertaken towards each other by Articles 4, 6, and 7 of the Declaration of today's date would remain intact.

Secret Article II

His Britannic Majesty's Government have no present intention of proposing to the Powers any changes in the system of the Capitulations, or in the judicial organisation of Egypt.

In the event of their considering it desirable to introduce in Egypt reforms tending to assimilate the Egyptian legislative system to that in force in other civilised Countries, the Government of the French Republic will not refuse to entertain any such proposals, on the understanding that His Britannic Majesty's Government will agree to entertain the suggestions that the Government of the French Republic may have to make to them with a view of introducing similar reforms in Morocco.

Secret Article III

The two Governments agree that a certain extent of Moorish territory adjacent to Melilla, Ceuta, and other *Présides* should, whenever the Sultan ceases to exercise authority over it, come within the sphere of influence of Spain, and that the administration of the coast from Melilla as far as, but not including, the heights on the right bank of the Sebou shall be entrusted to Spain.

Nevertheless, Spain would previously have to give her formal assent to the provisions of Articles IV and VII of the Declaration of today's date, and undertake to carry them out.

She would also have to undertake not to alienate the whole, or a part, of the territories placed under her authority or in her sphere of influence.

Secret Article IV

If Spain, when invited to assent to the provisions of the preceding article, should think proper to decline, the arrangement between France and Great Britain, as embodied in the Declaration of today's date, would be none the less at once applicable.

Secret Article V

Should the consent of the other Powers to the draft Decree mentioned in Article I of the Declaration of today's date not be obtained, the Government of the French Republic will not oppose the repayment at par of the Guaranteed, Privileged, and Unified Debts after the 15th July, 1910.
Done at London, in duplicate, the 8th day of April, 1904.

Lansdowne
Paul Cambon

The information in this appendix is drawn from J. A. S. Grenville and Bernard Wasserstein, *The Major International Treaties of the Twentieth Century: A History and Guide with Texts*, vol. 1 (London: Routledge, 2001), 43–45.

Appendix D

The Second Anglo-Japanese Agreement, 12 August 1905

The Governments of Great Britain and Japan, being desirous of replacing the Agreement concluded between them on the 30th January, 1902, by fresh stipulations, have agreed upon the following Articles, which have for their object:

The consolidation and maintenance of general peace in the regions of Eastern Asia and India;

The preservation of the common interests of all Powers in China by insuring the independence and integrity of the Chinese Empire and the principle of equal opportunities for the commerce and industry of all nations in China;

The maintenance of the territorial rights of the High Contracting Parties in the regions of Eastern Asia and of India, and the defence of their special interests in the said regions:

Article I

It is agreed that whenever, in the opinion of either Great Britain or Japan, any of the rights and interests referred to in the preamble of this Agreement are in jeopardy, the two Governments will communicate with one another fully and frankly, and will consider in common the measures which should be taken to safeguard those menaced rights or interests.

Article II

If, by reason of an unprovoked attack or aggressive action, whenever arising, on the part of any other Power or Powers either Contracting Party should be involved in war in defence of its territorial rights or special interests mentioned in the preamble of this Agreement, the other Contracting Party will at once come to the assistance of its ally, and will conduct war in common, and make peace in mutual agreement with it.

Article III

Japan possessing paramount political, military and economic interests in Corea, Great Britain recognizes the right of Japan to take such measures of guidance, control and protection in Corea as she may deem proper and necessary to safeguard and advance those interests, provided always that such measures are not contrary to the principle of equal opportunities for the commerce and industry of all nations.

Article IV

Great Britain having a special interest in all that concerns the security of the Indian frontier, Japan recognizes her right to take such measures in the proximity of that frontier as she may find necessary for safeguarding her Indian possessions.

Article V

The High Contracting Parties agree that neither of them will, without consulting the other, enter into separate arrangements with another Power to the prejudice of the objects described in the preamble of this Agreement.

Article VI

As regards the present war between Japan and Russia, Great Britain will continue to maintain strict neutrality unless some other Power or Powers should join in hostilities against Japan, in which case Great Britain will come to the assistance of Japan, and will conduct the war in common, and make peace in mutual agreement with Japan.

Article VII

The conditions under which armed assistance shall be afforded by either Power to the other in the circumstances mentioned in the present Agreement, and the means by which such assistance is to be made available, will be arranged by the Naval and Military authorities of the Contracting Parties, who will from time to time consult one another fully and freely upon all questions of mutual interest.

Article VIII

The present Agreement shall, subject to the provisions of Article VI, come into effect immediately after the date of its signature, and remain in force for ten years from that date.

In case neither of the High Contracting Parties should have notified twelve months before the expiration of the said ten years the intention of terminating it, it shall remain binding until the expiration of one year from the day on which either of the High Contracting Parties shall have denounced it. But if, when the date fixed for its expiration arrives, either ally is actually engaged in war, the alliance shall, *ipso facto*, continue until peace is concluded.

In faith whereof the Undersigned, duly authorized by their respective Governments, have signed this Agreement and have affixed thereto their Seals.

Done in duplicate at London, the 12th day of August, 1905.

Landsdowne
His Britannic Majesty's Principal Secretary of State for Foreign Affairs.
Tadesu Hayashi
Envoy Extraordinary and Minister Plenipotentiary of His Majesty the Emperor of Japan at the Court of St. James

The information in this appendix is drawn from G. P. Gooch and Harold Temperley, eds., *British Documents on the Origins of the War, 1898–1914*, vol. 4, *The Anglo-Russian Rapprochement, 1903–7* (London: His Majesty's Stationery Office, 1929), no. 155 (12 August 1905), 164–169.

Appendix E

Conventions between Russia and the United Kingdom Relating to Persia, Afghanistan, and Tibet, 31 August 1907

The Governments of Great Britain and Russia having mutually engaged to respect the integrity and independence of Persia, and sincerely desiring the preservation of order throughout that country and its peaceful development, as well as the permanent establishment of equal advantages for the trade and industry of all other nations;

Considering that each of them has, for geographical and economic reasons, a special interest in the maintenance of peace and order in certain Provinces of Persia adjoining, or in the neighborhood of, the Russian frontier on the one hand, and the frontiers of Afghanistan and Baluchistan on the other hand; and being desirous of avoiding all cause of conflict between their respective interests in the above-mentioned Provinces of Persia;

Have agreed on the following terms:

Article I

Great Britain engages not to seek for herself, and not to support in favour of British subjects, or in favour of the subjects of third Powers, any Concessions of a political or commercial nature—such as Concessions for railways, banks, telegraphs, roads, transport, insurance, etc.—beyond a line starting from Kasri-Shirin, passing through Isfahan, Yezd, Kakhk, and ending at a point on the Persian frontier at the intersection of the Russian and Afghan frontiers, and not to oppose, directly or indirectly, demands for similar Concessions in this region which are supported by the Russian Government. It is understood that the above-mentioned places are included in the region in which Great Britain engages not to seek the Concessions referred to.

Article II

Russia, on her part, engages not to seek for herself and not to support, in favour of Russian subjects, or in favour of the subjects of third Powers, any Concessions of a political or commercial nature—such as Concessions for railways, banks, telegraphs, roads, transport, insurance, etc.—beyond a line going from the Afghan frontier by way of Gazik, Birjand, Kerman, and ending at Bunder Abbas, and not to oppose, directly or indirectly, demands for similar Concessions in this region which are supported by the British Government. It is understood that the above-mentioned places are included in the region in which Russia engages not to seek the Concessions referred to.

Article III

Russia, on her part, engages not to oppose, without previous arrangement with Great Britain, the grant of any Concessions whatever to British subjects in the regions of Persia situated between the lines mentioned in Articles I and II. Great Britain undertakes a similar engagement as regards the grant of Concessions to Russian subjects in the same regions of Persia. All Concessions existing at present in the regions indicated in Articles I and II are maintained.

Article IV

It is understood that the revenues of all the Persian customs, with the exception of those of Farsistan and of the Persian Gulf, revenues guaranteeing the amortization and the interest of the loans concluded by the Government of the Shah with the "Banque d'Escompte et des Prits de Perse" up to the date of the signature of the present Arrangement, shall be devoted to the same purpose as in the past. It is equally understood that the revenues of the Persian customs of Farsistan and of the Persian Gulf, as well as those of the fisheries on the Persian shore of the Caspian Sea and those of the Posts and telegraphs, shall be devoted, as in the past, to the service of the loans concluded by the Government of the Shah with the Imperial Bank of Persia up to the date of the signature of the present Arrangement.

Article V

In the event of irregularities occurring in the amortization or payment of interest of the Persian loans concluded with the "Banque d'escompte et des Prits de Perse" and with the Imperial Bank of Persia up to the date of the signature of the present Agreement, and in the event of the necessity arising for Russia to establish control over the sources of revenue guaranteeing the regular service of the loans concluded with the first-named bank, and situated in the region mentioned in Article II of the present Agreement, or for Great Britain to establish control over the sources of revenue guaranteeing the regular service of the loans concluded with the second-named bank, and situated in the region mentioned in Article I of the present Agreement, the British and Russian Governments undertake to enter beforehand into a friendly exchange of ideas with a view to determine, in agreement with each other, the measures of control in question and to avoid all interference which would not be in conformity with the principles governing the present Agreement.

The information in this appendix is drawn from J. A. S. Grenville and Bernard Wasserstein, *The Major International Treaties of the Twentieth Century: A History and Guide with Texts*, vol. 1 (London: Routledge, 2001), 45–46.

Index

abandonment
  fears of, 25–26, 148, 179, 188–189
  reputation, and, 26, 54, 55n, 184
  Triple Alliance, and, 116, 121, 143, 178, 181, 185, 203
  Triple Entente, and, 99, 131, 138, 149, 162, 169, 202
Aehrenthal, Aloys, 93, 126, 153
  Agadir Crisis, and, 173
  meeting at Buchlau, 128
  view on Germany, 124
  views on Italy, 145, 146
Agadir Crisis, 34, 152–158
  Austrian reliability, and, 173–176, 180–181, 194
  British reliability, and, 158–165, 180, 193
  French reliability, and, 165–168, 180
  Italian reliability, and, 176–179, 180–181
  Russian reliability, and, 168–173, 180, 192, 195
Algeciras conference (1906), 92, 95, 155
  Austrian behavior, and, 18, 95, 111–113, 143, 185
  British behavior, and, 43, 96–97, 100, 123, 160
  consequences for England, 99–101, 103, 105, 167
  consequences for France, 105, 133
  consequences for Italy, 115–121
  consequences for Russia, 107–111, 153
  consequences for Austria-Hungary, 57, 113–114, 120
  French behavior, and, 103–105, 132, 166
  Italian behavior, and, 95, 112, 114–116, 118–119, 178, 185
  Russian behavior, and, 106–109, 111, 122–123
Alliance Treaty Obligations and Provisions (ATOP) dataset, 44
Anglo-French relations
  entente. *See* Entente Cordiale
  military talks (1905), 92, 102, 110, 149
  military talks (1910), 139, 152, 159, 201
  naval conventions, 152
Anglo-German relations
  alliance negotiations, 63, 65, 67–74, 87
  naval conventions (1910–11), 126
  reliability, and, 70–72, 74, 76, 89–90, 124
  secret convention (1914), 153
Anglo-Japanese alliance, 32, 74–78, 87, 184
  design of, 77–78
  France, and, 84–87. *See also* Entente Cordiale
  negotiations for, 63, 65, 74–75, 87
  reliability, and, 65, 75, 78–79, 89–90
  renewal of, 64, 66, 80–82
  treaty (1902), 86, 213–215
  treaty (1905), 221–223

Anglo-Russian relations
Bosnia-Herzegovina Crisis, after, 133, 136, 137
entente, 92, 100–101, 103, 122, 126
First Moroccan Crisis, after 95, 99, 100
implications of, 135, 195
in decline, 169
naval talks, 152, 153, 172
treaty (1907), 225–227
See also Triple Entente
Asquith, Herbert, 153, 159
assumptions, 38–42
Auffenberg, Moritz, 93, 116
Austria-Hungary
domestic problems, and, 112, 174
plans for Italian war, and, 117
seconding telegram, and, 112, 116
Austro-German relations
Agadir Crisis, after, 173, 175
Bosnia-Herzegovina Crisis, after, 142
military talks, 152, 173, 175, 194
Austro-Italian relations
naval conventions, 178, 195
plans to attack Italy, 117–118
tension over Bosnia, 144

Baghdad railway, 134, 160, 167, 194
balance of power theory. *See* balancing theories
balance of threat theory. *See* balancing theories
balancing behavior of states, 22, 183, 190, 200, 203
balancing theories
Agadir Crisis, and, 160, 164, 169, 171, 173–174, 175, 176–177
alliance formation, and, 21–22, 55–56
alliance termination, and, 26–27, 56
Anglo-German alliance, and, 69–70, 71
Anglo-Japanese alliance, and, 75–76, 81
Björko Treaty, and, 108–109
Bosnia-Herzegovina Crisis, and, 131, 133, 136, 138, 140–141, 141–142, 144–145, 146
Entente Cordiale, and, 85
First Moroccan Crisis, and, 98, 108–109, 113–114, 115–116, 117, 124
Balkan Wars (1912–13), 191, 194, 202
bandwagoning, 22, 56n57, 109, 183
Barrère, Camille, 127, 145, 154
Benckendorff, Alexander, 155
Berlin airlift, 197
Berlin Treaty (1878), 137
Bertie, Francis, 64, 93
France, and, 97, 105, 123, 165, 166, 167
Germany, and, 71–72, 167
view on Delcassé, 104
Bethmann Hollweg, Theobald, 154, 174, 202
binding theory, 56
Agadir Crisis, and, 164, 169, 171, 173–174, 175, 176–177
alliance formation, and, 21–22, 56
alliance termination, and, 26–27, 56
Anglo-German alliance, and, 70, 71
Anglo-Japanese alliance, and, 76, 81
Björko Treaty, and, 109
Bosnia-Herzegovina Crisis, and, 131, 133, 136, 138, 140, 142, 145, 146
Entente Cordiale, and, 85
First Moroccan Crisis, and, 98–99, 109, 114, 115–116, 117–118, 124
Björko Treaty, 92, 98, 107–109, 143, 170, 195
blank check, 129, 140, 191, 195
Boer War, 63, 65, 67
Bosnia, annexation of, 123–124, 128–130, 136–137, 139, 144, 146–147, 185
See also Bosnia-Herzegovina Crisis
Bosnia-Herzegovina Crisis, 32–34, 125, 126–130
Austrian reliability, and, 143
British reliability, and, 135–139
French reliability, and, 130–135, 171
German reliability, and, 139–143, 174
Italian reliability, and, 144–147
Russian reliability, and, 131
Brest-Litovsk, treaty of, 202
Buchlau
Russo-Austrian meeting, 126, 128–129
buck-passing, 21n73, 22, 148, 183
Bülow, Bernard, 64, 93, 127, 202
Austria-Hungary, and, 114, 140, 143, 174
Russo-Japanese War, and, 106
view on Italy, 119
views on England, 67, 136
views on France, 96, 132

Caillaux, Joseph, 154, 167, 201
Cambon, Jules, 154, 155
Cambon, Paul, 93, 97
England, and, 201, 220
view on Italy, 120
view on Russia, 106
Casablanca Agreement (1909), 126, 130–132, 139, 142, 155, 195
case selection, 31–34
Cecil, Robert, 64, 72

Central Powers, 101
  Italy, and, 115, 118, 150
  Triple Entente, and, 130, 134, 138, 158, 160, 194
  See also Triple Alliance
Chamberlain, Joseph, 64, 67
Churchill, Winston, 133–134, 153, 159
civil wars, 204–205
Clemenceau, Georges, 127, 131, 139, 154
Conference on Commerce and Navigation (1906), 115
Conrad, Franz, 127
  Germany, and, 140, 142
  views on Italy, 123n94, 146
Copeland, Dale, 18–19
Correlates of War (COW) capability scores, 56, 59–60, 81
  Agadir Crisis, and, 160–161
  Bosnia-Herzegovina Crisis, and, 131–132
  First Moroccan Crisis, and, 97–98
  in 1901, 68–69, 76
credibility
  compared to reliability, 3–4, 18, 103, 205
  required for deterrence, 2, 10–12, 49
Crowe, 166
Cuba
  Bay of Pigs, and, 197
  Missile Crisis, and, 2, 198
Curzon, George, 64, 72

Dardanelles Strait, 80, 128–129, 135–136
Delcassé, Theophile, 93, 97, 201
  resignation of, 92, 94–95, 103–105, 112, 191
deterrence, 10–12, 16–18, 203
  paradox of, 41, 158
Dogger Bank incident, 64, 80, 83, 106
Dual Alliance, 53n48, 63, 65, 68, 76, 84, 98, 106, 135
  Bosnia-Herzegovina Crisis, and, 150, 170–171
  England, and, 69, 79, 98–100
  First Moroccan Crisis, and, 103, 109–111, 133
  Germany, and, 109
  power of, 69, 98, 117
  Russo-Japanese War, and, 79, 86, 133, 179
Dubail-Wilson agreement, 152

Eckardstein, Hermann, 64, 67–68, 74
Edward VII, King, 60n63, 64, 77, 93, 97, 127, 153
Entente Cordiale, 63, 92
  Bosnia-Herzegovina Crisis, and, 139
  First Moroccan Crisis, and, 96–98, 102–103
  formation of, 65–66, 87, 185
  French dependence, and, 102, 107, 123, 139, 149, 186
  power of, 97–98, 109
  reliability, and, 84–86, 89–90, 190
  Russia, and, 98, 111
  secret articles, 219–220
  treaty, 217–220
entrapment, 25, 105, 138, 189
  British fears of, 83, 85, 201
  reputation, and, 54, 55n

Fashoda Crisis (1898), 43
Fearon, James, 10, 51n41, 53n47, 205
Fez, French occupation of, 155, 157, 166
First Moroccan Crisis, 33, 92–96
  Austrian reliability, and, 111–114
  British reliability, and, 43, 96–101, 122
  French reliability, and, 103–105
  Italian reliability, and, 114–121
  Russian reliability, and, 106–111
  See also Algeciras Conference
First World War
  alliances, and, 148, 179
  causes of, 32, 61, 65, 87, 182, 193, 196
  Germany, and, 195
  Italy, and, 47, 119, 177, 202
  Russia, and, 202
Franco-Russian relations. *See* Dual Alliance; Triple Entente
  military agreements, 152, 153
  naval conventions, 168, 171
Franz Ferdinand, 153, 174–175
Franz Joseph, Emperor, 60n63, 142

game theory, 12–16
  chain-store paradox, 15–16
  chicken game, 12
  prisoner's dilemma, 12–15
Germany
  alliance with England. *See* Anglo-German relations, alliance negotiations
  See also Björko Treaty; Potsdam convention; Triple Alliance
Goluchowski, Agenor, 93, 118
Goschen, Edward, 154, 167
Grey, Edward, 93, 127, 153
  Agadir Crisis, and, 156, 158, 162–163
  Anglo-French military talks, and, 102, 159

Grey, Edward *(continued)*
on need to support France, 96, 99, 103, 164, 166–167, 193, 201
Russia, and, 169, 172, 195
threatens resignation, 169
view on French reliability, 139

Haldane, Richard, 101, 153
visit to Berlin, 152, 159–160, 169, 194
Hardinge, Charles, 103, 127, 139, 153, 162
Holstein, Friedrich, 94, 116, 143, 190
Huth, Paul, 11–12, 19–20, 49n39
hypotheses
on alliance formation, 45–48
on alliance termination, 48–50
on alliance variation, 50–55
competing hypotheses, 55–58

India, 69, 72
Anglo-Japanese alliance, and, 75, 80, 84, 221–222
Russia, and, 173
interdependence of commitments, 10–12
interwar period, 47, 188, 202
Iraq War (2003), 199–200, 203, 206
Izvolsky, Alexander, 128–129, 141, 154
France, and, 136, 171
meeting at Buchlau, 128–129

Jervis, Robert, 10, 11, 41, 158
Joffre, Joseph, 154, 161

Komura, Jutaro, 64, 76–77, 89
Korea
Anglo-Japanese Alliance, and, 75, 78, 81
Russo-Japanese War, and, 79

Lamsdorf, Vladimir, 94, 101, 108
Lansdowne, Henry, 64, 93, 104, 220
view on France, 103
view on Japan, 77
views on Germany, 73, 74
Lascelles, Francis, 64, 73
learning, 41–42
Lloyd George, David, 153, 156
Mansion House speech by, 156, 157, 158, 162–163, 164, 166
Loubet, Émile, 93, 107
Louis, Georges, 154, 171
Louis XIV, King, 2, 40n18

Machiavelli, Niccolò, 9
Mansion House speech. *See* Lloyd George, David

Mercer, Jonathan, 45, 91, 206
Agadir Crisis, and, 157, 158, 160, 164–166, 167, 169–170, 172, 174, 176, 178
alliance behavior, and, 57
Anglo-German alliance, and, 70
Anglo-Japanese alliance, and, 82–83
Björko Treaty, and, 107, 109
Bosnia-Herzegovina Crisis, and, 132–133, 136–137, 138–139, 141, 142, 143, 145
critique of reputation, and, 3, 16–18, 66
definition of reputation, and, 35–38
Delcassé's dismissal, and, 103–105, 112, 201
Entente Cordiale, and, 85–86, 89
First Moroccan Crisis, and, 100, 103–105, 109, 112–113, 116, 120–121
resolve, and, 39, 42–43
military alliances, 44
dangers. *See* abandonment; entrapment
definition of, 20
See also specific alliances, such as Anglo-Japanese alliance; Dual Alliance; Entente Cordiale; North Atlantic Treaty Organization; Triple Alliance; Triple Entente
Moltke, Helmuth, 120, 127, 140
Monts, Anton, 94, 127, 154
views on Italy, 115, 116, 118, 147

Nelidov, Alexander, 94, 108, 128, 136
Nicholas II, Tsar, 60n63, 94
views on France, 106, 107
Nicolson, Arthur, 127, 154
view on Russia, 172
views on France, 139, 162–163, 166–167, 191
North Atlantic Treaty Organization (NATO)
9/11, after, 199
cold war, and, 27–29, 121, 182, 188, 196–199
reliability, and, 2, 34, 151
North Korea, 40, 42n25, 204

Open Door, 67
British support for, 68, 95, 97, 105, 191
China, and, 72, 97
Morocco, and, 95, 97
Persia, and, 168

Panther, 156–157
Persia, 225–226
Anglo-Russian relations over, 100–101, 111, 162, 166, 169, 172–173, 193–194

Russo-German relations over, 134, 162, 168
Pichon, Stephen, 93, 127
view on Italy, 120
view on Russia, 135
Poincaré, Raymond, 154, 163, 171, 193
Potsdam convention, 126, 152, 161, 168–169
effect on allies, 134–135, 169, 174, 195
theories about, 141–142
Press, Daryl, 3, 20, 58, 60n64, 66

Racconigi Agreement (1909), 126, 134, 144, 146, 147
reliability, 31, 42
benefits of, 14, 16, 62
development of, 18, 43
distinct from credibility, 4, 9, 18, 20, 32, 33n, 57
individual, 1, 5, 42
loss of, 17, 29, 43, 48, 49
perceptions of, 38, 44, 50
state behavior, and, 32–34, 44
See also specific alliances, crises, and wars, such as Agadir Crisis; Anglo-Japanese alliance; Russo-Japanese War
reputation
building one, 43, 158
in business, 4–6, 19, 35–36, 40, 42, 45–55, 183–184
conflict initiation, and, 189–193
definition of, 35–38
maintaining, 1, 9, 39
measurement of, 42–43
See also specific types of reputation, such as credibility; reliability
resolve. *See* credibility
Romania, 137n35, 146, 196n, 200n40
Rouvier, Maurice, 93, 95, 104, 108
Russo-German relations
alliance negotiations (1905), 92, 107
alliance negotiations (1906). *See* Björko Treaty
Russo-Japanese War (1904–5), 63, 79–80
Anglo-Japanese alliance, and, 32, 66, 79–84, 90, 128
consequences of, 59, 133, 135
Dual Alliance, and, 105–107, 110, 165
Entente Cordiale, and, 65, 85–86, 96, 179

Salisbury, Marquess of, 64, 72
Sazonov, Sergei, 155, 161–162
British relations, and, 173
Potsdam negotiations, and, 168
Schelling, Thomas, 11–12, 47n34
scope conditions, 58–62
Second Moroccan Crisis. *See* Agadir Crisis
security dilemma, 190, 204
Selborne, William, 64, 67, 77
Sino-Japanese War, 63, 74–75
"triple intervention," and, 75
splendid isolation, 31, 64, 87, 89, 90, 184
Stürgkh, Karl, 153, 178
Suez Canal, 80, 218
Suez Crisis, 197, 198
Szögyény-Marich, Ladislaus, 93, 118–119, 175

Tangier, 94, 116
Tardieu, André, 93, 100, 106, 127
Taylor, A. J. P.
Agadir Crisis, and, 155–156, 168
Delcassé's dismissal, and, 103–104
Mansion House speech, and, 162–163
Triple Alliance, 174, and, 179, 193
Triple Entente, and, 132, 139, 160–161, 166
terrorism, 3, 182, 199, 201, 204–207
tethering. *See* binding theory
Tittoni, Tommaso, 127, 147
Triple Alliance, 33, 63, 73
Agadir Crisis, and, 173–178
Bosnia-Herzegovina Crisis, and, 139–147
First Moroccan Crisis, and, 95, 111–120
military talks, 194
naval agreements, 153, 177
original treaty, 209–211
power of, 69, 76, 98, 132, 161
renewal of (1902), 63
renewal of (1907), 92, 112, 118, 119, 122, 124, 126, 128
renewal of (1912), 152, 173, 175, 177
See also Central Powers
Triple Entente, 92, 126
Agadir Crisis, and, 158–173
Bosnia-Herzegovina Crisis, and, 128, 130–139
fears of break-up, 142, 195
formation of, 33, 84–85, 87, 101, 124, 128, 185
power of, 132–133, 144, 161, 176
Tripoli, 94, 115, 144, 147, 202
Tschirschky, Heinrich, 93, 115

United States
alliances, and, 23, 121n
isolationism, and, 23, 65
most powerful state, as, 68–69, 203
NATO, and, 27, 28, 196–199

United States *(continued)*
  Open Door, and, 95, 105
  reputation, and, 2, 11, 41, 99, 197–198
  war on terror, and, 182, 188, 196, 199–200, 206
unreliability. *See* reliability; reputation

Victor Emmanuel III, King, 60n63
Vietnam War, 2, 40n17, 42n25, 198–199

war
  compared to crises, 32, 44, 66
  expectations of, 60–61
  See also specific wars, such as First World War, Russo-Japanese War, Sino-Japanese War, Vietnam War
Wilhelm II, Kaiser, 60n63, 64, 93, 127, 154
  Björko Treaty, and, 106–108
  First Moroccan Crisis, and, 94, 116, 185
  Potsdam convention, and, 134, 143
  view on England, 67
  view on Italy, 118–119
Witte, Sergei, 94, 110n61
World War I. *See* First World War

Yangtze Agreement, 63, 67, 72, 89

France's willingness to stand up to the Germans regardless of what the Germans thought about France's resolve.

In contrast, I found no clear evidence to suggest that Germany was emboldened to challenge France over Morocco because of a perception that Austria-Hungary was reliable (and we know Italy was not perceived to be a reliable ally). But Germany did believe that Russia would fail to support France and that England would do what it had done in the past and support the Open Door. A. F. Harrison contends that the forced resignation of Théophile Delcassé—and the Moroccan crisis itself—was brought about by Russia's weakened state rather than France's lack of resolve.[10] This suggests that Germany was emboldened to challenge France at least partly because of the lack of Russian reliability and also that France was forced to back down (at least over Delcassé's resignation) because the French were unsure of the level of support they would receive from their allies.

Mercer argues that France and Germany both explained allied support in situational terms and therefore would not count on future support.[11] Yet, not only did they challenge each other over Morocco again in 1911 but after Russia and England signed an agreement effectively creating the Triple Entente, Russia and Austria-Hungary squared off over Bosnia-Herzegovina in 1908.

Chapter 5 provides three observations that support my claim about the moral hazard problem of reliability. The first is Austria-Hungary's willingness to threaten Russia once they were provided with the German blank check. The second is Russia's willingness to challenge Austria-Hungary after it had signed an entente with a reliable England. On the other hand, Russia was unwilling to press the Bosnia issue once it recognized that France would not support a war over the Balkans. According to Arthur Nicolson, the British ambassador to Russia at the time, "had Russia . . . been able to rely with more confidence than is actually the case on material support from her ally France, she would, I am disposed to believe, have adopted a firmer attitude and employed sterner language."[12]

Not only does having a reliable ally embolden a state but believing that an adversary does not have reliable allies can also embolden. For instance, while lack of support from Italy did not prevent Germany in 1911,

10. A. F. Harrison, "Collapse of Russia (Germany and Morocco)," *Nineteenth Century* 58 (July 1905), 34–42, cited in Frank Anderson and Amos Hershey, *Handbook for the Diplomatic History of Europe, Asia, and Africa, 1870–1914* (Washington, DC: Government Printing Office, 1918), 337–338.

11. Mercer, *Reputation and International Politics*, 109.

12. Nicolson to Grey, in G. P. Gooch and Harold Temperley, eds., *British Documents on the Origins of the War, 1898–1914*, vol. 5, *The Near East: The Macedonian Problem and the Annexation of Bosnia, 1903–9* (London: His Majesty's Stationery Office, 1928), no. 752 (23 March 1909), 726–727, cited in Mercer, *Reputation and International Politics*, 145.

or Austria in 1914, from challenging the Triple Entente, it may have emboldened France and Russia to stand up to the Triple Alliance under the belief that they could count on Italian unreliability. Chapter 6 illustrates additional examples of this trend. Russia's weak support for France during the Agadir Crisis encouraged Germany to continue challenging the Entente.[13]

Based on the above examples from my cases, I posit that perceptions of reliability will influence the initiation of crises, especially if a state and its adversaries have different perceptions of its allies' reliability. (Table 7.2 illustrates the components of this argument, where A and B are allies and A and C are adversaries; think of state A as France, state B as Russia, and state C as Germany.) Columns refer to a state's perception of its ally's reputation. The rows refer to the ally's reputation from the point of view of an adversary. Not only does this argument suggest when crises are more or less likely but it also provides testable hypotheses concerning which state is most likely to initiate the conflict.

The most dangerous situation is one in which a state believes its ally is reliable (either because of its past behavior or because of institutional changes that bind them more closely together) and is therefore more emboldened, while the adversary does not believe the state's ally is reliable (because of its past behavior and the fact that states often are unaware of the internal changes made within other alliances) and is therefore unlikely to back down when challenged. When this holds true for both sides in a crisis, then escalation to war is most likely. In contrast, the safest situation is the one in which a state believes its allies are unreliable but they are thought to be reliable by its adversaries. In such situations, neither side will risk challenging the other.

Table 7.2. A reputation theory of conflict initiation (where states A and B are allies and states A and C are adversaries)

State C's perception of state B	State A's perception of state B (its ally)	
	Reliable	**Unreliable**
Reliable	Dangerous (A likely to challenge; C likely to back down)	Doubly Safe (A unlikely to challenge; C likely to back down if challenged)
Unreliable	Doubly Dangerous (A likely to challenge; C likely to stand firm)	Dangerous (A unlikely to challenge; C likely to stand firm if challenged)

13. Ima Barlowe, *The Agadir Crisis* (Chapel Hill: University of North Carolina Press, 1940), 246–247.

increased perceptions of allied reliability, thus emboldening one or both of the superpowers to challenge the other.

The War on Terror

A great deal has been made of the states that supported the 2003 invasion of Iraq and the U.S. allies that failed to provide support. However, if we focus first on the immediate response to 9/11, it is clear that U.S. allies should have benefitted from improved reliability. NATO, for the first time, invoked Article V of the North Atlantic Treaty, which stipulated that an attack on one member of the alliance would be considered an attack on all members.[35] The alliance also deployed airborne warning and control system (AWACS) surveillance flights on 9 October 2001 as part of Operation Eagle Assist to help protect the U.S. homeland,[36] enacted Operation Active Endeavor on 26 October 2001 to use NATO air and sea assets to patrol the eastern Mediterranean,[37] and created the Partnership Action Plan against Terrorism on 21 November 2002.[38] In addition, on 11 August 2003, NATO took command of the International Security Assistance Force (ISAF) in Afghanistan, for which it oversees roughly eighty thousand troops from all twenty-eight NATO members as well as sixteen other states.[39]

As a result, I would expect the United States to view its allies favorably, which ironically may have given the United States more confidence to invade Iraq (if the argument on moral hazard made earlier in this chapter is correct). That several states did not support the invasion of Iraq is also useful, because even though no state was required to support it, U.S. relations with those who did provide consistent support—for example, England, Italy, Poland, Australia—appeared much stronger afterward than its

Pakistan not only withdrew from the organization in 1973 over the lack of allied support against India, but it grew closer to Communist China. France also withdrew in 1974. The alliance finally fell apart in 1976, just one year after the Vietnam War ended. At least with this cursory examination, we can see evidence of reputation influencing not only the creation of the organization but also the behavior of states withdrawing from the agreement when its members proved to be unreliable. Whether U.S. relations with SEATO members reflected different levels of reliability is a more extensive project than I can address here, but it would be useful to examine the question to further advance our understanding of reputation.

35. Suzanne Daley, "For First Time, NATO Invokes Joint Defense Pact with U.S.," *New York Times*, 13 September 2001.

36. Suzanne Daley, "Europeans Pledge Troops, if Necessary," *New York Times*, 9 October 2001; Eric Schmitt, "NATO Planes to End Patrol of U.S. Skies," *New York Times*, 2 May 2002.

37. "Operation Active Endeavor," http://www.nato.int/cps/en/natolive/topics_7932.htm, accessed 10 March 2010.

38. "The Partnership Action Plan against Terrorism," http://www.nato.int/cps/en/SID-2D8D5965–998324AA/natolive/topics_50084.htm, accessed 10 March 2010.

39. "NATO's Role in Afghanistan," http://www.nato.int/cps/en/natolive/topics_8189.htm, accessed 10 March 2010; see also the ISAF website, http://www.isaf.nato.int/.

relations with those states that did not support it. For example, an agreement was signed under President George W. Bush for a U.S. missile defense system in Europe to be located in Poland.[40] The United States also helped Poland upgrade its armed forces. In contrast, states that failed to support the United States paid a price.[41] Therefore, even though several U.S. allies supported the war on terror, those that failed to support the United States in Iraq saw relations strained, whereas those that supported the United States both in Afghanistan and in Iraq were more likely to see their relations with the United States improve.

Comparing the importance of reputation in earlier periods to its role in a unipolar system is interesting. But because the war on terror deals primarily with a nonstate actor, it is not clear that we should take the assessment too far. Yet there appears to be evidence that states in a unipolar system still pay attention to whether or not their partners live up to their expected obligations. This case is particularly challenging because it is ongoing and therefore requires some predictive ability. However, based on the findings of this book, I can make a couple of important points.

First, because a hegemonic state does not need its allies to ensure its security, it should be less concerned about its own reliability as an ally (whether or not it is punished by its allies for being unreliable). Second, if theories about hegemonic stability are valid, then as a hegemon's power increases we should see it demanding more reliability from its allies and punishing those states that do not live up to their commitments. At the same time, a hegemon in decline should refrain from inflicting too much punishment on its unreliable allies for fear of losing those allies (possibly to a balancing coalition). Whether or not the United States is in decline, and whether or not these expectations hold true, are questions for other research projects. The point is that incorporating reputation into our studies of alliances provides us with a novel view of state behavior, regardless of the nature of the international system.

Additional Applications of Reputation

Although I have shown that reliability is a factor in state alliance choices, sometimes in unanticipated ways, this book leaves a number of unanswered

40. Thom Shanker and Nicholas Kulish, "U.S. and Poland Set Missile Deal," *New York Times,* 15 August 2008. This plan was shelved by President Barack Obama on 17 September 2009, and another plan was implemented to put the missile interceptors in Romania. Peter Baker, "White House Scraps Bush's Approach to Missile Shield," *New York Times,* 18 September 2009; Nicholas Kulish and Ellen Barry, "Romanians Accept Plan for Basing of Missiles," *New York Times,* 5 February 2010.

41. Ron Hutcheson, "Administration Deals Payback to Leaders Who Crossed Bush on Iraq," *Knight Ridder/Tribune Business News,* 7 May 2003; Mark Steyn, "Payback Time for the Axis of Weasels," *Sunday Telegraph* (UK), 13 December 2003.

questions. I address some of those questions here, as well as discuss how my argument is applicable to other areas of international relations scholarship and how it may be useful for policymakers. Specifically, I discuss whether state reputations survive a change of leadership, the role of reputation in nonmilitary agreements, the possibility that reputation helps explain the difficulty of resolving internal conflicts, and the value of reputation for responding to terrorism.

Reputation and Political Change

This book does not directly deal with the question of whether reputations are assigned to states or to individual leaders. I assume for the sake of simplicity that both have reputations, but there is evidence from my cases that perceptions of a state's reputation can change as a result of new leadership. Some initial work has been done on the differences between national and individual reputations,[42] but more is needed. Despite the relatively few changes in leadership in that time, the pre–First World War period does provide some interesting observations about the relative importance of individual versus national reputations. The British fear prior to the First Moroccan Crisis was that Delcassé would lead France to war with Germany, thus entangling Britain in an unwanted war. Mercer suggests that the resignation of Delcassé because of German requests was a sign of France being irresolute. However, British fears of entrapment were decreased, which not only suggests that reputations of individuals are somewhat relevant for the state but also that the British were more willing to bind themselves to France after Morocco because there was a new person in charge of French foreign policy. Similarly, I briefly discussed in chapter 6 the effect that the pacifist Joseph Caillaux had on Anglo-French relations and how it altered not only British perceptions of France but also French perceptions of its allies.

In a couple of cases, I even found evidence to suggest that a political party was perceived to have its own reputation. According to L. W. Fuller, "the French Government had been somewhat concerned at the accession of the Liberals to power in England, knowing their traditionally pacifist views. Paul Cambon, therefore, approached Edward Grey with a view to the continuation of the military conversations and, if possible, the securing of a definite pledge of aid in case France were involved in war with Germany."[43] Although this complicates studies of reputation if different parties

42. Alexandra Guisinger and Alastair Smith, "Honest Threats: The Interaction of Reputation and Political Institutions in International Crises," *Journal of Conflict Resolution* 46, no. 2 (April 2002), 175–200.

43. L. W. Fuller, *The Effect of the First Moroccan Crisis on Anglo-German Relations* (Colorado Springs: Colorado College Publication, 1932), 27.

hold specific reputations, it is still compatible with my hypotheses. When a potentially less reliable party came to power in England (or at least a party whose reliability was so far untested), the French sought a more binding commitment from that new party. In much the same way, each domestic group within Germany had a preferred ally and adversary, and this divide influenced each group's perception of the reliability of states.[44]

In another instance, if we expand our focus to include other types of reputation, it is clear that the perceptions of England, France, and Russia concerning a growing German threat did not change when Bethmann-Hollweg took over as chancellor from von Bülow in 1909. This change had little influence on Germany's reputation as an aggressive state, or at least it was not considered significant because of the reputations of the other German leaders who remained in power.

That individual or group reputations may outweigh a state's reputation provides a possible explanation for the continued ability of Italy to find allies during the interwar years. Despite Italy's poor reputation leading up to the First World War, it was approached by numerous states seeking alliances before the Second World War. Alliances during this period are also described as being much more flexible than those prior to the First World War, so my suggestion is that, overall, the reliability of allies should have even more influence on state behavior. This would explain British reluctance to ally with either France or the Soviet Union, as well as French unwillingness to ally with the Soviets. Their main concern with the Soviet Union was not just about allying with a communist state; they should also have been influenced by Russia's actions during the First World War, abandoning England and France to sign a separate peace treaty with Germany on 3 March 1918 (the Treaty of Brest-Litovsk).

The obvious puzzle is why anyone, especially the Germans, would have wanted to ally with Italy. Not only did Italy fail to support its allies in repeated crises before the First World War but it also exploited German preoccupation over Morocco in 1911 to launch its own war against Turkey to gain Tripoli (which resulted in a weakening of the Ottoman Empire, allowing the Balkan states to begin their own wars).[45] According to George Manhart, "in general, it is thought here that neither the Triple Entente nor the Triple Alliance can count on the loyalty of Italy."[46] Nevertheless, the Italians were kept within the Triple Alliance until they abandoned their allies yet again during the First World War. However, despite this obvious

44. Taylor, *Struggle for Mastery*, 519.

45. "Turkey and Italy," *Times* (London), 28 September 1911; "The War," *Times* (London), 2 October 1911.

46. George Manhart, *Alliance and Entente, 1871–1914* (New York: F. S. Crofts & Co., 1932), 64.

junctures will enable the spatial structure to be clarified and to reduce deficits in the functional structure of suburbia. (Grochulska-Salak M., 2017).

Urban farm development can be implemented in various ways, including as a multifunctional building complex that crystallizes space. An important conclusion that can be drawn from the research work is to point to the need to implement "self-sufficient hybrid urban units". The analysis of the implementation of urban farms in the city leads to the conclusion that the cultivation of plants can be combined with various functions of public buildings. The implementation of self-sufficient multifunctional building complexes and smart buildings in the city is in line with the principles of sustainable development. In a publication presenting the results of research on the pro-environmental cities development model, a team of scientists from the Faculty of Architecture of the Warsaw University of Technology summarizes *"In order to improve the efficiency of urbanized areas, it is necessary to program "sustainable "and self-sufficient urban units constituting multi-element units of cooperating systems, that is "hybrid urban units". These units should be characterized by optimized development parameters integrated with biologically active surfaces, they should combine public utility and production functions, implemented in multi-purpose buildings that are "environmentally friendly" through passive design, low-carbon materials, high energy efficiency and the use of materials such as greenery as a biologically active surface integrated with the building."*(Grochulska-Salak M., Zielonko-Jung K., Zinowiec-Cieplik K., 2018).

The research works involved analysis of the issues concerning the use of plants for the needs of a self-sufficient hybrid urban unit. As a result, another type of urban farms - algae farms - was distinguished. Factors such as the method of land development, buildings and building elements implemented for the cultivation of algae, which are aquatic plants, were analysed. The cultivation and use of algae are varied and have not yet been fully defined. There are numerous studies on the possibility of using algae, as biofuels, catalysts, for wastewater treatment, for the production of oxygen, hydrogen and as food products, dietary supplements and in cosmetics. As such, algae display a high capacity to absorb nitrogen oxides, one of the most dangerous components of exhaust fumes and smog. At the same time, research is conducted on the use and selection of appropriate mosses species to improve air quality in the city. However, algae seem to have a significant yield and more secondary applications.

Research concerning the use of algae and algae farms in the city is being conducted, among other researchers, by scientists from the Jacobs University and the Jülich Research Center. The algae farm are intended to be used to produce biomass. The algae biomass will be split into two important objectives: for bioethanol and methane.

Algae are used as automotive fuel and as fuel for heat production. Research is being conducted on the use of algae and the processing of algae into biofuel and biogas or hydrogen fuel. Hydrogen combustion does not cause emissions of dust or carbon dioxide, whereas water is the product of this reaction. Researchers are working on effective hydrogen production methods. A team of researchers from the University of Turku in Finland has presented studies showing that underwater algae - algae - are able to produce photosynthesis hydrogen instead of oxygen if left in anaerobic conditions. It is possible, therefore, to obtain a "farm" of hydrogen, *which will not only build organic matter in the photosynthesis process and accumulate carbon dioxide, but also will provide a simple renewable fuel. This method basically provides even renewable, biological fuel cells that only need water and proper light to stimulate function.* (Janiszkiewicz M., Red. GLOBEnergia, 2018). During EXPO 2015 in Milan, EcoLogics Studio presented an algae farm, the result of six years of work conducted by two designers - Claudia Pasquero and Marco Poletto - in cooperation with Taiyo Europe. The presented algae farm, a hybrid of architecture, technology and biology, produced as much oxygen per day as does 37 square kilometers of forest. It comprised a roof that provides shelter from the sun to city dwellers, and in its interior there is water in which algae live. Management of the farm via an electronic system enabled the researchers to control efficiency of photosynthetic by algae. The algae farm allows for the production of oxygen and biomass that can be used to obtain energy. (EcoLogics Studio, 2015). In 2016, the idea of introducing algae plantations into city centers, bio-reactors in the city in which algae grow was presented. The idea was developed by architects from the Howeler + Yoon studio and digital designers from the Squared Design Lab studio. Plastic containers called Eco-Podami would be attached to the free walls of buildings.

The proposed vertical garden should include algae cultivation (for the production of renewable energy) and plants (for the ecosystem and biodiversity in housing).

Vincent Callebaut, the Belgian futurist architect, also works on the implementation of green infrastructure and biomass in the city. In 2016, he presented the concept of "green Paris 2050". The concept included vertical parks growing in buildings equipped with algae bioreactors and bamboo towers of urban vegetable farms. Wind turbines, photovoltaic panels and heat exchangers for heating water in buildings were included in the project. Rainwater was supposed to hit the inverted hydroelectric pumps to create more clean energy.

For the needs of the development of innovative technologies, a Polish-German-US scientific-research group was formed, chaired by the Prorector of the University of Zielona Góra, prof. Andrzej Pieczyński. The research team will be working to